Sewing

FOR

DUMMIES®

3RD EDITION

Sewing

FOR

DUMMIES®

3RD EDITION

by Jan Saunders Maresh

Wiley Publishing, Inc.

Sewing For Dummies®, 3rd Edition

Published by
Wiley Publishing, Inc.
111 River St.
Hoboken, NJ 07030-5774
www.wiley.com

For general information on our other products and services, please contact our Customer Care Department within the U.S. at 877-762-2974, outside the U.S. at 317-572-3993, or fax 317-572-4002.

For technical support, please visit www.wiley.com/techsupport.

Wiley also publishes its books in a variety of electronic formats. Some content that appears in print may not be available in electronic books.

Library of Congress Control Number: 2010930968

ISBN: 978-0-470-62320-6

Manufactured in the United States of America

10 9 8 7 6

WILEY

About the Author

Jan Saunders Maresh is a nationally known sewing journalist, interior redesigner, and certified staging professional. After graduating from Adrian College in Michigan, she became the education director of one of the largest sewing machine companies in the country, and then the director of consumer education for the largest fabric chain in the country. Both professional experiences give her a solid foundation in the home sewing industry, which she continues to serve with her many writing, marketing, and industry consulting projects.

In addition to writing for several home sewing publications, she is a best-selling author for several publishers, with 16 books to her credit. Her most recent title is *Home Staging For Dummies* (Wiley) which she co-authored with Christine Rae. Many of her titles have been chosen as main selections for the *Crafters' Choice Collection,* a division of the Book-of-the-Month Club.

To promote her projects, Jan has been a frequent guest on several PBS television shows. Jan has also made regular appearances on the Home Shopping Network and is the local expert featuring lifestyle tips and decorating techniques in western Massachusetts.

When she's not writing, Jan keeps busy teaching and motivating consumers to create beautiful and sustainable homes. She's also a Certified Trainer for the Live Green Live Smart Institute. Since being transferred to New England, Jan's latest venture has been renovating a 1959 ranch with her husband, using all the green and sustainable renovation products and practices the industry (and their budget) has to offer.

Jan currently resides in Longmeadow, Massachusetts (near Springfield), with her husband, dog, and a collection of books, sewing equipment, fabric, and green building products stashed neatly in every available corner of her home.

Dedication

This book is dedicated to my husband, Ted Maresh, and son, Todd Moser. After so many nights of pizza and cereal for dinner, they deserve all the credit for putting up with my crazy writing projects all these years. Thanks, guys.

Author's Acknowledgments

At age 7, I learned to sew under the watchful eye of my grandmother. When I had finished hand-stitching the set-in sleeves of a doll jacket, I cried and cried because it didn't look right. Grandma gently took the jacket from me and turned the sleeves "inside out." It was a miracle — the jacket looked just like the one in the store. From that moment on, I was hooked on sewing. It's been an intimate part of who I am ever since. Thank you, Grandma, for being my first teacher.

A big-time thank you also goes to my parents, Ray and Bernice Saunders. Although I grew up on a strict budget, there was always money for fabric and plenty of praise for my handmade creations. Dad is gone now, but I'm sure the many hours of looking over his civil-engineer shoulders as he reviewed the latest blueprints for the job helped me think three-dimensionally — crucial for what I do today.

I have the most wonderful network of friends who have influenced what I've done in my life and career. You provide inspiration, knowledge, encouragement, and expertise, and I thank each of you from the bottom of my heart. Without you, this book would have been written by someone else. Thank you, Robbie Fanning, for teaching me so much about writing, sewing, and keeping life in perspective. Thank you, Jackie Dodson, for your incredible sense of humor, for your sewing help on a tight deadline, your creative genius, and friendship. Thank you, Gail Brown, for your constant encouragement and market savvy. Thank you, Karyl Garbow, for being a kindred spirit for almost 30 years. Thank you, Sue Hausmann, for your dedication to sewing education in our industry and for always sharing your wisdom with me no matter the time of day. Thank you, Judy Raymond at Simplicity Pattern Company, for your help and support of this project and for publishing and promoting the *Sewing For Dummies* sewing patterns. Many more people have the courage to try sewing for the first time because of your efforts. Finally, thank you Cindy Cummins at DIYStyle for your friendship and assistance with some of the projects in this book and your diligent research that makes the appendix a very helpful and up-to-date sewing resource for readers everywhere.

Thank you, Lisa Reed, for your tremendously talented hand and critical eye in illustrating this 3rd Edition. And thank you, Mike Lewis, Elizabeth Rea, and Caitie Copple, the team of incredible editors at Wiley Publishing who helped my words sound brilliant and encouraged my sense of humor about this craft I love so much. You are all truly amazing at what you do and how you do it.

Publisher's Acknowledgments

We're proud of this book; please send us your comments at http://dummies.custhelp.com. For other comments, please contact our Customer Care Department within the U.S. at 877-762-2974, outside the U.S. at 317-572-3993, or fax 317-572-4002.

Some of the people who helped bring this book to market include the following:

Acquisitions, Editorial, and Media Development

Project Editor: Elizabeth Rea

Acquisitions Editor: Michael Lewis

Copy Editor: Caitlin Copple

Assistant Editor: Erin Calligan Mooney

Senior Editorial Assistant: David Lutton

Technical Editor: Diane E. Burns

Editorial Manager: Michelle Hacker

Editorial Assistants: Jennette ElNaggar, Rachelle Amick

Art Coordinator: Alicia B. South

Cover Photos: ©iStockphoto.com/YinYang

Cartoons: Rich Tennant (www.the5thwave.com)

Composition Services

Project Coordinator: Patrick Redmond

Layout and Graphics: Timothy C. Detrick, Kelly Kijovsky

Illustrations: Lisa Reed

Photography: Matt Bowen, DIYStyle, Tom Reed/Kreber, Colleen Green/Kreber (styling)

Proofreader: Betty Kish

Indexer: Estalita Slivoskey

Publishing and Editorial for Consumer Dummies

Diane Graves Steele, Vice President and Publisher, Consumer Dummies

Kristin Ferguson-Wagstaffe, Product Development Director, Consumer Dummies

Ensley Eikenburg, Associate Publisher, Travel

Kelly Regan, Editorial Director, Travel

Publishing for Technology Dummies

Andy Cummings, Vice President and Publisher, Dummies Technology/General User

Composition Services

Debbie Stailey, Director of Composition Services

Contents at a Glance

Introduction 1

Part I: Getting Ready to Sew 5
Chapter 1: The World of Sewing 7
Chapter 2: Assembling Your Sewing Kit 17
Chapter 3: Selecting Fabric, Findings, and Interfacing 37
Chapter 4: Working with Patterns 55

Part II: Mastering Basic Sewing Skills 75
Chapter 5: Kicking Off Your Sewing Adventure 77
Chapter 6: Securing Sensational Seams 103
Chapter 7: Fast and Easy Hems by Hand and Machine 125

Part III: Fashion Sewing Fun-damentals 139
Chapter 8: Shaping Things Up 141
Chapter 9: Zippers, Buttons, and Other Closure Company 171
Chapter 10: Sleeves: The Long and the Short of It 197
Chapter 11: Pockets Full of Ideas 215

Part IV: Sewing for Your Home 225
Chapter 12: Do-It-Yourself Decorating: Home Décor Sewing 227
Chapter 13: Quick-Change Table Toppers 247
Chapter 14: Praiseworthy Pillows 257
Chapter 15: Adding Wow to Your Windows 273
Chapter 16: Giving Your Bed a Makeover 289

Part V: Making Alterations and Quick Fixes for a Sustainable Wardrobe 303
Chapter 17: When Clothes Are Too Short, Too Long, Too Tight, or Too Loose 305
Chapter 18: Making Repairs on the Run 321
Chapter 19: Eco Fashion: Giving Existing Garments New Life 331

Part VI: The Part of Tens 345
Chapter 20: Ten Tips for Mixing Prints 347
Chapter 21: Ten Rookie Sewing Mistakes to Avoid 351
Chapter 22: Ten Important Sewing Fundamentals 355

Appendix: Sewing Resources 361

Index 367

Table of Contents

Introduction 1

About This Book 1
Conventions Used in This Book 2
Foolish Assumptions 2
How This Book Is Organized 2
    Part I: Getting Ready to Sew 2
    Part II: Mastering Basic Sewing Skills 3
    Part III: Fashion Sewing Fun-damentals 3
    Part IV: Sewing for Your Home 3
    Part V: Making Alterations and Quick Fixes
      for a Sustainable Wardrobe 3
    Part VI: The Part of Tens 3
Icons Used in This Book 4
Where to Go from Here 4

Part 1: Getting Ready to Sew 5

Chapter 1: The World of Sewing 7
Figuring Out What Comes First: The Idea or the Tools? 8
    The pleasure of using good tools 8
    Understanding fabrics and fibers 9
    Getting the sewing notion 10
    Pondering the pattern 10
Sizing Up the Sewing Process 11
    Preshrinking fabric 11
    Finding the right pattern pieces 12
    Laying out the pattern on the fabric 12
    Pinning and cutting 12
    Marking 12
    Interfacing 12
    Pressing for the best shape 13
Moving On to the Needle and Thread 13
    Finishing the edges first 13
    Shaping 13
    Seaming 14
    Closing 14
    Hemming 14
Adding Fashion Detail with Sleeves and Pockets 15
Sewing for the Home Is Where the Saving Is 15
Doing Your Part for the Planet with a Sustainable Wardrobe 16

Chapter 2: Assembling Your Sewing Kit 17

Making Sure Your Sewing Measures Up 18
Cutting Up (Without Cracking Up) 20
Making Your Mark 22
Pinning Down Your Projects 23
Getting to the Point with the Right Needles, Thimbles, and
    Seam Rippers 23
    Selecting needles for hand sewing... 23
    Selecting needles for sewing machines...................................... 24
    Fortify your fingertips with thimbles 24
    As ye sew, so shall ye rip 25
Selecting Thread for Your Project.. 25
Pressing Issues... 26
Real Machines: Sewing Machines and Sergers 28
    Working with a sewing machine 29
    Finding your way around a serger... 35

Chapter 3: Selecting Fabric, Findings, and Interfacing 37

Choosing the Right Fabric for Your Project................................... 37
    Figuring out fiber... 38
    Getting to know common fabric types 39
    Taking fabric nap into consideration 43
    Considering fabric width and yardage needed 45
    Reading labels and bolt ends 45
Getting Notions about Findings 46
    Bias tape basics... 46
    Bonkers for braid 47
    Getting elastic... 47
    Loving lace 48
    Piping up for piping and cording 49
    Running with ribbons 50
    Refreshing with rickrack and twill tape 50
    Getting the lowdown on drapery headers 51
    Adding zip with zippers 51
Investigating Interfacing 52
Preshrinking Your Fabric 53

Chapter 4: Working with Patterns 55

Shopping for Patterns 55
Sizing Things Up for Fashion Sewing 56
Deciphering the Pattern and Its Parts... 58
    Checking out the front of the pattern envelope............................ 59
    Reading the back of the pattern envelope.................................. 59
    It's what's inside that counts 60
    Decoding the pattern pieces 60

Laying Out the Pattern...63
   Getting to know your fabric................................63
   Preparing the fabric...64
   Knowing right from wrong.................................64
   Placing the pattern pieces on-grain.....................64
   Laying out plaids, stripes, and one-way designs ...66
Pinning and Cutting Out the Pieces.........................70
Making Your Mark...71
   Marking what matters..71
   Using the right tool at the right time...................72

Part II: Mastering Basic Sewing Skills 75

Chapter 5: Kicking Off Your Sewing Adventure 77

Threading the Needle..77
   Hand needles..78
   Machine needles 79
Tying a Sewing Knot...80
Choosing and Using the Right Hand Stitches.............82
   The securing stitch..83
   The hand-basting stitch 83
   The running stitch 84
   The even backstitch 84
   The blind hemming stitch...................................85
   The slant hemming or whip stitch........................85
   The hemming slipstitch......................................86
   The even slipstitch..86
Working with Machine Stitches..................................87
   Examining the basic machine stitches..................87
   Selecting a stitch type.......................................89
   Choosing the length of the stitch........................89
   Setting the stitch width......................................90
   Stitching in the ditch...90
   Topstitching 91
Starting and Stopping..92
   . . . with your sewing machine............................92
   . . . with your serger..93
Basting Projects for a Better Fit...............................94
Pressing Matters...96
   Why press and iron as you sew?.........................96
   When and where to press 96
   Pressing napped fabrics.....................................97
Repurposed Shirt Pillow...98

Chapter 6: Securing Sensational Seams 103
   Finishing the Edges First..103
      Pinking your edges 104
      Using your sewing machine or serger.........................104
   Securing Your Seams 105
      Backstitching or not 106
      Tying off threads 106
   Fleece Throw with Colorful Fringe 107
   Seaming Fabrics 111
      Sewing straight seams.......................................111
      Turning corners 113
      Sewing ¼-inch seams..114
      Serging ¼-inch seams 115
   Ripping into Seam Mistakes 116
   Shaping Up the Seams..118
      Starting by stitching the seam on your sewing machine.....118
      Clipping the curve with your scissors 122

Chapter 7: Fast and Easy Hems by Hand and Machine 125
   Marking the Hem's Placement 126
      If you're the hem-ee 126
      If you're the hemmer 126
   Deciding on the Hem Allowance 127
   Finishing the Raw Edges of the Hem 128
      Using a straight stitch 128
      Using a three-step zigzag or overlock stitch 130
      Using a serger 130
   Securing the Hem...131
      No-sew hemming..132
      Pinning up the hem for hand or machine hemming.........133
      Hand blind hemming 133
      Machine blind hemming 134
   Sewing Tapered Hems..135
   Hemming Knits with Twin Needles 136

Part III: Fashion Sewing Fun-damentals.....................**139**

Chapter 8: Shaping Things Up 141
   Darting Around 141
      Sewing the straight dart.....................................142
      Sewing the contour dart.....................................144
      Finishing the dart..145

Gathering Fabric from One Piece into Another 145
    Gathering with two threads..146
    Gathering over a cord 147
Ruffled Apron 148
    Cutting out the apron parts..149
    Finishing the apron side seams......................................150
    Gathering and attaching the ruffle strip 151
    Tying up the apron strings 152
Completing Pleats..154
    Defining the types of pleats 154
    Making a pleat 155
Adding Stretch and Comfort with Elastic...156
    Inserting elastic in a casing 157
    Attaching elastic on an edge 160
Cuffed Pajama Pants..163
    Laying and cutting out your pj's....................................164
    Sewing your pj's together 166
    Sewing elastic at the waist 167
    Cuffing each leg...168

Chapter 9: Zippers, Buttons, and Other Closure Company **171**
Welcoming Easy Ways to Put in Zippers 171
    Putting in a centered zipper...172
    Putting in an invisible zipper.......................................176
Mastering Buttonhole Basics 180
    Sizing buttonholes 181
    Marking buttonholes 182
    Sewing beautiful buttonholes 183
    Cutting open buttonholes 183
    Figuring out button placement......................................185
    Attaching buttons 186
Checking Out Other Fasteners...191
Fold-Over Clutch with Button Closure...192
    Choosing the materials 193
    Sewing the clutch...194

Chapter 10: Sleeves: The Long and the Short of It **197**
Finishing Sleeveless Armholes...197
    Facing sleeveless armholes 198
    Binding sleeveless armholes 201
Rarin' to Sew Raglan Sleeves 203
Taking On Set-In Sleeves..206
    Using easestitch-plus to prepare traditional set-in sleeves 207
    Setting sleeves in flat..209
    Setting sleeves in the round 210
Protective Laptop Sleeve..212

Chapter 11: Pockets Full of Ideas 215

Putting Together Patch Pockets 215
   Making unlined patch pockets with square corners 216
   Making unlined patch pockets with curved corners 218
   Attaching patch pockets 221
Using Your Own Pocket Patterns 222
Coordinating Pocket-Collage Shirt 224

Part IV: Sewing for Your Home 225

Chapter 12: Do-It-Yourself Decorating: Home Décor Sewing 227

Overcoming Décoraphobia 227
   Understanding color 228
   Unmasking your home's complexion 228
   Determining your color odds 229
Homing In on Home Décor Fabric 230
Tackling Trim 231
   Braving braid basics 231
   Conquering cord 232
   Figuring out fringe 233
   Dealing with decorator trims 234
Attaching Piping, Cording, and Fringe 235
   Making your own piping 236
   Cutting bias strips for covering cable cord 237
   Sewing on piping and fringe 240
   Attaching and joining cord-edge trim 244
Reversible Table Runner 245

Chapter 13: Quick-Change Table Toppers 247

Selecting Fabric for Table Toppers 247
Making Easy Napkins 248
   Figuring out fabric yardage 248
   Sewing basic table napkins 249
   Serging napkins with narrow rolled edges 251
Party-Ready Lapkins 253
Hip to Be Square Tablecloth 255

Chapter 14: Praiseworthy Pillows. 257

Selecting Materials for Pillows 257
A Basic Cover Fit for a Pillow Form 258
   Measuring your pillow form and cutting the pillow
     front and back 258
   Sewing the seams 259
   Wrapping the corners 260
   Stitching the closure 261

The Easiest Reversible Pillow Cover Ever.............................262
15-Minute Flanged Pillow Cover 264
Plush Pet Bed 265
    Making the bolster...266
    Creating the fleece pillow cover 267
    Putting the bed together...269
Box-Edged Pillow 270

Chapter 15: Adding Wow to Your Windows 273
The Wide World of Window Treatments 273
    Dealing with draperies and curtains 274
    Exploring the anatomy of windows and rods...................276
Determining Window Treatment Dimensions........................278
    Measuring the finished width and length 279
    Calculating cut fabric length and width...........................279
Custom Draperies...282
    Determining how much fabric you need...........................283
    Putting the drapery together..284
    Heading off rips with the drapery header 286

Chapter 16: Giving Your Bed a Makeover 289
Saving Money by Crafting a Bedding Set 289
Pleated Bed Skirt 290
    Measuring the box spring..291
    Buying your fabric 292
    Cutting the fabric 292
    Double hemming the skirt and pleats 294
    Attaching the skirt and pleats to the base fabric 296
    Positioning the bed skirt on the box spring....................297
Custom Duvet Cover 298
    Cutting out the front of the duvet cover 299
    Constructing the back of the duvet cover 299
    Putting everything together 300

Part V: Making Alterations and Quick Fixes for a Sustainable Wardrobe 303

Chapter 17: When Clothes Are Too Short, Too Long, Too Tight, or Too Loose 305
When It's Too Short...305
    Cutting off pant legs and re-hemming them 306
    Letting down and facing the hem 306
    Adding ribbing into an opening 308

When It's Too Long 310
    Moving the button on a sleeve cuff 310
    Removing the cuff to shorten the sleeve 311
    Shortening jeans 313
When It's Too Tight 315
    Moving the buttons over on a jacket 315
    Adding room to the waistband 315
When It's Too Loose 317
Crossover Belt 318

Chapter 18: Making Repairs on the Run......................321

Repairing a Split Seam 321
    Repairing a seam on woven fabrics 321
    Repairing a seam on knit fabrics 322
Patching Holes and Rips 323
    Covering holes with patches 323
    Patching with appliqués 325
Mending Tears in Fabric 326
Replacing a Fly-Front Zipper 327

Chapter 19: Eco Fashion: Giving Existing Garments New Life......331

Felted Wool Hat 332
    Sourcing and preparing the wool 332
    Felting the wool 333
    Laying out and cutting the hat pieces 333
    Assembling the hat 335
(Almost) Instant Party Dress 339
    Finding the perfect bra and fabric 339
    Cutting out the skirt and straps 340
    Making the skirt 340
    Sewing the straps 343
    Hemming the dress 344

Part VI: The Part of Tens 345

Chapter 20: Ten Tips for Mixing Prints.......................347

Stick with One Base 347
Run a Background Check 347
Go Solid and Save Money 348
Mix 'n' Match Manufacturers 348
Stare Down Your Prints 348
Weigh the Scales 348
Try Before You Buy 349

Rely on a Collection...349
Buy More, Use Less 350
Consult a Pro..350

Chapter 21: Ten Rookie Sewing Mistakes to Avoid.............351

Attempting a Project Beyond Your Skill Level.....................351
Choosing Difficult Fabrics to Work With 352
Choosing an Unflattering Style....................................352
Using the Wrong Fabric for the Pattern...........................352
Laying Out the Fabric Incorrectly 353
Neglecting to Use Interfacing 353
Failing to Press as You Sew 353
Using an Old, Beat-Up Sewing Machine 353
Neglecting to Use a New Needle on Every Project 354
Refusing to Cut Yourself Some Slack 354

Chapter 22: Ten Important Sewing Fundamentals 355

Buy the Best Fabric You Can Afford................................355
Understand Your Fabric Terminology 356
Know the Difference between Right and Wrong.......................356
Put Your Foot Down before Sewing 357
Stop and Start Sewing the Right Way...............................357
Righty, Tighty; Lefty, Loosey 358
Test-Stitch First...358
Sew from the Bottom Up and from the Center Out....................359
Press Seams Together and then Open or to One Side.................359
Clip with the Tips of Your Scissors...............................360

Appendix: Sewing Resources...................................... *361*

Sewing Organizations..361
Sewing Publications 361
Sewing Community Web Sites..362
Sewing Machine Manufacturers......................................362
Pattern Companies 363
National Fabric Stores..363
Regional Fabric Stores 364
Notion Companies 365
Fabric and Notion Mail-Order Companies............................366
Thread Manufacturers 366

Index *367*

Introduction

· ·

I love to sew. Period. First I get the immediate gratification of completing a project using beautiful fabrics and great timesaving tools. Then I can bask in the personal recognition — I get to admire my work and hear praise from my family and friends. On top of that, I save money sewing because I can make things (and make them right) instead of purchase them (and pay to have them altered, if necessary). Wow, what a hobby!

I'm betting that after you have a couple of projects under your belt you'll love to sew as much as I do.

About This Book

Sewing For Dummies, 3rd Edition, is a book for both absolute beginners and experienced sewers. If you're a stone-cold beginner, you may appreciate that I explain everything necessary to sew beginning-level projects and I don't assume that you've ever even picked up a needle and thread before. If you're not a complete stranger to needle and thread (or sewing machine and pedal), *Sewing For Dummies,* 3rd Edition, still has something to offer — I give you tips and tricks that it took me years to pick up. All sewers can enjoy the projects in this book, no matter what their level of experience.

With the "greening" of the world on everyone's mind these days, I've taken a new approach to the projects in this edition. Many of the projects start with a used ready-to-wear garment that, with a little sewing sleight of hand, gets a refreshed new life. The rest of the projects have been redesigned and modernized to reflect the latest fashion trends and our more streamlined, uncluttered lives. The most significant improvement to the edition is the addition of over 100 new instructive illustrations. A picture says a thousand words, so the clearly written, no-nonsense instructions *For Dummies* books are famous for are enhanced with exceptional illustrations to ensure your success. As always, this all-new edition includes my favorite sewing techniques and the innovative shortcuts learned over my career. Remember, I've made every sewing mistake known to man (or woman), so you don't have to!

Conventions Used in This Book

As you sew, you're going to rely heavily on the tools in your sewing survival kit, which I describe in Chapter 2. Keep it handy and well stocked. You need it for just about every project listed in this book, and I wrote this book assuming that you have and use these tools.

You also see instructions throughout the book that can be completed by using a sewing machine or a serger. A *serger* is a specialized machine that saves a lot of sewing time; it sews the seam, overcasts the edge, and then cuts off the excess fabric from a seam allowance — all at the same time. I think of a serger like the microwave oven of sewing — you don't usually make an entire project on a serger, but it sure speeds up the process.

Foolish Assumptions

As I wrote this book, I made some assumptions about you and your needs:

- ✔ You don't yet know how to sew or are looking for a refresher course.
- ✔ You want to master the fundamentals of sewing.
- ✔ You're looking for tips and tricks to make your sewing projects easier and more fun.
- ✔ You want to start sewing as soon as possible.

If this sounds like you, you've come to the right book!

How This Book Is Organized

I organized this book into six parts so it's easy for you to find exactly the information you need.

Part 1: Getting Ready to Sew

In this part I run through the tools you need for sewing and tell you how to work with them, including your sewing machine, fabric, thread, needles, pins, iron, and patterns.

Part II: Mastering Basic Sewing Skills

Read the chapters in this part to find out how to do some of the more fundamental tasks involved in sewing, including threading a needle, tying a knot, sewing a seam, and hemming.

Part III: Fashion Sewing Fun-damentals

When you sew clothing, you usually start out with a pattern and a set of instructions for putting the project together. For a beginner, these pattern instructions can sometimes be a little intimidating; the instructions may tell you to do something (like sew a dart or apply a zipper) that you don't know how to do. The chapters in this part help you decipher techniques like putting in buttons and zippers, adding sleeves, and sewing pockets that are essential to successful fashion sewing.

Part IV: Sewing for Your Home

Sewing your own home fashions means that you get exactly what you want and save money — a winning combination! This part of the book lets you turn a little sewing knowledge into untold savings for your home. I show you how to sew pillows, a duvet cover, a bed skirt, draperies, napkins, a table runner, tablecloths, and more. Using the chapters in this part, you can quickly and inexpensively create coordinated looks for almost every room in your home.

Part V: Making Alterations and Quick Fixes for a Sustainable Wardrobe

Are you suffering from the *terrible toos* — clothes that are too tight, too loose, too long, or too short? This part is a lifesaver when you need creative solutions to fix what ails your clothing and get a little more wear from them before sending them off to the landfill. I also show you how to do some basic repairs on holes, rips, and other mishaps.

Part VI: The Part of Tens

In this part I share tips for avoiding common mistakes when you start sewing. I include the all-important guidelines for sewing smarter and faster along with tips for mixing fabrics without creating fashion faux pas or home décor havoc. I also include an appendix of resources and popular Web sites to help you find the materials you need.

Icons Used in This Book

Throughout this book I guide you toward important points by using the following icons:

Some sewing tools are essential to sewing, and others aren't essential but are still nice to have as you sew. Try out the tools mentioned next to this icon — you may find one that helps you quite a bit with the sort of projects you like to do.

Next to this icon you find information that you should keep in the back of your mind as you sew. These points are key to creative and efficient sewing.

The information next to this icon tells you how to do something in the quickest and best way possible.

Make sure to read the text next to this icon. It can save you a lot of blood, sweat, and tears.

Where to Go from Here

If you're new to sewing, I suggest that you start by reading the chapters in Parts I and II. You can find some fundamental information on sewing in those parts. After that, you can skip around from chapter to chapter in the book, reading about the types of sewing and the projects that interest you.

I wrote this book to be your sewing companion. Instead of putting it on the bookshelf for future reference after you finish reading it and making the projects, use it actively each time you sew — whether at home or in one of the many sewing classes available at your local sewing machine dealer or fabric store. Keep it handy so that when pattern guide sheet instructions direct you to do something, you can check out this book to find the fastest, most efficient way to accomplish the task.

I've spent my professional lifetime amassing these sewing methods (and more), and they fuel my love affair with the craft every time I sit in front of the machine. My fervent hope is that after spending a little time with this book, a beautiful piece of fabric, and your beloved sewing machine, your own love affair with sewing will blossom. Enjoy!

Part I
Getting Ready to Sew

The 5th Wave   By Rich Tennant

"It's a beginner's sewing kit I put together for you. There's scissors, needles, bandaids, gauze, antiseptic..."

In this part . . .

To end up with a successful sewing project, you need to start out with good materials. These materials include your sewing machine, needles, thread, fabric, and pattern, among other things. I tell you about the very best tools for your sewing projects in this part. In addition, I tell you how to work with those tools after you have them, including how to navigate a sewing machine and how to lay out a pattern.

Chapter 1

The World of Sewing

In This Chapter

▶ Discovering why you should sew

▶ Taking a look at the sewing process, seaming, and adding details

▶ Understanding how sewing can save money and resources

*W*hy sew? Simply put, it's fun. You also get the gratification of making something useful and beautiful and the personal recognition from friends and family who are in awe of your raw, natural talent. Not to mention that what you learn about fabrics, fibers, and fashion helps you in other areas of your life.

You may think of sewing as a hobby in which you make clothes. But as you move from place to place in your busy life, start paying attention to how much fabric is used everywhere. You can sew Halloween costumes, teddy bears, prom dresses, and purses. Think of the fashions in home décor. A tablescape isn't complete without some great-looking linens — that you can make, of course. You can update your house by making a wardrobe of pillows with a set of covers for every season or by sewing a new duvet cover. Need a gift? Make a throw or fill a basket with a set of napkins. It's all possible when you sew. My friend and editor, Robbie Fanning, called this collection of possibilities "the world of sewing."

Because the topic of sewing is so extensive and I have only so many pages in this book, I thoughtfully organized the world of sewing for you. I first walk you through the sewing process used in making clothing and then move on to ways to sew for your home and repair and remake existing clothing for a more sustainable wardrobe. My hope is that after you get to know more about this creative endeavor and have some success with the projects in this book, you'll spread your wings and investigate the larger world of sewing.

Figuring Out What Comes First: The Idea or the Tools?

My family was on a strict budget when I was growing up, so I'd read my *Seventeen* magazine and head off to the mall to see what all the kids were wearing. After seeing just what I wanted and knowing it was too expensive, I'd pore over the pattern catalogs for the latest junior fashions that I could "knock off."

Next stop — the fabric store. There I combed though the bolts for just the right fabric, color, and texture, and went on to the notions wall to find the right-sized buttons. Little did I know that I was shaping the skills I now use to create something trendy for myself, my family members, and my home.

So to answer the question of whether the idea or the tools come first, for me the idea or inspiration is first, and then the adventure of hunting for just the right project pattern and fabric starts me on my journey. After I find everything, I take it all home and put it together with tools — but not just any tools; tools that are a pleasure to use. Read on to understand what I mean.

The pleasure of using good tools

You can cook a five-course gourmet meal for eight by using nasty old pots and pans and cooking over an open fire, but it's not a lot of fun. The same is true for sewing — you can make a project by sewing everything together with a hand needle and thread, but it takes a lot of time and patience and you may not like the results. For me, the joy of sewing is having quality tools at my fingertips. No scurrying around the house to find a pair of shears that haven't been used in my husband's workshop or pins that have been pulled off packaged dress shirts. Sure, good tools are an investment, but if you're serious about learning to sew, nothing gets you closer to success than the pleasure of using a quality tool that works perfectly every time you use it. Not sure if you'll like sewing but still want to try it? Take a sewing class at your local fabric store or sewing machine dealer where you can use great tools and quality equipment.

I spend some time in Chapter 2 sharing my favorite tools with you, so check it out. Besides the fabric and pattern, here's what will make your sewing experience a real pleasure:

- **Measuring tools for small and large areas of a project.** I love my 6-inch adjustable sewing gauge, my flexible vinyl tape measure, and the see-through O'Lipfa ruler with ¼-inch increments.

- **Cutting tools for cutting out your project.** I use 8-inch bent-handle dressmaking shears, 5-inch scissors for trimming smaller areas, and embroidery scissors for clipping and ripping out unwanted stitches. For long straight cutting, the pizza cutter–type rotary cutter is the best.

✔ **Marking tools to show you how to turn a flat, shapeless piece of fabric into something useful.** You need a marking tool for dark-colored fabrics and one for light-colored fabrics. My favorites are disappearing dressmaker's chalk that washes out with water and air-soluble markers.

✔ **Pinning tools both for pinning and to hold pins.** My favorite pins for 90 percent of the sewing I do are 1¼-inch glass-head pins. To keep my pins from ending up all over the place, I use three magnetic pin catchers (one for the ironing board, one on the cutting table, and one next to my sewing machine). I also like a wrist pin cushion with a felt cushion so my pins are portable.

✔ **New hand and machine needles.** After some use, needles wear out and need to be discarded. As far as hand needles go, specialty needles are available for just about every hand-sewing task. I most often use self-threading needles for basic hand sewing and easy repairs — I used these even before I needed reading glasses because the thread just clips into place, no squinting and poking thread ends through a microscopic eye required.

✔ **Thread to hold everything together.** Be sure not to skimp on the thread — when you see three spools for $1, run (away from the store, not to it!). The quality of that thread isn't worth the spool its wound on. Read more about choosing quality thread in Chapter 2.

✔ **A good sewing machine to enjoy the sewing experience.** I said you need a good one, not an expensive one — and it doesn't have to be new. Just buy it from a reputable sewing machine dealer that can offer you reliable service and lessons if you need them.

✔ **A serger —** *if* **you discover that you like to sew and want to take your newfound skill to a new level.** If you're new to sewing, you don't need a serger, but after you have some experience, it makes the sewing process faster and more streamlined (like the microwave oven does for cooking).

Understanding fabrics and fibers

Among other perks of learning to sew, one cool thing is that you gain more knowledge about fabrics, fibers, how they respond to washing (or not), wearing, and pressing, and ultimately this knowledge makes you a savvier shopper of ready-to-wear garments. And because your time and effort is worth something, spend your sewing time wisely by buying the best fabric you can afford and the best fiber for the project you're making. So what's the difference between *fiber* and *fabric?*

Fabrics are woven or knitted yarns, which are created by twisting fibers together. Whether the fabric is all wool or a cotton-polyester blend, each fiber has its unique advantages and disadvantages, which makes one better than others for a particular project. (See more specific information about the most common types of fibers and fabrics in Chapter 3.)

If you aren't sure about your fabric choice, the sales associate at your local fabric store is a great resource for locating just the right fabric for the project. Most have knowledge it would take you years to learn, so don't be shy. Ask for help, tell her what you want to make, and ask for her best advice. This can save you time and guide you on your way to success.

Getting the sewing notion

In most fabric stores you find a notions wall that's full of specialty tools and sewing stuff that can be packaged and hung up. Notions range from pins, needles, scissors, shears, and measuring tools, to buttons, bra hooks, collar stays, and iron-on knee patches. The list of notions needed for a particular project is listed on the back of your pattern envelope, so when in doubt, find what you need on the notions wall. Don't be afraid to ask for help — what you need may be hidden in plain sight.

Pondering the pattern

Fabric stores have catalogs of patterns that you can browse through, but you only need to do a quick Internet search for "sewing patterns" and the world of sewing is at your fingertips. Looking for a particular project? Type in the project you want to make then "sewing pattern" after it to find even more choices. The Internet brings pattern catalogs home and puts the right project just a keystroke away. It also makes investigating independent pattern designers easy.

Choose a pattern designed for your skill set. If a pattern says it's easy, the instruction writers often still assume you have some knowledge of sewing, so if you're a true beginner, choose patterns for beginners. If you don't, you may become discouraged and never sew again! Simplicity Pattern Company helps beginners find appropriate patterns with their line of "Sewing For Dummies" patterns. Check it out at www.simplicity.com.

When the pattern has been chosen, check out the front and back of the envelope for very important information: what fabric works best to achieve the results pictured on the front of the envelope, how much fabric to buy for the sized garment you're making, what you need in the way of trims and notions (see above), and the front and back views shown in easy-to-read line drawings.

Inside the envelope you find an instruction sheet commonly referred to as the *pattern guide sheet*. The pattern guide sheet shows you which pattern pieces you need to use for a specific version of the pattern (several versions or views may be packaged in one pattern), shows you how to lay out the pattern pieces on the fabric, and gives you step-by-step instructions showing you how to put the project together. Even though I've been sewing for years, I still refer to my pattern guide sheet to be sure that I haven't forgotten to do something. You can read more about working with patterns in Chapter 4.

Use this book to supplement the pattern guide sheet instructions. Many times pattern instruction writers assume you know how to make a dart or sew in a zipper and may leave out information essential for your success. If you don't understand what the instructions tell you, look up how I recommend you complete a particular technique. I'm confident that trying it my way will get 'er done and that you'll pick up the skills and the lingo as you work though the project. So where to begin? In the following section I break it down and give you a general idea of where you're headed — think of this as your sewing GPS at the mile-high view.

Sizing Up the Sewing Process

Like any new endeavor, sewing has its very own vocabulary, skill set, and process. After you decide on a project, select your pattern and fabric, and collect the notions and tools you need, the sewing process follows the basic steps outlined in this section to complete a project.

As you look over the rest of this chapter, it may occur to you that a lot happens before you start actually sewing things together. Have you noticed that it takes a long time for road crews to prepare to lay a new road and then almost overnight it's in and you're cruising smoothly along your merry way? That's how it is with sewing. When you get your fabric and pattern; lay out, pin down, cut, and mark your pattern pieces; fuse on the interfacing; and finish the fabric edges; you're two-thirds of the way finished. But I'm ahead of myself. Here's a quick breakdown of the sewing process and the creative journey you're about to take.

Preshrinking fabric

After getting home from fabric shopping, preshrink your washable fabrics so the finished project won't shrink any more after it's washed. (You can find the whys and hows of preshrinking in Chapter 3.)

If life gets in the way and you have to set your project aside temporarily, still preshrink the fabric when you first bring it home. That way you don't have to wonder if the fabric is "needle ready" when you are.

Finding the right pattern pieces

Most patterns have a couple of variations included. Each variation is called a *view* and requires specific pattern pieces. Check out the pattern guide sheet to see what pattern pieces are needed for the view you're making, then cut those pattern pieces apart from the large sheet of printed pattern paper and set them aside. Read more in-depth about this in Chapter 4.

Laying out the pattern on the fabric

The pattern guide sheet has a suggested pattern-piece layout for the width of the fabric you are using (see "Understating fabrics and fibers" above). This is the most important step because if you lay out and cut something crookedly or incorrectly, no amount of sewing, ironing, begging, or pleading will make the fabric behave the way you want it to. Learn the do's and don'ts in Chapter 4.

Pinning and cutting

When you have the pattern pieces arranged on the fabric, pin each pattern piece to the fabric ready for cutting. As you cut out each pattern piece, notice if there are special markings such as a dart or a larger than normal dot. If so, place the cut pieces that need to be marked in one stack and those that don't in another. Read on to learn why.

Marking

Even though you may not know what the random pattern markings mean, as you proceed through the project the guide sheet instructions will tell you. When in doubt, transfer the mark from the pattern paper to the fabric. Chapter 4 gives you several methods to do this. If you don't, you'll waste a bunch of time sifting through pattern paper you've removed from the fabric to find and mark something you should have done in the first place. (Trust me here — I make the mistakes so you don't have to.)

Interfacing

After cutting out the pattern pieces and marking them, your guide sheet may tell you to cut interfacing for several of the pattern pieces. Some patterns even give you separate paper pattern pieces for the interfacing. So what is it and why should you care?

Certain places on a project need a little extra stability — like a collar, sleeve cuff, waistband, or down the front of a shirt or jacket with buttons and buttonholes. If what you're wearing has a waistband, take a look at the two separate pieces of fabric creating the outside and inside of the band. Inside and between these two layers of fabric is a third piece of fabric called *interfacing* that keeps your waistband from stretching out of shape and that keeps the hooks and eyes, buttons, or snaps from pulling off the fabric. So even though this may seem like an unnecessary step and extra expense, interfacing gives your project a professional finish and provides excellent wear. Read more about interfacings and how to use them in Chapter 3.

Pressing for the best shape

One my tailoring professors at the New York Fashion Institute of Technology said, "as you sew, have a love affair with your iron." By that time I had been sewing for 14 years and didn't give my iron much thought, but she was right. The best way to get a very professional-looking project is to press every seam and press it well. Learn more about this pressing subject in Chapter 5.

Moving On to the Needle and Thread

Pieces of fabric are joined by using a needle and thread to stitch them together in a way that fits a form. Stitches are done by hand or machine, and some stitches work better than others for a specific job. See Chapter 5 for the breakdown of the most common hand and machine stitches.

Finishing the edges first

If you use a fabric that ravels, you need to treat the edges of the fabric in some way to stop it from raveling. This treatment is called *finishing* the edges and is done before the seams are sewn. You can finish the edges either with pinking shears, for that delightful zigzag cut that's impervious to unraveling, or by sewing the edges with a machine or serger. Discover what works best for your project in Chapter 6.

Shaping

Shaping a piece of fabric to fit a form is done by nipping in a little here or letting out a little fabric there. So before you sew most pattern pieces together, you need to shape them with a dart, gathers, or tucks so they conform to the particular body part they cover.

To both nip in and let out at the same time, you sew a *dart* — a little triangle-shaped wedge of fabric that's wide at one end and is stitched to a point at the other end. After the dart is pressed it turns that flat, lifeless piece of fabric into something that conforms to the shape of your waist, bust, knee, or elbow so the fabric can move with you and be comfortable.

Need a nip here and a lot more fullness there? Then sew a tuck — it has a similar purpose as a dart except that the fabric is taken in, stitched in a straight line, and is open (rather than coming to a point) on one or both ends. Adding gathers and elastic are other ways of putting shape where you want it. Learn all about these shape-shifting techniques in Chapter 8.

Seaming

The place where two pieces of fabric come together is called a *seam*. Seams can be straight, curved, or turn a corner. After seams are sewn they're pressed and ironed into submission so that flat piece of fabric can be transformed into something that follows the contours of your body or a piece of furniture. What happens if you make a mistake? No worries. Unwanted stitches can be ripped out in several ways. You can find out more about seaming, pressing, and ripping in Chapter 6.

Closing

After your garment is made, you need a way to keep it on, and you typically accomplish this with a zipper or buttons and buttonholes. Besides being practical, both closure methods can be incorporated as design elements. There are some tricks to sewing them well, though, and pattern guide sheets rarely provide the instructions you need. Check out Chapter 9 for step-by-step guidance when installing zippers and to find out how sewing on a button can be a creative endeavor, too.

Hemming

Unless you want to pay someone every time you need to have a hem altered, learning how to hem is a life skill — like sewing on a button. You probably know what a hem is (just in case, it's the folded over and finished edge of a project), but did you know you can sew wide hems, narrow hems, cuffed hems, straight hems, curved hems, double hems, and blind hems? When you know how to hem and what hems look best on what projects, you're on your way to hemming success. Get the scoop on this life skill in Chapter 7.

Adding Fashion Detail with Sleeves and Pockets

Even though fashions change, the basic how-tos of sewing sleeves and pockets remain the same. Sleeves come in many flavors and often add the detail that makes the outfit. They can be short, long, raglan, set-in, faced, split, cuffed, tapered, batwing, or butterfly; gathered, puffed, tucked, cuffed, or padded. (Phew!) Armholes can be finished off with a decorative binding or faced with a matching fabric (read more about facings in Chapter 10). Stay tuned to find out what fashion will do to sleeves, but know this: When you learn the basics and feel comfortable with conventional sleeves, you have conquered the toughest part. When fashion changes, you'll be ready to tackle whatever trend comes a-knocking.

While pockets are far less fickle, they're a detail that can define a garment. Take a jeans back pocket, for example. Who knew derrières from every walk of life could don so many designs? Read more about theses little patches of inspiration in Chapter 11.

Sewing for the Home Is Where the Saving Is

If you're a fan of home-interior makeover TV shows, you can hardly tune into a show without seeing someone using a sewing machine. What I love about sewing for my home is that I get the look I want and for so much less than custom made. And the sewing goes fast because most projects involve cutting and sewing straight lines.

What's different about sewing for your home versus sewing clothing is that you need more room to spread out and cut the fabric. You also use a ½-inch seam allowance rather than a ⅝-inch seam allowance used in typical garment construction. Home décor fabrics are usually a little heavier and wider than apparel fabrics, and a whole set of trims and notions are specific to home décor projects.

If you're new to sewing projects for your home, try your hand at making the smaller projects for your table or throw pillows for your family room found in Chapters 12, 13, and 14. If new widow treatments or a bedroom makeover are on your to-do list, then Chapters 15 and 16 are instrumental in your decorating success.

Doing Your Part for the Planet with a Sustainable Wardrobe

My mom and grandma were always sewing. Besides making a lot of my clothes, both women fixed everyone else's clothes by hemming, rehemming, fixing split seams, replacing zippers, sewing on buttons, and adding embellishments. Adjusting and updating clothing was just a normal thing.

Fast forward to the '80s, '90s, and early 2000s; the economy was cooking and ready-to-wear clothing was inexpensive and easier to discard than repair. Thanks goodness that now we've come to our senses and see the value in repairing, recycling, and repurposing things. Chapters 17, 18, and 19 give you the thrill of saving ill-fitting or damaged garments from the trash. You can make something fit and look better and get the satisfaction of completing it in one short sitting. Though these chapters come late in the book, repair work may be some of the first sewing you do, and hopefully you'll discover right away that sewing is great fun. It's a creative outlet for creating something useful, beautiful, or practical. It's also a hobby you can enjoy for a lifetime, so welcome to the world of sewing. I'm glad you're in it with me.

Chapter 2

Assembling Your Sewing Kit

In This Chapter

▶ Finding out what tools you need for sewing and why you need them

▶ Taking a look at tools that are helpful but not necessary

▶ Determining the best pressing tools

▶ Getting to know your sewing machine and its parts

*L*ike most hobbies, successful sewing projects begin with a few good tools and a little know-how. Sure, you can find some of these tools around your household — those old scissors from the garage, the ruler from your desk drawer, pins scavenged from freshly opened dress shirts — but you'll have a better sewing experience by using the tools intended for the job.

In this chapter I list and explain the necessities — the tools I use just about every time I sew and that are essential for creating the projects in this book. I also give you some tips about additional tools that come in handy as your skills improve. Consider these tools part of your sewing survival kit.

Keep your sewing survival kit in a small fishing tackle box or use one of the many sewing or craft organizers available through your local fabric or craft store. Choose an organizer that has a handle and a secure latch so you can easily carry it without dumping stuff all over the place.

Use the following checklist when you round up the tools for your sewing survival kit. The items are pictured in Figure 2-1, and the rest of this chapter explains the items in more detail and offers additional suggestions of tools that are nice to have but not as necessary as the ones that follow.

❑ Tape measure

❑ Seam gauge

❑ Dressmaker's shears

❑ Trimming scissors

❏ Fabric markers for light and dark fabrics

❏ Glass-head pins and pincushion (wrist, magnetic, or both)

❏ Hand needles and thimbles

❏ Sewing machine needles

❏ Seam ripper

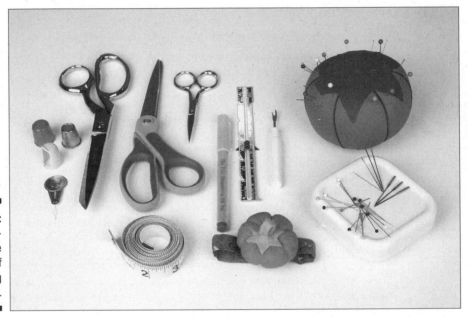

Figure 2-1:
The indispensable contents of a sewing survival kit.

Making Sure Your Sewing Measures Up

"Measure twice, cut once" isn't just an old adage; it's essential to your sewing success. I use the following measuring tools every time I sew. Each one has a specific purpose based on how and what you are measuring.

✔ **Tape measure:** You use a *tape measure* for taking your own measurements, checking measurements on a pattern, and other measuring tasks. (See Chapter 4 for more information on patterns.)

I recommend that you use a plastic-coated fabric tape measure. It doesn't stretch, so you always get accurate measurements. Most tapes are ⅝-inch wide, the width of a standard seam allowance (see Chapter 6 for more on seams), and 60 inches long, like the tape measure in Figure 2-2. Many tapes come with both metric and U.S. customary measurements and are two-toned so you notice when the tape is twisted.

When I'm laying out a pattern, I prefer the type of tape measure I can drape around my neck rather than one in a retractable case so that it's on hand whenever I need to check a measurement or see if the pattern is on-grain. (See Chapter 4 for more about laying out your pattern.)

⁵/₈" (1.5 cm)

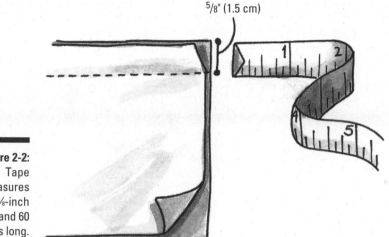

Figure 2-2:
Tape measures are ⅝-inch wide and 60 inches long.

✔ **Seam gauge:** A tape measure suffices for most measuring jobs, but for measuring small and narrow things, such as hems and buttonholes, use a *seam gauge*. This 6-inch ruler has an adjustable slide that moves up and down the length of the ruler, allowing you to check that hems or buttonholes are the desired size.

✔ **Ruler:** The straight edge and quarter-inch increments on rulers are helpful when you need to mark even strips of fabric (as in many home décor projects). I have two clear O'Lipfa rulers — one that's 24 inches long and 5 inches wide, and another that's 36 inches long and 4 inches wide. A ruler and a cutting mat (see the section "Cutting Up (Without Cracking Up)" to find out more) work together like a T-square — helpful when marking and cutting perfect 90-degree squares or rectangles and for cutting strips, plus the fabric is easier to cut when the ruler provides a guide for a rotary cutter to run along. Look for rulers with a lip edge, which will hug the mat so the ruler doesn't wiggle around. You can find a lot of clear rulers of varying length on the market, and you may find, like I do, that you want to use a ruler almost every time you sew.

Cutting Up (Without Cracking Up)

If I could have only two cutting tools, I'd use the following:

- ✔ **8-inch bent dressmaker's shears:** Shears are the best tool for cutting fabric. They have one straight and one bent-angle blade, a round thumb-hole, and an oblong finger hole for comfortable, accurate cutting. The bent-angle blade gives your index finger a place to rest when you have a long cutting job and allows you to cut without lifting the fabric off the table, ensuring a more accurate cut.

- ✔ **5-inch trimming scissors:** These scissors have straight blades and two round holes for your finger and thumb. They come in handy for trimming smaller areas on a project and for clipping threads.

When shopping for shears or scissors, make sure you test them on a variety of fabrics. Good ones cut cleanly all the way to the tips of the blades.

Some brands of scissors and shears are made of lightweight aluminum alloy. The lightweight models generally fit more comfortably in your hand, are usually a little cheaper than other models, and can be resharpened several times, though with some brands, the lighter-weight blades may not cut as easily through heavy fabrics or multiple fabric layers. Fiskars makes light-weight, good quality, ergonomically comfortable cutting tools.

Steel scissors and shears are heavier, which means they easily cut through heavier fabrics and more fabric layers. Being heavier though, they may not be as comfortable to use as their lighter-weight counterparts and are generally more expensive. Because each blade is made of one solid piece of steel, you can resharpen heavy scissors and shears more times than the lightweight variety, and they often stay sharper longer. A brand to look for is Gingher.

Regardless of the weight, scissors and shears with a screw joining the blades generally cut heavier fabrics and more layers than those that are riveted.

After you plunk down money for a good pair of scissors and shears, don't let the family get ahold of them and cut plastic, cardboard, wire, or anything you don't normally cut when sewing. These materials cause the blades to become rough and dull, and rough blades not only chew or snag your fabric but also wear out your hand when you try to use them.

I also often use a pair of 3-inch *embroidery scissors.* The pointed, thin blades are perfect for cutting out unwanted stitches and trimming laces, appliqués, and hard-to-reach places.

Keeping your shears and scissors sharp

Dull scissors can make cutting a real drag: You have to work twice as hard to use them, and the results aren't nearly as good. Keep your shears and scissors sharp so they're a pleasure to use. After all, cutting is a big part of sewing, and if it's a chore, you won't like to sew.

Most sewing machine dealers sharpen scissors and shears. In addition, many fabric stores have a scissors-sharpener who visits the store periodically. After the pro finishes sharpening your shears or scissors, check that they cut all the way to the point of the blades.

After you decide you like to sew, treat yourself to a *rotary cutter,* which looks like a pizza cutter, and a *cutting mat,* which protects the table and helps keep the rotary blade sharp. You use these tools, shown in Figure 2-3, without lifting the fabric off the cutting mat, so you can cut lines very accurately. Rotary cutters come in several sizes — I like the largest model because you can cut more, faster. But don't discard your shears; you need them for cutting intricate pattern pieces.

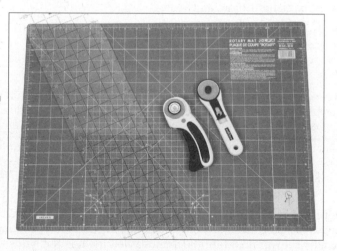

Figure 2-3:
Cut fabric fast and accurately with a rotary cutter, cutting mat, and ruler.

Cut edges can mean frayed edges, but you can put a stop to that with *seam sealant,* a liquid that dries soft and clear so that you don't see any residue on the fabric and it won't snag or scratch. It comes in a small, plastic bottle with a tip for easy aim. In addition to using sealant along cut edges of fabric, dot it on knots of thread to prevent them from coming out and dribble a bead at the cut edges of ribbons to prevent fraying.

Making Your Mark

When you sew, you must match up the pieces of your project precisely — otherwise you get the left sleeve in the right armhole and end up feeling like you're walking backwards. To help you match up your fabric pattern pieces exactly the right way, the pattern for a project includes *match points,* called notches and dots, which are printed on the pattern tissue paper (Chapter 4 has everything you need to know about patterns). You use fabric markers to transfer these match points to the fabric.

Fabric markers made especially for sewing make transferring match points from the pattern tissue to the fabric a quick and easy task. Use one of the following markers (some of which appear in Figure 2-1), depending on the kind of fabric you want to mark:

- **Disappearing dressmaker's chalk:** Excellent for marking dark fabrics, dressmaker's chalk disappears in about five days or when you wash or iron over the mark.

- **Wash-out pencil:** This pencil shows up well when marking dark fabrics and erases with a drop of cold water. It looks like a regular pencil with white, pink, or light blue lead.

- **Vanishing marker:** Best for marking light-colored fabrics, this felt-tipped marker usually has pink or purple ink that disappears in 12 to 24 hours, unless you live in a humid climate where marks can disappear in minutes.

- **Water-erasable marker:** This felt-tipped marker for light- to medium-colored fabrics has blue ink that disappears with water. This marker works better than the vanishing marker if you sew in a humid environment.

The ink in vanishing and water-erasable markers uses a chemical that may react to the dyes and chemicals in synthetic fabrics. Always test markers on a scrap of fabric to make sure that you can remove the mark and that it doesn't come back when you press the fabric.

- **Invisible or removable transparent tape:** These are useful but not essential marking tools. Invisible tape has a cloudy appearance that you can easily see on most fabrics. Removable tape has the same adhesive as sticky notes and doesn't pull off the *nap* (fuzz) from velvet, corduroy, or velour. I use ½-inch-width invisible or removable tape as a stitching template for sewing in a zipper (covered in Chapter 9), as a guide for straight stitching (I talk about stitches in Chapter 5), and for a lot of other little jobs. Hide it from your family, though, or it may disappear when you want it.

Pinning Down Your Projects

You need pins to sew. Period. You use them to pin the pattern to the fabric, pin the pieces of fabric together before sewing them, and for several other jobs. Because pins are such a constant companion when you sew, buy some that keep your fingers happy.

I recommend using long, fine, glass-head pins. The glass head fits comfortably in your fingers when you pin through multiple layers of fabric, and the extra length makes pinning more secure. Plus, if you accidentally press or iron over the glass heads, they don't melt like the plastic ones may.

You also need a place to keep your pins. Some pins come packaged in convenient plastic boxes that make great pin holders. But to save time, I wear a wrist pincushion (a pincushion attached to a strap that fastens snugly around your wrist) so that my pins stay with me wherever I go.

A magnetic pincushion, available in a wrist or tabletop model, is handy in your cutting area and at the ironing board. Besides pins, small scissors and a seam ripper also stick to the magnetized surface. A magnetic pincushion is wonderful for picking up pins and stray metal objects that fall on the floor.

Avoid getting a magnetic pincushion near computerized sewing machines. They aren't as likely these days to be affected by magnets as they were in the past, but you don't want to risk wiping out the machine's memory.

Getting to the Point with the Right Needles, Thimbles, and Seam Rippers

Needles come in hand and machine varieties, and you can find many shapes, sizes, and types within each variety. The needle you select depends on the fabric you use and the project you want to sew.

Generally, the finer the fabric you work with, the finer the needle, and the heavier the fabric, the heavier the needle.

Selecting needles for hand sewing

When selecting hand needles, a variety pack supplies you with what you need for most basic hand-sewing projects. Variety packs vary from brand to brand but generally have from five to ten needles of various lengths and thicknesses. Some even have different-sized eyes (the holes that the thread goes through to keep it attached to the needle).

I also like to use self-threading needles, which have two eyes. The top eye has an open notch in it with a one-way hook. The notch lets you snap the thread into the eye from the top while the hook prevents the thread from coming out of the needle. The second eye is used like a conventional needle so if you're in the middle of hand sewing and the self-threading feature breaks, you have a backup plan. The top of a self-threading needle can be a little uncomfortable if you aren't using a thimble, but even so, once I discovered self-threading needles I never went back. Look for the different types of hand needles in your local fabric store.

In a pinch, you can use any hand needle as long as the point can easily penetrate the fabric and the eye isn't so small that it shreds the thread.

Selecting needles for sewing machines

For machine needles, size #11 (in American sizing) or #12/80 (in European sizing) works well for general sewing on about 80 percent of today's fabrics.

To make sure that you have the right size needle for the fabric, read your sewing machine's operating manual or ask your local sewing machine dealer. Some needles offer different point types designed to handle different stitching techniques and fabric types. For most projects, though, a multipurpose or Universal point works beautifully. Buy a package or two of #11 American multipurpose or #12/80 Universal European sewing machine needles and you're all set.

When shopping for sewing machine needles, take the make and model number of your machine with you. Some models can use only their brand of needle without causing harm to the machine. When in doubt, ask your local sewing machine dealer what to buy.

During the course of a project, a sewing machine needle gets used and abused, and when the needle becomes bent, blunt, or burred (like the hooked end of a burr on a thistle), the needle skips stitches and can snag the fabric. Unlike hand needles, your machine needle needs to be replaced frequently. The best machine needle for any project is a new one, so start each project with a new needle.

Fortify your fingertips with thimbles

Fingers are fabulous tools, but they leave a little to be desired when it comes to pushing a needle through heavy thicknesses of fabric. Protect the soft pads of your fingers from potential pain with a thimble, which is kind of like a little hard hat for your finger.

Thimbles come in a variety of sizes, so choose a thimble that comfortably fits the middle finger on your dominant hand. Try on a variety of thimbles until you find one that's just right — then use it! You can save your fingers a lot of wear and tear.

As ye sew, so shall ye rip

If you sew, you must rip out the occasional stitch. When you make mistakes, you correct them by ripping out the stitches, or unsewing (see Chapter 6 for instructions).

Make ripping out stitches as pleasant as possible. Buy a sharp *seam ripper*, a little tool with a point that lifts the stitch off the fabric and cuts the thread with a blade (refer to the ripper in Figure 2-1).

I've put too many unwanted holes in a project with a dull ripper because I had to push too hard to cut a stitch and ended up tearing right past the stitches into the fabric. When your seam ripper gets dull, throw it away and buy another one. You can't resharpen them.

Selecting Thread for Your Project

All-purpose sewing thread is the type and weight of thread that works well for most fabrics. You can find several all-purpose brands at your local fabric store or sewing machine dealer.

Some all-purpose threads are a cotton-covered polyester; other all-purpose threads are 100-percent polyester or 100-percent cotton. Ask your sewing machine dealer what thread brand works best in your machine. After you select the appropriate thread, unwrap a little bit from the spool and look closely at it. Check that it has a smooth, even appearance. Take that unwrapped strand of thread and place it on your fabric. You want the thread color to be slightly darker than your fabric for a good match.

If you see five spools of thread for a dollar, run the other way. This "bargain" is promotional thread made with short fibers, which get lumpy and fuzzy very quickly. The lumps cause uneven thread tension, creating puckered seams that you can't press flat, and the extra fuzz lodges under the needle and may cause skipped stitches. So use good thread and frequently clean out fabric lint where it collects for smooth, trouble-free sewing (see your operating manual for cleaning directions).

A serger, a special sewing machine used for certain tasks, uses its own type of thread. (You can find out about sergers in the later section "Real Machines: Sewing Machines and Sergers.") All-purpose polyester, cotton, or cotton-covered polyester serger threads are fine, two-ply threads available in a few basic colors on cones that can hold 1,000 yards of thread or more. (A *ply* is a finer, slightly twisted strand used to make the thread.) When three, four, or five separate threads are used to serge a stitch, the finer serger thread creates a smoother seam finish than the three-ply all-purpose sewing thread used on a conventional sewing machine. Because it's a finer thread, serger thread should be used only on the serger and not for all-purpose sewing with your sewing machine. You can see examples of both types of thread in Figure 2-4.

Figure 2-4: Quality thread for the sewing machine and cone thread for the serger are specifically engineered for each machine.

Pressing Issues

Why are you delighted when someone asks if your pie is homemade but insulted when someone points to your dress and asks, "Did you make that?" In sewing, if someone can immediately tell that your project is homemade, it's probably because something just looks . . . wrong. Usually this happens because the project wasn't properly pressed during construction. Good pressing tools mean the difference between a project that looks good and a project that looks great.

The following list covers essential pressing tools and some points to consider when choosing them:

✔ **Iron:** You need a good iron. I didn't say an *expensive* one — just a good one. Choose an iron that has a variety of heat settings and can make steam. Some irons automatically turn off after a few minutes, which is great when you're done pressing a shirt but a real pain when you're sewing because you have to wait for the iron to heat up every time you press a seam. So choose one that doesn't have the automatic shut off feature. Also, choose an iron that has a smooth *soleplate* (the part that heats up) and is easy to clean.

If you use *fusible products,* such as iron-on patches that melt when heated, you can easily gum up the iron. A nonstick soleplate is easy to clean and provides a smooth, slick surface for trouble-free pressing and ironing.

✔ **Ironing board:** Make sure you have a padded ironing board. Without the padding, seams and edges press against a hard surface that scars the fabric. This scarring shadows through to the visible side of the fabric, so when a seam is pressed open it can look like ski tracks on either side of the seam. And hard surfaces can also cause the finished project to have a shiny, overpressed look that's tough — if not impossible — to remove.

Choose a muslin or nonreflective ironing board cover. The silver, reflector-type covers are too slippery and sometimes get too hot, causing unnecessary scorching on some synthetic fabrics.

✔ **Press cloth:** A *press cloth* is essential for pressing a variety of fabrics, from fine silks to heavier woolens and wool blends. You place the press cloth between the iron and the fabric to help prevent shine and over-pressing. Use a clean, white or off-white, 100-percent cotton or linen tea towel or napkin, or purchase a press cloth.

If you're considering a print or color-dyed fabric for a press cloth — don't do it. Dyes can bleed through and ruin your project. Terry cloth isn't a good choice, either. The napped surface of a terry cloth towel can leave its bumpy texture on the fabric.

A professional dressmaker friend of mine uses a cloth diaper for a press cloth. The diaper is white and holds as much or as little moisture as needed for the job, can be doubled or tripled depending on the use, and is a good size.

After you decide to make sewing a regular hobby and you feel comfortable investing a little extra money into your projects, consider purchasing the following tools shown in Figure 2-5:

✔ **Seam roll:** This fabric cylinder measures about 12 inches long by 3 inches in diameter. You place the roll underneath seams you're pressing, and the seam allowance (the fabric on the inside of the project that is on either side of the seam) falls down the sides of the seam roll, away from the iron. This prevents the iron from creating ski tracks on either side of the seam that show up on the visible side of the fabric.

✔ **Tailor's ham:** This stuffed, triangular-shaped cushion has several curves on it that simulate the curves on your body. You use the ham to press and shape seams along the side of the waist, sleeves, bust darts, and other curved areas on a garment.

When purchasing both the seam roll and the tailor's ham, be sure that each has a 100-percent cotton cloth side made out of heavy muslin-type fabric for pressing high-temperature fabrics such as cotton and linen, and a wool side for pressing lower-temperature fabrics such as silks and synthetics.

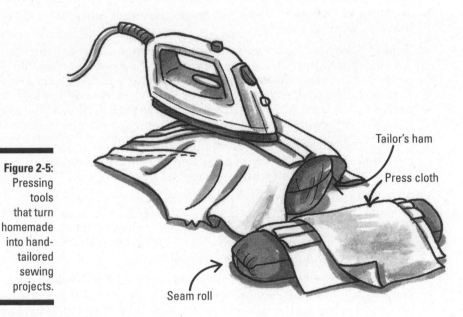

Tailor's ham

Press cloth

Figure 2-5: Pressing tools that turn homemade into hand-tailored sewing projects.

Seam roll

Real Machines: Sewing Machines and Sergers

If you want to boil water for tea, you have a couple of choices: You can use a kettle on the stovetop or put a cup in the microwave. In the world of sewing, too, some tasks can be accomplished with two different machines:

✔ A sewing machine

✔ A serger (sometimes called an overlock machine)

A sewing machine makes a stitch called a *lock stitch* with two separate threads — one threaded through the needle and one threaded on a bobbin that rests in the bobbin case under the needle (read more about the parts and working pieces of the sewing machine in the following section). With a sewing machine you have optimum maneuverability and can sew straight seams and curves, sew on buttons, and make buttonholes. You can also sew into corners, apply elastic, appliqué, embroider, and finish raw fabric edges. Some tasks, though, are time-consuming and tedious with a sewing machine and almost instantaneous with a serger.

A serger is a compact commercial-looking machine. The most common sergers uses three or four threads to sew a ¼-inch seam, overcast the edge by "knitting" the thread over the fabric edge using loopers, and cut off the excess fabric all in one quick step. (Look at an inside seam on what you're wearing; chances are the stitches were made by a serger.) Because the stitch formation is more complicated and the bed of the machine is smaller than a sewing machine, the fabric is less maneuverable using a serger. So the serger is great for sewing seams, finishing raw edges, and sewing wide curves; with practice, you can even blind hem and apply elastic with it, but it's much more limited than the sewing machine. And although you can make a project from beginning to end using a sewing machine, that's more difficult and sometimes impossible to do with a serger.

In the following sections you take a closer look at both machines to get a better understanding of each one.

Working with a sewing machine

Just like your car, you want your sewing machine to be dependable. It doesn't need to be brand new, and it doesn't need every modern convenience known to man; it just needs to work well. If you inherited Aunt Millie's old machine, have a knowledgeable dealer assess its condition to see if you can realistically count on using it. If you want to purchase a new machine, some dealers will allow you to test machines in the store or rent one to try.

Acquainting yourself with the parts of the sewing machine and knowing how it works keeps you and your sewing machine out of trouble. Consider this section of the book your road map to navigating a sewing machine. I tell you all about the parts on a typical machine (shown in Figure 2-6) and what you use them for.

Of course, your sewing machine may look a little different from what you see in Figure 2-6, or you may be working on a serger (in which case, check out the section "Finding your way around a serger" later in this chapter). If things on your machine don't correspond exactly to what I show you, consult the operating manual that comes with your machine to see how the parts compare.

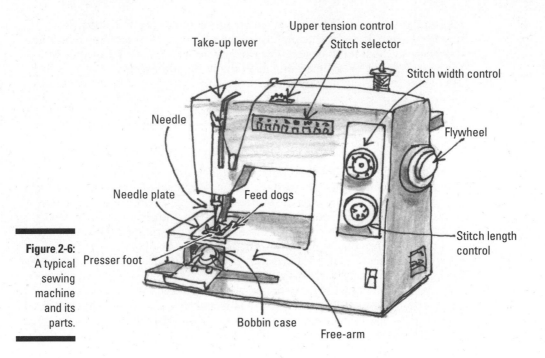

Upper tension control

Stitch selector

Take-up lever

Stitch width control

Needle

Flywheel

Needle plate   Feed dogs

Stitch length
control

Figure 2-6:
A typical
sewing
machine
and its
parts.

Presser foot

Bobbin case

Free-arm

Needle

The most important part of the sewing machine is the needle. It's so important that I devote a section to the needle, "Selecting needles for sewing machines," earlier in this chapter.

Always start a new project with a new sewing machine needle. A new needle won't skip stitches or snag the fabric, and changing your needle regularly may save you from an unnecessary trip to the dealer just to find out that all you need is a new needle. (Ask me how I know this.)

Presser foot

Sometimes referred to as a pressure foot, the *presser foot* holds the fabric firmly against the feed dogs (check out the section "Feed dogs," later in this chapter, to . . . well, find out about feed dogs) so that the fabric doesn't flap up and down with each stitch.

For most machines, you can buy different presser feet for specialty jobs. Most machines come with four or five of the most useful variations, including the following (shown in Figure 2-7):

 ✔ **All-purpose foot:** This foot, which is usually metal, works well on a lot of fabrics. The foot is often available with a Teflon coating for an even smoother sewing experience.

✔ **Embroidery foot:** Sometimes referred to as the *appliqué foot,* the embroidery foot is often made of a transparent material. The high, wide groove carved out on the underside allows the foot to glide over satin decorative stitches without smashing them into the fabric.

✔ **Blind hem foot:** This foot helps stitch a truly invisible hem (you can read more about hems in Chapter 7). The presser feet mentioned above have evenly-sized toes on either side of the needle. The blind hem foot usually has a wide toe on the right and a narrow toe and guide (which may be adjustable) on the left (check out Figure 2-7 to see the difference).

✔ **Button-sewing foot:** This foot usually has very short toes and a nylon or rubber gripper designed to hold a button firmly in place (see Chapter 9 for clever ways to sew on buttons by machine and hand).

✔ **Quilting or edge guide:** This bar slides or screws on behind the ankle of the presser foot. The guide rides over the previous row of stitching for parallel rows of quilting or next to an edge for perfectly positioned top-stitching. (See Chapter 5 to find out about topstitching.)

✔ **Zipper foot:** Not surprisingly, you use this foot to sew in a zipper (see Chapter 9 for the details on zippers). The foot has one toe, and you can adjust it either by sliding the foot over or by attaching it on the other side of the ankle.

Figure 2-7:
Typical
sewing
machine
presser feet.

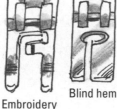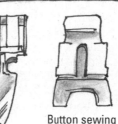

All-purpose   Embroidery   Blind hem   Zipper   Button sewing   Quilting guide

Presser foot lever

Located near the back side of the needle, the *presser foot lever* is used to raise the presser foot. Doing so releases the upper tension so that you can remove the fabric.

The timesaving knee-lift feature, common on commercial sewing machines, is available on some brands of household sewing machines. The knee lift allows you to lift the pressure foot without using your hands, keeping them free when removing the fabric from under the presser foot or when pivoting the fabric around a corner.

Feed dogs

Feed dogs, sometimes referred to as *feed teeth,* are saw-shaped teeth or pads that move the fabric through the machine. You sandwich the fabric between the presser foot and the feed dogs, and as the needle stitches up and down, the feed dogs grab the fabric and move it under the foot.

Most machines allow you to sew with the feed dogs up or down. You do most sewing with the feed dogs in the up position; you use the down position mostly for button sewing, or for mending and free-machine embroidery, in which you move the fabric freely under the needle as it stitches.

Needle plate

Sometimes referred to as a *throat plate,* the *needle plate* rests on the bed of the machine and fits over the feed dogs. It has either a small round hole or an oblong hole that the needle passes through. The needle plate often includes a series of lines that run in ¼-inch increments from the needle. These lines guide you as you sew a seam allowance, which you can read more about in Chapter 6.

For most sewing, you use the needle plate with the oblong hole so that the needle has the clearance it needs and doesn't break when you use a stitch that zigzags from side to side.

Bobbin and company

A *bobbin* is a small spool that holds about 40 to 70 yards of thread. The machine uses the needle thread and the bobbin thread to make a stitch. Machines usually come with three to five bobbins that are specially made for the machine's make and model. Bobbins are wound (filled with thread) using a part of the machine called a *bobbin winder.* Check your operating manual for proper bobbin-winding and threading instructions. After you wind the thread around a bobbin, the bobbin fits into a *bobbin case,* and the thread can be pulled up through the needle plate, ready for stitching.

If you're winding a bobbin that has a hole in its side, fold over about an inch of thread and twist the thread end at the fold. Then poke the folded end of the thread through the hole from the inside of the bobbin out. Place the bobbin on the winder, holding the thread end tightly. Start winding until the thread breaks off. This way, when you get to the end of a bobbin, the wrong end of the thread doesn't accidentally get caught in the stitch.

When winding a bobbin, don't overfill it if you want smooth sewing and the best stitch quality.

Free-arm

A *free-arm,* sometimes called an *open arm,* is a squared-off cylinder on the bed of the machine that lets you stitch around tubular areas, such as pant legs, sleeves, cuffs, and armholes, without ripping out a seam.

Flywheel

The right end of the machine has a *flywheel,* or *hand wheel,* that turns when you sew. The flywheel drives the needle up and down and coordinates the needle movement with the feed dogs when creating a stitch. On certain machines the flywheel allows you to manually control the needle, which helps you pivot fabric under the needle when sewing corners.

To pivot your fabric under the needle, simply turn the flywheel so that the needle is down in the fabric, lift the presser foot, pivot the fabric, lower the presser foot, and then continue sewing. Some machines have a needle-up/needle-down function (discussed later in this chapter) that makes pivoting even easier.

Depending on the machine model, some flywheels have a *clutch* or button that you must release when winding a bobbin. Consult your operating manual for specific instructions on bobbin winding.

Stitch-length control

The *stitch-length control* determines the distance the feed dogs move the fabric under the needle. When the feed dogs move with shorter strokes, the machine sews shorter stitches. When the feed dogs move with longer strokes, the stitches are longer. Your stitch-length control gives stitch lengths in one of the following two ways, depending on the make and model of the machine:

- Millimeters (mm)
- Stitches per inch (spi)

Throughout this book I give you stitch length settings in millimeters (mm) and stitches per inch (spi).

The average stitch length for mid-weight fabrics is 2.5 to 3 mm/10 to 12 spi. For fine fabrics, use 1.5 to 2 mm/13 to 20 spi. (Anything shorter is almost impossible to rip out when you make a mistake.) For heavier fabrics, basting, or topstitching, use 3.5 to 6 mm/4 to 5 spi. (You can read more about basting and topstitching in Chapter 5.)

Stitch-width control

The *stitch-width control* sets the distance the needle moves from side to side. You always measure this distance in millimeters (mm). Some sewing machines have a maximum stitch width of 4 to 5 mm. Others create stitches as wide as 9 mm. A 5-mm width does the trick for most utility sewing. (Throughout *Sewing For Dummies,* I give stitch-width settings in a range that works for most sewing machines.)

Needle position

Needle position refers to the position of the needle in relationship to the hole in the needle plate. In center needle position, you center the needle over the oblong hole in the needle plate. In left needle position, you set the needle to the left of center. In right needle position, you put the needle to the right of center.

A few older, less-expensive models have either a permanent left needle position or a permanent center needle position. Most models made in the last 25 years or so have an adjustable needle position, which comes in handy when you topstitch, sew on buttons, and sew in zippers. Instead of manually positioning the fabric under the needle, you simply move the needle into the right spot. The needle position control is usually near or part of the stitch-width control. If you can't locate it, read your operating manual.

Stitch selector

If your sewing machine does more than straight stitch and zigzag, it has a way for you to select a stitch. (See Chapter 5 for more information on basic sewing machine stitches.) The *stitch selectors* on older machines are dials, levers, buttons, or drop-in cams. Newer, computerized models have keys or touch pads that not only select the stitch but also automatically set the stitch length and width.

Upper tension control

In order to make uniform stitches, your machine requires a certain amount of tension on the thread as it sews. You adjust the tension using the *upper tension control,* which is usually located on the top or front of the machine.

The upper tension is usually marked in numbers — the higher the number, the tighter the tension, and the lower the number, the looser the tension. Some makes have the upper tension marked with a plus sign (+), meaning more tension, and a minus sign (–), meaning less tension.

The old adage "If it ain't broke, don't fix it" definitely applies to the upper tension control. Unless you have major problems with the fabric puckering or the thread looping, leave the tension alone. If you experience these problems, consult your operating manual or a qualified sewing machine dealer for advice on adjusting the tension.

Pressure adjustment

The *pressure adjustment,* which you can usually find above the bar that holds the presser foot, controls how much pressure the foot exerts against the fabric.

For most sewing projects you want to leave the pressure on the *full* setting. This way, the fabric doesn't slip and slide around under the foot, creating crooked seams while you sew. For some jobs, like sewing through very heavy fabrics or through multiple thicknesses or stitching complicated embroidery designs, lighter pressure works better. Consult your operating manual for specifics on your machine's pressure control and when to adjust it.

Take-up lever

The *take-up lever* is very important in the threading and normal operation of the sewing machine. This lever pulls just enough thread off the spool for the next stitch.

Needle-up/needle-down function

Newer machines have a needle-up/needle-down function that automatically stops the needle in the up or down position without your having to manually turn the flywheel. Set this function on the up setting, and the needle stops out of the fabric — you don't unthread the needle with the next stitch. Set it for the down function, and the needle stops in the fabric for easy pivoting around corners.

Speed control

Most newer machines have a *speed control* (check your operating manual to see if you have this feature on your machine and where it's located). It works like the cruise control in your car by limiting how fast you can sew. You adjust the speed control to the fastest sewing speed that feels comfortable.

Reverse button

At the beginning and end of seams, you often want to lock the stitches in some way so that they don't come out. You can tie off each seam by hand (ugh) or use your reverse button. Simply sew three or four stitches, touch the *reverse button,* and the feed dogs back up the fabric a couple of stitches. Release the button, and the machine resumes stitching forward. The stitches are then locked off and secure.

Finding your way around a serger

A *serger* is to sewing as a microwave oven is to cooking. I love my serger because it really speeds up the sewing process by sewing a seam, finishing the edge (to keep it from fraying), and then cutting off the excess fabric in one step. You can use a serger to stitch a wide variety of fabrics and it works much faster than a standard sewing machine, but isn't as versatile. For instance, you can't sew a buttonhole or adjust the seam allowance.

A serger, shown in Figure 2-8, has most of the same parts and pieces as a sewing machine. But rather than using a bobbin, the serger uses loopers, threaded through the machine from a cone of thread, that essentially knit the thread over the raw edges of the fabric and gives the inside of the garment that factory-made look.

If you want to give a serger a test drive before deciding whether to buy one of your own, visit your local sewing machine dealer and try one or sign up for a class.

Most beginners start off on standard sewing machines. However, in case you want to sew on a serger, I give you special instructions where you need them throughout this book.

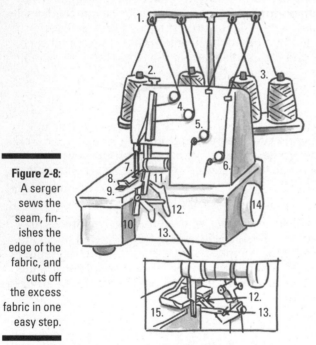

Figure 2-8:
A serger sews the seam, finishes the edge of the fabric, and cuts off the excess fabric in one easy step.

1. Telescoping thread guide
2. Pressure regulator
3. Spool rod
4. Needle thread tensions
5. Upper looper tension
6. Lower looper tension
7. Needles
8. Presser foot
9. Feed dogs
10. Lower knife
11. Upper knife
12. Upper looper
13. Lower looper
14. Flywheel
15. Needle plate

Chapter 3

Selecting Fabric, Findings, and Interfacing

In This Chapter

▶ Finding fabulous fabric

▶ Discovering sewing notions

▶ Choosing interfacing

▶ Preshrinking everything in sight

*R*emember how much fun you had shopping for back-to-school stuff when you were a kid? That's how I feel every time I start a new sewing or decorating project. I envision the finished project, get excited about walking though a fabric store selecting just the right items for my project, and imagine the compliments I'll get from my friends and family when it's completed. And because everything you sew is chosen by you and custom-made, you never have to return something because it isn't exactly what you wanted.

This chapter covers what you need to know about fabric and the materials involved with sewing, including info on fiber content (not the type that aids digestion, but the type that makes fabric), buying good fabric, what to consider when picking out decorative trims and findings, and the purpose of a mysterious item called *interfacing*.

Choosing the Right Fabric for Your Project

Have you ever bought a good-looking, great-fitting pair of pants on sale, thinking that you were getting a smokin' deal — only to find that after the first washing, the pants fell apart, shrank more than a full size, or suffered from terminal wrinkling? Chances are that those bargain pants were plagued with poor fiber content.

You may wonder what makes a good piece of fabric and how to know whether you're getting the most for your fabric-buying dollar. This section educates you on the advantages and disadvantages of common fibers so that you can make the best choice for every project.

You can often find a list of recommended fabrics on the back of pattern envelopes. This information about fibers and fabric comes in handy when selecting fabric and also when buying clothes off the rack. Don't stray from the advice about the choice of fabric on the back of a pattern envelope — you may get the color you want, but I promise that the final product won't look as good or fit as well as you intended.

Figuring out fiber

Fibers are the raw ingredients used to make fabric. Fibers are important because they determine a fabric's characteristics, including

- ✔ **Feel:** In the biz we call this the *hand* of the fabric. Is it comfortable to wear? Does it drape well and keep its shape?

- ✔ **Weight:** Is it too heavy? Too light?

- ✔ **Care:** Is it wash-and-wear, or does it need to be dry-cleaned?

- ✔ **Durability:** How does it hold color after being washed or dry-cleaned?

Fibers break down into the following four categories:

- ✔ **Natural:** These fibers include cotton, silk, and wool. Natural fibers breathe, take dyes well, and drape beautifully. On the downside, they also have a tendency to shrink, fade when washed or dry-cleaned, wrinkle, and stretch out of shape with moderate wear.

- ✔ **Man-made:** Acrylic, acetate, and rayon are high-profile members of the man-made fiber group, which uses materials from plants that make cellulose. Acrylic is soft, warm, and resistant to oil and chemical stains, but acrylic fibers may stretch out of shape and *pill* (form little fuzz balls) with wear. Acetate doesn't shrink, is moth-resistant, and drapes well; however, it can lose its color and shred with wear, perspiration, and dry cleaning. Rayon (which has been referred to as the poor man's silk) breathes, drapes, and dyes well. Rayon also wrinkles and shrinks, so it must be dry-cleaned or hand-washed and pressed rigorously.

- ✔ **Synthetic:** Nylon, polyester, spandex, and microfibers are among the hundreds of synthetic fibers, which are produced from refined petroleum or natural gas. Nylon is exceptionally strong, elastic when wet, abrasion resistant, lustrous, and easy to wash with low moisture absorbency. Polyester doesn't shrink, wrinkle, stretch, or fade. It's stain- and chemical-resistant, dyes easily, and is easy to wash. But unless you buy all-polyester garments that are chemically engineered to breathe, you find that polyester is best when blended with natural fibers. Spandex (including Lycra, a widely recognizable brand of spandex) is lightweight, smooth, and soft, and stronger, more durable, and just as elastic as rubber. Microfibers take dyes well, are washable and durable, have incredible strength, and drape well.

✔ **Blends:** Fibers can be blended so the finished fabric has the advantages of the blended fibers. For example, a cotton/polyester blend washes, wears, and breathes because of the cotton, and it wrinkles less than 100-percent cotton because of the polyester. Popular fabrics for sportswear are cotton/spandex blends that allow for a snug, comfortable-fitting garment that moves and bends without strangling your legs or waist.

You want fabric fibers to fit your needs and lifestyle. For example, my mom doesn't like ironing or taking things to the dry cleaners, so synthetic, easy-care fibers that are machine washable, dryable, and don't wrinkle are her fabrics of choice. My husband likes the breathable characteristics of cotton, linen, and wool. He doesn't mind going to the dry cleaners and paying the price to have his shirts laundered and his suits cleaned and pressed, so (you guessed it) he's a natural-fiber guy.

Getting to know common fabric types

Millions of fabrics are produced worldwide every year. Most are used by manufacturers to make everything from the latest runway fashions to car seats, and only a very tiny percentage makes its way into your local fabric store. Even so, you have so many fabrics available by the yard to choose from that you may be overwhelmed. In this section I give you an overview of the most common types of fabric, but first you need to get familiar with the two basic categories of fabrics: woven and knit.

Finding out about woven fabrics

Woven fabrics are made on a loom similar to the one you may have used as a child to make potholders. The lengthwise yarns are called the *warp* and are the strongest yarns in the fabric. Crosswise yarns are called the *woof, weft,* or *filler.* Woven fabrics are stable in the lengthwise and crosswise directions but stretch a little when pulled on the *bias* — the diagonal between the lengthwise and crosswise grains.

Fabrics can be woven loosely or tightly. For a loosely woven, plain-weave fabric, think gauze or cheese cloth. When you hold these fabrics up to the light, you can almost see through them. For a closely woven, plain-weave fabric, think of boat canvas. It's evenly woven and heavier than the gauze because its yarns are very closely or tightly woven together.

Knowing more about knits

Knits are constructed with a series of lengthwise loops called *ribs* and cross-wise stitches called *courses*. Because of this looped construction, you treat knits differently when sewing than you treat woven fabrics. Most knits have crosswise stretch and lengthwise stability, so they move and conform to the body. Like woven fabrics, there are various types of knits; the most common are single knits, which curl to one side when stretched across the grain, and double knits, which don't.

Taking a look at common fabrics

The following list describes some of the most common fabrics available by the yard. Note that most are woven or knit, but some fabrics can come in either variety.

- **Broadcloth:** A light- to mid-weight, evenly woven cotton, silk, or wool fabric used in men's shirts and fine suiting.

- **Brocade:** Originally made of heavy silk with an elaborate pattern of silver or gold threads, affordable brocade is now made from synthetic fibers and has a heavy, embossed appearance. Brocades are used both in apparel and in home décor projects.

- **Canvas:** A heavy, close and evenly-woven fabric usually made of cotton and used for director's chair backs and seats, tote bags, and other projects that require strong, tough, and long-wearing use.

- **Chambray:** A light- to mid-weight, evenly woven cotton or cotton blend you find in work clothes, shirts, and pajamas. Chambray, which resembles denim but is lighter weight, is usually made with a colored warp yarn and a white filler yarn.

- **Chenille:** Derived from the French word for *caterpillar,* chenille is a plush, fuzzy yarn used to create fabrics for upholstery and bedding.

- **Chintz:** A closely woven, plain-weave cotton or cotton/polyester blend often used in curtains and draperies. This fabric is printed with figures — most commonly flowers — and has a smooth, shiny, or glazed finish.

- **Corduroy:** A mid- to heavyweight, cotton *weft pile* (fuzzy ribbed) fabric that is woven creating the distinct ribs on the lengthwise grain. Corduroy comes in various rib widths, solid and printed, and is commonly used in children's clothing and casual sportswear (not to be confused with "active" sportswear used for a gym workout).

- **Crepe:** A pebbly-surfaced woven or knitted fabric. Because of the pebbly surface, crepes snag more and don't wear as well as even weaves like poplin. Crepe is most often used in women's dress clothing, such as suits, dresses, and blouses.

✔ **Damask:** Flatter than brocade and reversible with a different pattern color on the opposite side. The designs are usually elaborate and were originally woven in silk. Today's damasks are made of cotton or linen and may be blended with synthetic or man-made fibers.

✔ **Denim:** A strong mid- to heavyweight, twill-weave fabric in which the warp yarn is a color (usually blue) and the filler yarn is white or off-white. Denim is available in many weights, depending on the end use, and is great for jeans, jackets, skirts, and home décor projects.

✔ **Double knit:** A mid-weight, knitted fabric in which both sides are knitted identically. Double knit keeps its shape and has good recovery. Use double knit to make dresses, tops, skirts, and jackets.

✔ **Doupioni:** A flat-finished silk with a very subtle linen-look of *slubbing* — little irregularities in the fiber that give the fabric a noticeable texture. Because silk dyes beautifully and has such a supple hand, doupioni is used in apparel and in home décor. It's a fairly fragile fabric, so when using it in home décor projects, keep it out of direct sunlight to prevent it from breaking down.

✔ **Duck:** A heavyweight, tightly woven cotton or linen fabric available in plain or twill weaves. Duck and canvas are used interchangeably and make great aprons and slipcovers. (Don't try adding a raspberry glaze to this duck.)

✔ **Eyelet:** An embroidered cotton available by the yard for blouses and dresses or in narrower widths as trim. The distinct embroidery has holes that are overcast with zigzag stitches.

✔ **Fake fur:** A heavy pile fabric that has the look, hand, and almost the warmth of animal fur but is far less expensive. Fake furs are usually made from modacrylic fibers (those used to make deep-pile fabrics, like for plush toys) blended with other synthetic or natural fibers and have gotten so good that many high-end versions are dead ringers for their real animal counterparts. Most faux furs are made on a knit backing which means they won't ravel, are washable or dry-cleanable, and won't get you in trouble with the animal rights folks.

✔ **Flannel:** A light- to mid-weight, plain or twill-weave cotton or wool fabric. Cotton flannel that's brushed has a soft, fluffy surface and is used for work shirts and pajamas. Wool flannel isn't usually brushed and is used as suiting.

✔ **Fleece:** A light- to heavyweight, *hydrophobic* (water-hating), double-sided polyester knit used in pullovers, jackets, mittens, booties, blankets, slippers, and scarves. A common trade name for this type of fleece is Polarfleece. You can also find sweatshirts in fleece made with cotton and cotton/polyester blends. See "Taking special care when working with fleece" later in this chapter.

- **Gabardine:** A strong, mid- to heavyweight, twill-weave fabric made from several fibers or fiber blends. You see it in sportswear, suiting, raincoats, and pants.

- **Interlock:** A fine lightweight knit used in T-shirts and other sportswear. Interlock is generally made of cotton and cotton blends and is very stretchy.

- **Jacquard:** Damasks, tapestries, brocades, matelasse, and upholstery fabrics with elaborate figures are all jacquard fabrics woven on a loom named for its inventor, Joseph Jacquard.

- **Jersey:** A fine, light- to mid-weight knit used in better quality sportswear, tops, and dresses. Jersey comes in solid colors, stripes, or prints.

- **Matelasse:** A French word meaning *to cushion or pad,* it refers to fabric with a quilted surface produced on a jacquard loom. Matelasse blankets are popular in modern bedding.

- **Microfiber:** This fine-quality polyester fabric is called a *microfiber* because the fiber itself has a smaller diameter than silk. Microfiber fabrics come in varying weights from lightweight dressmaking fabrics to heavier twill, faux suede, and velvet. Because it's made of polyester, microfiber doesn't breathe very well, so when choosing a pattern, choose one that fits loosely.

- **Poplin:** A mid- to heavyweight, tightly woven fabric with a fine horizontal rib. Poplin is usually made of cotton or a cotton blend and is wonderful for sportswear, children's clothing, and outerwear.

- **Satin:** This term refers to a fabric's weave. Satin can be made of cotton, silk, synthetic fibers, and blends. Many types of satin fabrics are used on both clothing and home furnishings, but all have a distinct shiny appearance because of the way the fabric is woven.

- **Toile de Jouy:** Often just called *toile,* this typically cotton or linen fabric is printed in a single color on a solid background with scenes, landscapes, and people, depicting life in 18th-century France. It's currently a very popular fabric in French Country home décor.

- **Tricot:** A fine, sheer, single knit with vertical ribs on the right side of the fabric and crosswise ribs on the wrong (back) side of the fabric. Stretch the fabric across the grain (see Chapter 4 for more on grainlines and why they're important) and it curls to the right side of the fabric. Use tricot for making lingerie. Tricot is also made into fusible interfacing. (See "Investigating Interfacing" in this chapter for the details.)

- **Tulle:** Open netting made of knotted, geometrically shaped holes. Made in several weights, tulle ranges from very fine, used in bridal and dance wear, to heavy nylon netting, used in other crafting projects. Tulle is made of silk or nylon and ranges in width from 45 inches to 120 inches.

✔ **Velour:** A woven or knitted fabric with a thick, short pile (fibers that stand up on the surface of the fabric and give it a soft, fuzzy texture) and usually dyed into deep, dark colors. Use knitted velour for tops and robes and woven velour in home décor projects. Velour is a more casual fabric than velvet (see next bullet). Velour requires a *with nap* layout (see the next section).

✔ **Velvet:** A woven silk or synthetic fabric with a short pile (fibers that stand up on the surface of the fabric and give it a soft, fuzzy texture). Use velvet for eveningwear, tailored suits, and home décor projects. Velvet requires a *with nap* layout (see the next section).

✔ **Velveteen:** A woven cotton fabric with a short pile (fibers that stand up on the surface of the fabric and give it a soft, fuzzy texture), made similarly to corduroy but without the ribs. Use velveteen in children's clothing, home décor projects, and eveningwear.

✔ **Worsted:** A fine, closely woven wool fabric with a hard, smooth surface. Worsteds make great suiting because they're very closely woven and look great over years of wear.

Taking fabric nap into consideration

Fabric has shine, texture, design, color, and pattern to give the project interest. These factors create the *nap* and may require you to buy more fabric and to take extra care when laying and cutting out the pattern.

Determining whether the fabric has nap

Your fabric has nap if it falls into any of the following categories:

✔ **Contains a one-way design:** With a directional floral design, if you cut out some of the pattern pieces in one direction and other pattern pieces in the opposite direction, you find your flowers right side up on part of the project and upside down on another part of the same project. You need extra fabric so that you can get all your flowers going (or growing) in the right direction.

✔ **Has a fuzzy texture:** Fuzzy fabrics include velvet, corduroy, Polarfleece, and some sweatshirt fleeces. When brushed in one direction, the fabric is smooth; in the other direction, it's rough. This texture difference translates into a color difference, so you need more fabric to cut out the pattern pieces in the same direction.

✔ **Contains an uneven stripe:** To match the stripes at the seams, you need extra fabric because you have to lay out the pattern in the same direction. See the section "Laying out plaids, stripes, and one-way designs," later in this chapter, for more information.

✔ **Contains an even or uneven plaid:** The color bars in a plaid must match both vertically and horizontally. If the color bars have the same spacing and are in the same order in both directions along the selvage (the long, finished edge of the fabric when it comes off the loom; see Chapter 4 for more on selvages), the plaid is even, which means you can lay out the pattern pieces in both directions. If the color bars aren't symmetrical in one or both directions, the plaid is uneven, so you need to lay out all the pattern pieces going in the same direction. You need more fabric to make either kind of plaid match. Check out Chapter 4 to find out more about working with plaids.

Taking special care when working with fleece

Treat it right, and fleece (often referred to as Polarfleece) provides you with durable projects that look as good as they feel. But as great as fleece is for home décor projects and clothing, it does require some special treatment.

Here are a few general do's and don'ts to help you get the best results when working with fleece:

✔ **Do know the right from wrong side of the fleece.** As fleece wears, the color ages differently on the right and the wrong sides of the fabric. This is no big deal unless you use two different sides for one project. To figure out which side is which, stretch it on the selvage (the long finished edge of the fabric when it comes off the loom — see Chapter 4 for more on selvages). The fleece curls to the right side. When stretched across the grain, it curls to the wrong side.

✔ **Do mark the wrong side of the fabric by using a dressmaker's pencil or chalk after cutting out your pattern.** Mark the center front with a single hash mark and the center back with a double hash mark. If the front and back pattern pieces look similar to one another, you can tell them apart by the markings. Dressmaker's chalk or pencil mark fleece easily and don't smudge.

✔ **Do mark notches with a chalk pencil instead of clipping into the seam allowance.** Most fleece projects use ½-inch seam allowances, and if you clip too far into the seam allowance, the snip is hard to fix.

✔ **Do wash your finished project by turning it inside out.** Use lukewarm water, the gentle wash cycle, and powdered detergent. Liquid detergents can damage the chemical finish on the lighter-weight fleeces, impairing their moisture-wicking capabilities.

✔ **Don't prewash fleece.** Prewashing is not necessary. Fleece is usually made of polyester or a polyester blend that doesn't shrink. You won't damage the fabric if you do preshrink it, you just don't need to.

✔ **Don't press fleece, not even after you sew seams.** Placing a hot iron directly on the fabric crushes the nap and can melt the fibers. If somewhere down the road you find yourself with a pesky fleece seam that needs shaping, set the iron for *steam* and hold it 3 to 4 inches above the seamline, letting the steam penetrate the fibers. Finger-press the seam in shape by holding and patting your hand over it until the fabric cools.

Considering fabric width and yardage needed

Fabric comes in different widths, and when you're buying fabric for your latest sewing project, you may need to do some conversion because the pattern you're using calls for something different than what you see in the store. Table 3-1 converts the yardage you need from one fabric width to another. For example, if your pattern calls for 1 yard of 60-inch wide fabric and the fabric you want to use is only 45 inches wide, the table tells you that you need 1⅜ yards of the 45-inch width fabric to make the project.

Table 3-1 Fabric Yardage Conversion Table

35 inches	*45 inches*	*50 inches*	*54 inches*	*60 inches*
1¾	1⅜	1¼	1⅛	1
2	1⅝	1½	1⅜	1¼
2¼	1¾	1⅝	1½	1⅜
2½	2⅛	1¾	1¾	1⅝
2⅞	2¼	2	1⅞	1¾
3⅛	2½	2¼	2	1⅞
3⅜	2¾	2⅜	2¼	2
3¾	2⅞	2⅝	2⅜	2¼
4¼	3⅛	2¾	2⅝	2⅜
4½	3⅜	3	2¾	2⅝
4¾	3⅝	3¼	2⅞	2¾
5	3⅞	3⅜	3⅛	2⅞

Reading labels and bolt ends

In the fabric store, you see the fabric wrapped around *bolts* — cardboard flats or round tubes. Flat bolts of fabric stand at attention on tables, and tube-type bolts are stored upright in a rack or threaded with a wooden dowel and hung horizontally on a rack for easy viewing. At the end of flat bolts or on a hangtag, you find a label like the one you see in Figure 3-1 that tells you many important things about the fabric, including the fiber content, width of the fabric, care instructions, price per yard, and often the manufacturer.

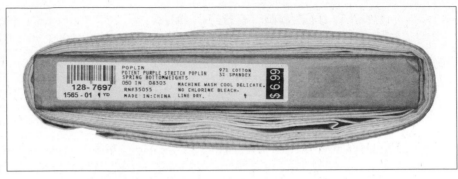

Figure 3-1: Read the end of the bolt to find out necessary information about the fabric.

The fabric's width determines how much fabric you need to purchase for a particular project. Reading the back of your project's pattern envelope helps determine how much fabric to buy based on the fabric width. (See Chapter 4 for more information on reading pattern envelopes.)

The most common fabric widths are as follows:

- **45 to 48 inches wide:** Most woven cotton, cotton blends, novelty prints, dressmaking, and quilting fabrics come in this width.

- **54 to 60 inches wide:** Many knits, woolens, and home décor fabrics come in this width.

Occasionally you find a fabric that is 72 inches wide, and sheer fabrics, such as bridal tulle, come up to 120 inches wide.

Getting Notions about Findings

Tapes, trimmings, ribbons, piping, laces, elastics, and zippers are all lumped together under the category of *sewing notions* or *findings* — presumably because you need to find and gather them together before making a project.

The back of your pattern envelope tells you exactly which findings and notions you need for a particular project. (Chapter 4 tells you more about pattern envelopes.)

Bias tape basics

Bias tape is a long, continuous strip of woven cotton/polyester blend fabric used to finish or cover up a raw fabric edge. Because the tape is cut on the bias, it conforms to a straight edge, such as a seam allowance, and can be easily shaped to fit a curve or hem edge. (Read more about what *bias* means in Chapter 4.)

Bias tape comes in several configurations, including single fold, extra wide, double fold, hem facing, and hem tape. Your project's pattern envelope tells you which type of bias tape you need.

Bonkers for braid

You use braid to cover an edge or to embellish a fabric's surface. Braids come in a variety of types. *Fold-over braid* is used to trim the edges. *Middy* and *soutache braids* are flat, narrow braids often seen on sailor suits and band uniforms. Middy braid has several fine ridges that run the length of the braid, and soutache braid has one deep groove in the center that runs the length of the braid.

Getting elastic

Take a look at Figure 3-2 and see the many different types of elastics — and these are just a few of the popular types. The type and width you use for a specific project are determined by how you use it:

- **Drawstring elastic:** This knitted elastic has a drawstring running through the center of it — perfect for use in drawstring shorts and sweat pants.

- **Elastic braid:** Looks like middy braid but stretches. Use it in a casing at the wrist or waist (see Chapter 16 for more information on casings). Swimwear elastic is an elastic braid treated to resist wear in salt and chlorinated water.

- **Elastic cord:** This cord is heavier than elastic thread and can be zig-zagged over for a soft, stretchy wrist treatment.

- **Elastic thread:** Use this for shirring fabric (see Chapter 16), for hemming swimwear (see Chapter 7), and for other decorative applications.

- **Knitted elastic:** This elastic is soft and extremely stretchy. When you stretch knitted elastic while sewing, the needle slips through the loops of the knit so that the elastic doesn't break down or grow larger than the cut length during the application.

- **Non-roll waistband elastic:** This elastic works wonderfully through a waistline casing or at the waistline of pull-on shorts, pants, or skirts. The ribs of this elastic keep the elastic rigid so that it doesn't bend or curl in the casing.

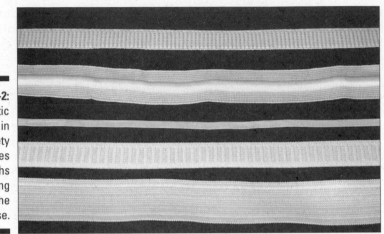

Figure 3-2:
Elastic
comes in
a variety
of types
and widths
depending
on the
end use.

Loving lace

Lace shown in Figure 3-3 is sold by the yard and comes in these varieties and many, many more:

- ✔ **Hem lace:** This lace is flimsy and straight on both edges like lace insertion (see later in this bulleted list). Because it's used on the inside of a garment at the hem edge, hem lace doesn't have to be expensive or sensational to do the job.

- ✔ **Lace beading:** This machine-made lace trim has straight edges and a row of openwork holes running down the center so that ribbon can be woven through it. It's often used as a channel for a ribbon drawstring.

- ✔ **Lace edging:** It can have either a straight edge or a scalloped edge. You use lace edging to trim a hem or cuff edge, most often in heirloom sewing (sewing done with old-fashioned styling). You also use lace edging to trim the edge of tucks. (Check out Chapter 9 for more about tucks.)

- ✔ **Eyelet lace:** Eyelet lace is made of woven cotton or linen and features *eyelets,* little holes in the fabric, which are finished with short, narrow zigzag stitches called *satin stitches.* Eyelet lace can also be gathered onto a band and used as a hem edge.

✔ **Lace insertion:** This narrow lace has straight edges so that you can easily insert it between two other pieces of lace or fabric. Insertion lace is most often used on heirloom garments.

Figure 3-3:
These are just a few common laces available.

Piping up for piping and cording

Piping and cording, like those shown in Figure 3-4, have lip edges and are sandwiched between two pieces of fabric at the seamline. A *lip edge* is a flat flap of fabric or braid that's attached to the edge of the cording for easy application. The most common types of piping and cording include the following:

✔ **Cord-edge trim:** You use this trim mostly in home décor projects. One edge of this trim has a twisted cable cord; the other edge is a lip edge. The lip edge is stitched to the cable cord, and you can remove it by pulling one end of the chain stitch thread. (See Chapter 12 for more information on using cord-edge trim in your home décor projects.)

✔ **Filler cord:** This cord fills the center of piping that's wrapped and stitched with fabric. Filler cord comes in a wide range of widths.

✔ **Piping:** Piping is purely decorative. You use it to trim the edges of slipcovers, pillows, and cushions. In clothing, use piping at the edge of pockets, cuffs, collars, and yokes in seamlines.

Figure 3-4:
Look for
these when
you need
cord edge
trim, filler
cords, and
piping.

Running with ribbons

You can use ribbons for everything from trimming apparel to decorating floral arrangements. They come in hundreds, if not thousands, of configurations, fiber contents, widths, colors, finishes, textures, and edges. I list three common types of ribbon here, but you have a whole world of ribbons to explore:

- **Grosgrain ribbon:** This ribbon — which is pronounced *grow*-grain — has a ribbed texture and is very easy to sew. Use it for trim on something tailored or, because it doesn't snag easily, on children's clothing.

- **Satin ribbon:** It has a smooth, shiny texture. Use it on more formal projects and where you need a dressier look.

- **Silk ribbon:** Great for hand or machine embroidery, silk ribbon comes in various widths and is a popular ribbon for adorning handmade projects.

Refreshing with rickrack and twill tape

Rickrack, a narrow zigzagging braid like you see in Figure 3-5, comes in many widths and colors. Use it on the surface of a garment to disguise a hem crease that you can't press out, or use it to peek out at the edge of a pocket in a seam allowance for extra interest.

Twill tape as shown in Figure 3-5 is made with a twill weave. It comes in narrow, medium, and wider widths and is very stable. Because of its stability, you can use twill tape to stabilize shoulder seams and other areas in a garment that may stretch or droop out of shape.

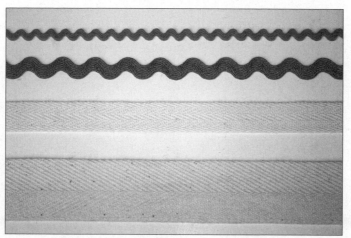

Figure 3-5:
Rickrack
and twill
tape come
in many
widths and
colors.

Getting the lowdown on drapery headers

Drapery header tape is used at the top of a drape to provide stability, stiffness, and sometimes a place to slip in drapery hooks (see Chapter 15 for more on making a drape and using drapery header). It usually comes in limited widths (from 4 to 5 inches) and can be made from woven or nonwoven material.

Adding zip with zippers

Zippers come in a variety of types and configurations, including the following (see Chapter 9 for all things zipper-related):

- **Conventional nylon coil zipper:** The cool thing about this zipper, shown in Figure 3-6, is that it can heal itself — if the zipper splits, you simply zip the pull up and down, and the split *heals.* The zipper can handle only a few such splits, so use a coil zipper in nonstress areas of garments for adults.

- **Invisible zipper:** When sewn in properly, an invisible zipper (see Figure 3-6) ends up looking like a seam.

   To sew in an invisible zipper you need a special presser foot. So when you buy your first invisible zipper, remember to take the make and model number of your sewing machine with you so you buy the right invisible zipper presser foot.

- **Molded-tooth zipper:** This zipper has individual zipper teeth made either of metal or nylon. The molded-tooth zipper (shown in Figure 3-6) is quite durable, which makes it great for kids' clothing, outerwear, backpacks, jackets, and sleeping bags.

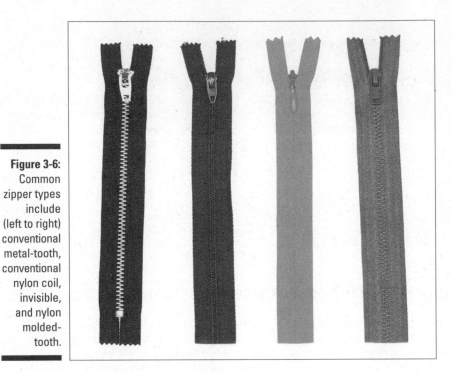

Figure 3-6:
Common
zipper types
include
(left to right)
conventional
metal-tooth,
conventional
nylon coil,
invisible,
and nylon
molded-
tooth.

Investigating Interfacing

Interfacing is an additional layer of fabric used to give high-wear areas of a garment more shape and durability. Use interfacing inside cuffs, waistbands, neck facings, and front plackets (the parts of shirts where the buttons and button holes sit) so those areas hold their shape.

If you think you can save some time and money by omitting the interfacing called for in the pattern, think again. Your project is sure to look, well, *awful*. Without interfacing, the fabric just doesn't hold up, the collar and cuffs on a garment wrinkle and pucker . . . you get the picture.

Interfacing comes in the following forms:

✔ **Knitted:** Made of nylon tricot, this interfacing is wonderful for use with knit fabrics because it has the same stretchy quality as the fabric. Lay out the pieces so the stretch goes in the same direction as the fabric pieces.

✔ **Nonwoven:** This interfacing is the easiest to use because you can lay it out any way you please.

> ✔ **Woven:** You lay out this interfacing along the same grainline as the fabric pieces. If your fabric pattern piece is cut on the lengthwise grain, the interfacing pattern piece should be cut on the lengthwise grain as well. (See Chapter 4 for the details on cutting out patterns.)

You can also choose between *fusible* interfacing, which you iron onto the fabric, and *sew-in* interfacing, which you apply the old-fashioned way — by sewing it onto the garment. I love fusible interfacing. After properly fused, it stays where you want it, and because fusible interfacing is used frequently in ready-to-wear garments, you get a more professional finish on your hand-made originals.

What's the best type of interfacing to use? It depends on the fabric. If in doubt, consult the sales associate at the fabric store for help on selecting an interfacing that's compatible with your fabric.

Preshrinking Your Fabric

Before laying and cutting out your project and before sewing a stitch, you must *preshrink* your fabric. Preshrinking allows you to see how your fabric behaves — it shows you how much your fabric shrinks, whether or not the colors run, how much it wrinkles, and other important characteristics.

The only exceptions are fleece, dry-clean-only fabrics such as wool and silk or wool and silk blends, and home décor fabrics and trims.

> ✔ Fleece doesn't shrink when washed, so preshrinking isn't necessary (see "Taking special care when working with fleece" earlier in this chapter).
>
> ✔ For dry-clean-only fabrics, trims, and zippers, set your steam iron for high steam. Hold the iron above the surface of the fabric, letting the steam penetrate the fibers, but without soaking the fabric or zipper. Line-dry the fabric and then iron the fabric flat with a dry iron (not set on the steam setting).
>
> ✔ Home decor fabrics and trims can become dull-looking and limp when they're preshrunk — so don't do it. Check out the care instructions on the trim, hang tags, and bolt ends for more complete care instructions.

As soon as you get back from the fabric store, preshrink your fabric. If you preshrink and put off the project, you don't have to wonder later, "Did I preshrink my fabric already?"

Preshrinking fusible interfacing

If fusible interfacing isn't fused according to the manufacturer's instructions, it can shrink after you wash the project, causing a rippled bubbly appearance. It can also detach from or become too crisp for the fabric, resulting in a stiff, boardy look that screams H-O-M-E-M-A-D-E.

Preshrinking woven or knitted fusible interfacing reduces the chances of such disasters. I preshrink these types of interfacings by soaking them in hot tap water until they're completely wet and then letting them air or line-dry.

Fusible tricot, which is a wonderful lightweight knitted interfacing, curls terribly when you preshrink it. So instead of preshrinking it, I cut out my interfacing pattern pieces on the bias (see more about the bias in Chapter 4), and the tricot behaves beautifully in the finished project. Other fusible interfacings that work well without preshrinking are the nonwoven variety, provided that you follow the manufacturer's instructions for application printed on the plastic interleafing wrapped around the interfacing. These directions tell you everything you need to know about using the product, including important information such as how to cut out the pattern pieces, how hot to set your iron, and how long to leave the iron on the fabric.

For washable fabrics, preshrink your fabric by washing it as you would the finished project. For example, if you plan to wash your finished garment in the washing machine with regular-strength detergent and then dry it in the dryer, wash and dry your fabric in the same way to preshrink it. To prevent nonstop raveling of woven fabrics, finish off the raw edges first using one of the sewing machine or serger stitches shown in Chapter 6. After preshrinking, press your fabric smooth and flat. Now the fabric is ready for the layout and cutting process (see Chapter 4).

Also preshrink any trims, tapes, and piping you plan to use with your project. Wrap them around your hand and remove your hand from the trim, creating a *hank*, or coil. Put a rubber band around the hank and wash it along with the project's fabric.

Chapter 4

Working with Patterns

In This Chapter

▶ Finding the pattern you want

▶ Reading the pattern and the pattern envelope

▶ Laying out, pinning, and cutting out the pattern

▶ Transferring important marks to the fabric

*B*esides starting with a good piece of fabric and a pattern that fits your figure type, laying out, cutting, and marking the pattern pieces correctly are the foundations to your sewing success, as you see in this chapter. After you understand these important steps, you'll zoom toward a finished project.

Shopping for Patterns

Patterns are marketed through pattern magazines, which you can find on the newsstands at your local bookstore, fabric store, or grocery store. A number of independent pattern designers market their patterns via their Web sites and/or the online store www.etsy.com. (Think of Etsy as the eBay for anything handmade.) You can also find patterns in pattern catalogs at fabric stores that carry fashion fabrics (fabrics that are made into clothing as opposed to fabrics that are made into home décor, craft, or quilting projects). Common commercial pattern companies that put out catalogs include Burda, Kwik Sew, McCalls, Simplicity, Stretch & Sew, and Vogue/Butterick. Besides catalogs, fabric stores also display some specially priced or promotional patterns on spinner racks for easy access, or have racks specifically dedicated to one type of pattern such as window treatments.

In most pattern catalogs, projects are grouped by category, ranging from dresses and children's clothing to crafts and home décor. Within those categories, you often find patterns with different degrees of difficulty, usually with emphasis placed on easy-to-sew projects.

Even a pattern labeled *easy* or *quick* may be difficult and time-consuming for a rookie. Many pattern-instruction writers assume that you have a certain amount of general sewing knowledge. If you're a real beginner, look for patterns with few seams and simple lines.

The *Sewing For Dummies* patterns, published by Simplicity Pattern Company, are a perfect choice (see Figure 4-2 later in this chapter). They have stylish projects and the easiest-to-follow sewing directions you can find. If you can't figure out whether you're ready for a particular pattern, have a sales associate at the fabric store help you.

Sizing Things Up for Fashion Sewing

Determining your pattern size for a garment can be a humbling experience. Patterns for adults usually run smaller than ready-to-wear sizes you find in clothing stores — sad but true. That means, for example, that if you usually wear a size 10 dress, you may find yourself buying a size 12 pattern. However, patterns for children have the opposite problem and run larger than ready-to-wear sizes. Note that patterns often come with three or more sizes printed on the pattern paper. You simply cut out the pattern on the specified cutting line for your size.

And I have more bad news: For measurement accuracy, someone else must take and record your measurements. You just can't get accurate measurements by yourself, so don't even try it. Find someone you trust, swear them to secrecy, and start measuring. (See Chapter 2 if you're in the market for a measuring tape to take your vital statistics.)

To take your measurements and decide your pattern size and figure type, you need to locate your *natural waistline,* which is not necessarily where you wear your pants. To do so, dress in your underwear or a leotard and tie a piece of narrow ribbon or elastic around your waist. Don't cinch the ribbon too tight. Wiggle around until the ribbon or elastic finds your natural waistline — usually the narrowest part of your torso, about 7 to 9 inches above the fullest part of your hips.

Have your helper take the following six measurements. Figure 4-1 shows you the exact placement of each measurement:

- Height: _____
- Full bust circumference: _____
- High bust circumference (measured halfway between the collarbone and the full bust measurement): _____
- Waist circumference: _____
- Back waist length (measured from the bone at the back of the neck to the waistline): _____
- Hip circumference: _____

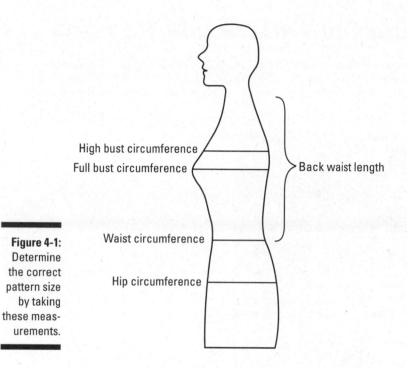

High bust circumference

Full bust circumference

Back waist length

Waist circumference

Hip circumference

Figure 4-1:
Determine
the correct
pattern size
by taking
these meas-
urements.

If you're shopping for a pattern in a fabric store that carries fashion fabric and pattern catalogs, somewhere in the front or back of the pattern catalog you can find measurement charts. Using your height and back waist length, determine your figure type (Junior, Misses/Miss petite, Child, Unisex, and so on), and then compare your other measurements with the charts to find the size that comes closest to your measurements. That's your pattern size. Write your size, the brand name of the pattern, and the number of the pattern you want to sew (usually a four-digit number) on a piece of paper and head to the retailer's pattern drawer. Stores file patterns numerically by brand. So after you find the brand, the pattern number, and your size pull the pattern from the drawer. Find your size on the chart on the back of the pattern envelope to see how much fabric you need to buy.

Online pattern shopping is convenient and very similar to finding patterns in a store. Each pattern company's site differs slightly, but they all organize patterns by category. If you have a local pattern retailer, comparison shop before you buy — unless the site is having a sale, you can often buy patterns cheaper at your local retailer. Each online retailer has a mountain of information regarding sizing, so carefully review this information to find the right pattern. Check out the appendix in this book for the most popular pattern company Web sites.

Deciphering the Pattern and Its Parts

Nothing can be more intimidating than trying to figure out all the hiero-glyphics on the various parts of a pattern envelope, shown in Figure 4-2. In this section I tell you just what you need to know about pattern parts.

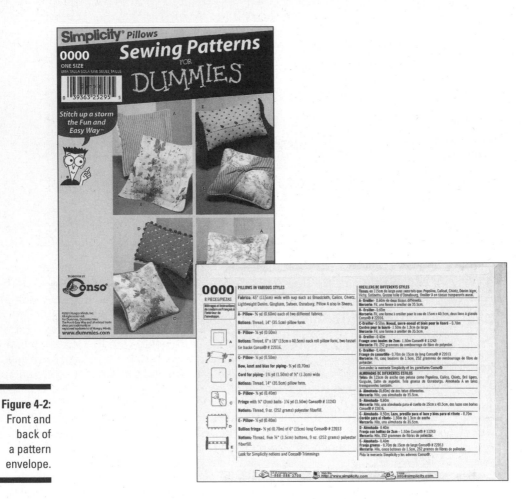

Figure 4-2:
Front and
back of
a pattern
envelope.

Checking out the front of the pattern envelope

On the front of the pattern envelope you often see several style variations of the same project. In the world of sewing, people call these style variations *views.* One view may have a collar, long sleeves, and cuffs. Another view may have a V-neck and short sleeves.

In home décor patterns, you may have several views in one pattern for a basic window treatment. Other patterns may have several pillow views or several options for chair covers. Views simply give you style options for creating the same basic project.

Reading the back of the pattern envelope

The back of a pattern envelope contains the following information about your project:

- **The back of the project in detail:** The front of the pattern envelope usually just shows the front of your project, and the back of the envelope shows you the back of the project. A line drawing shows you the details like kick pleats or a back zipper and the seamlines that you may not be able to see from the photograph on the front— information that you want to know about before choosing the pattern.

- **A description of the project by view:** Drawings and photographs can deceive, but this written description tells you exactly what you're getting so you can determine if it's within your skill set or not. For example, as a beginning sewer, a pattern with a raglan sleeve is easier to make than one with a set-in sleeve. (Find more about sleeve types in Chapter 10.)

- **How much fabric to buy:** This information is based on the width of the fabric you choose, the view you make, your size, and whether your fabric has nap (see Chapter 3 for info on fabric width and nap). The fabric is measured and priced by the yard as it comes off the bolt. So if you need 2 yards of fabric that is 54-inches wide but the fabric you choose only comes in 45-inch width, you need 2½ yards for the same yield. Check out the fabric conversion chart in Chapter 3 to make sure you buy just the right amount of fabric you need.

- **List of notions needed for specific views:** This list may include information such as the number and size of buttons, the zipper length and type, elastic width and length, shoulder pad style and size, hooks and eyes, and so on.

It's what's inside that counts

Inside your pattern envelope, you find the following items necessary for your project:

- ✔ **Pattern pieces:** Some pattern pieces are printed on large pieces of tissue paper. Others are printed on sturdy pieces of white paper called *master patterns.*

- ✔ **Key and glossary:** These references help you decipher the markings on the pattern pieces.

- ✔ **Pattern layout:** This guide shows you how to lay out the pattern pieces on the fabric yardage for each view.

- ✔ **Step-by-step instructions for putting the project together:** Depending on your knowledge of sewing, you may find this *pattern guide sheet* clear as day — or as mud. Don't worry, though — this book tells you what you need to know to decipher the instructions.

The project instructions may run more than one page. If they do, staple the pages together so you don't lose any. Post the instructions in front of you or next to your sewing machine as you sew so you can easily check off each step as you finish it.

Some home décor projects, such as pillow patterns, include tissue or paper pattern pieces. Others, such as sofa slipcovers and some window treatments, don't include a paper pattern because they don't use a standard size or style of sofa or window. In these patterns, you find just the step-by-step instructions.

Decoding the pattern pieces

When you look at your pattern pieces and see only one sleeve, half of a front top, half of a back top pattern, half of a collar, and so on, you may think that the company forgot to print the whole pattern. Not so. Because you fold the fabric in half the long way (usually with the right side of the fabric to the inside), you lay out the pattern pieces and cut them on a double fabric layer. So you usually need only half of the pattern to make a complete garment.

All pattern pieces have the following information printed on or near the center of each pattern piece:

- ✔ **Pattern number:** If you accidentally mix together pattern pieces of different projects, these numbers can help you figure out which pieces belong to which projects.

- ✔ **Name of the pattern piece:** These names are pretty straightforward — sleeve, front pant, and so on.

- **Letter or number of the pattern piece:** These identifiers help you find all the pattern pieces for the view you're making (see the previous section "Reading the front of the pattern envelope" for information about views).

- **Size:** Many pattern pieces show several sizes. Each size is marked clearly, so you shouldn't have too much trouble keeping them straight.

- **Number of pieces you need to cut:** Often, you need to cut more than one of each pattern piece. For example, on the sleeve pattern you may see *cut 2* so you end up with both a right and left sleeve. If you lay and cut out the sleeve on a double layer of fabric, it counts as two sleeves.

The pattern markings listed below and shown in Figure 4-3 appear around the periphery of the pattern pieces:

- **Cutting line:** This heavy, outer line on the pattern piece lets you know where to cut and may feature scissors symbols.

- **Seamline or stitching line:** You usually find this broken line ¼ to ⅝ inch inside the cutting line. Multiple-sized patterns may not have a seamline printed on the pattern. Read the pattern guide sheet to determine the width of the seam allowance. (Chapter 6 tells you more about seams.)

- **Notches:** You use these diamond-shaped match points on the cutting line for accurately joining one pattern piece to another. You may find single notches, double notches, and triple notches all on one pattern.

- **Circles, dots, triangles, or squares:** No, this isn't a geometry lesson. These shapes indicate additional match points that aid in the construction, fit, and ease of putting the project together. For example, large dots on the pattern may indicate where you gather a waistline. The corresponding instruction on your pattern guide sheet says something like, "Gather from large dot to large dot."

- **Place-on-fold brackets or symbols:** Use these symbols to lay out the pattern piece exactly on the fold of the fabric, which is usually along the lengthwise grain of the fabric. When you cut out the pattern piece and remove the paper pattern, the fabric unfolds into a single piece that is twice the size of the pattern.

- **Lengthen or shorten directives:** Based on your measurements, your body may be longer or shorter than the paper pattern piece. These double lines show where you can cut the pattern apart to lengthen it or fold up the pattern piece to shorten it.

- **Darts:** Darts help shape the flat piece of fabric into a form-fitting one that fits the curves of the human body (see Chapter 8). Broken stitching lines meet at a point to create the dart. Some patterns also have a solid line that runs the length of the dart showing where you fold the fabric to create the dart.

- **Center back and center front:** These directions are clearly labeled with a solid cutting line or place-on-fold symbol (refer to that item earlier in this list). If the pattern has a solid cutting line, it means the garment has a seam down the center front or center back. If, instead, you place the center front or center back on the fold, you don't have a seam down the center front or the center back.

- ✔ **Zipper position:** This symbol shows the zipper placement. The top and bottom markings (usually dots) show you the length of the zipper. (Chapter 9 covers putting in a zipper.)

- ✔ **Grainline:** The most important pattern marking, the grainline symbol is a straight line that may or may not have arrowheads at each end. The grainline parallels the *selvages* (finished edges) of the fabric. See the section "Placing the pattern pieces on-grain" later in this chapter to find out why this marking is critical for your sewing success.

- ✔ **Directional-stitching symbols:** These symbols, which often look like small arrows or presser feet symbols, indicate the direction you sew when sewing the seam.

- ✔ **The hemline:** This direction on the pattern shows the recommended finished length of the project, which varies from person to person. But, even though the hemline may vary, the *hem allowance* (the recommended distance from the hemline to the cut edge) doesn't. See Chapter 7 for more information on hem depths.

Figure 4-3 shows the full gamut of markings you may find on a pattern piece.

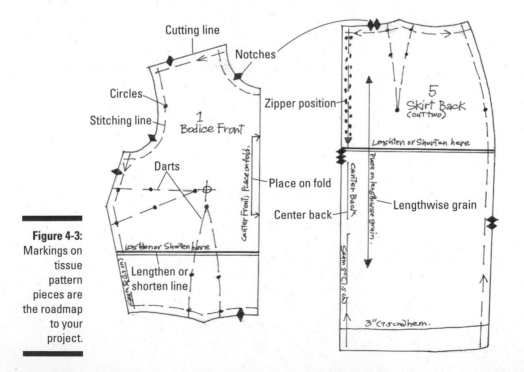

Figure 4-3: Markings on tissue pattern pieces are the roadmap to your project.

Laying Out the Pattern

Before laying out the pattern on the fabric, you need to understand some basic fabric terminology. Understanding the parts of the fabric and cutting your pattern pieces on-grain means that seams stay pressed and straight, pant legs and sleeves don't twist when you wear them, and the creases in your pants and the stripes, plaid, and prints stay perpendicular to the ground.

Getting to know your fabric

If you hear the word *grain* and think of oatmeal, you're not quite ready to lay out your pattern. Knowing your way around a piece of fabric is crucial to your sewing success. Take a look at Figure 4-4 to acquaint yourself with fabric's four key facets:

- **Selvages:** The finished edges where the fabric comes off the looms, the selvages are parallel to the lengthwise grain.

- **Lengthwise grain or grainline:** The grainline runs the length of the fabric, parallel to the selvages. On knit fabrics, the lengthwise grain is usually more stable and less stretchy than the crosswise grain.

- **Crosswise grain:** This grain runs across the width of the fabric, from selvage to selvage and perpendicular to the lengthwise grain. On knit fabrics, most of the stretch is usually across the grain.

- **Bias:** 45 degrees between the lengthwise and crosswise grains. When you pull a woven fabric on the bias it stretches and is very malleable. This is why bias tape (see Chapter 3) and trims that are cut on the bias can be easily shaped to follow a curved edge.

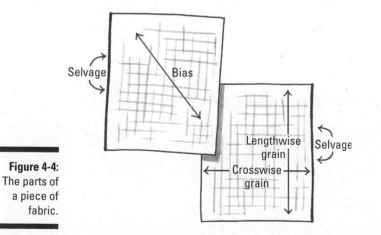

Figure 4-4:
The parts of
a piece of
fabric.

Preparing the fabric

Using fabric straight off the bolt is a little like eating an unbaked apple pie: You can do it, but the results won't be so good. You skip an important step if you don't preshrink and press your fabric before you begin. (See Chapter 3 for more information on preshrinking; you're on your own for the apple pie.)

Even after preshrinking and pressing your fabric, you may notice a crease where the fabric was folded on the bolt. You can press this pesky crease out of most fabrics by sprinkling equal parts of white vinegar and water on a press cloth and then laying the press cloth on the crease between the iron and the fabric, pressing until the fabric dries.

After you press the fabric, let it dry completely and then refold it to the original bolt fold so that the selvages are even. Then take a look at the fabric: When you fold it in half so the selvages are together, are the raw edges perpendicular to the selvages and the selvages parallel to one another? If not, the fabric may have been cut off the bolt unevenly, or the fabric needs to be pulled back on grain. To do so, unfold the fabric again, pull it on the bias (refer to Figure 4-4), and straighten it. If you have a large piece of fabric, get a helper to pull the yardage from one corner while you pull on the yardage from the opposite corner.

Knowing right from wrong

The *right side* of the fabric is the pretty side that everyone sees. Most fabrics are folded or rolled on the bolt with the right side folded to the inside to keep it clean. The *wrong side* of the fabric is the inside that nobody sees when you wear the project. When you lay out the pattern for cutting, be sure that you lay out all the pattern pieces as shown in your pattern guide sheet instructions.

The pattern guide sheet shows the right side of the fabric shaded in a darker color than the wrong side of the fabric so you can see what's going on in the step-by-step illustrations.

Placing the pattern pieces on-grain

Each pattern piece shows a grainline (which can also be the place-on-fold symbol) which is also the lengthwise grain. See the section "Decoding the pattern pieces" earlier in this chapter for more information on the chicken scratches you find on pattern pieces.) The grainline allows you to cut the piece *on-grain,* meaning that the pattern piece lines up with the lengthwise grain of the fabric.

If you don't have a large table or countertop to cut on, buy a foldable cutting board. It's a large, flat sheet of corrugated cardboard with a fold or two in the middle, and usually comes with a grid of inches and centimeters printed on it. Lay it on a small table and you have an instant workable cutting space. When you finish using it, fold it up and slide it under your bed or behind your dresser.

Follow these steps to lay the pattern pieces on the fabric:

1. **Find and cut apart the paper pattern pieces you need to make your project view; set them aside.**

   If you're using a multisized master pattern and want to preserve the option of making the project in a different size in the future, trace the pattern size you need on pattern tracing paper, remembering to transfer all the pattern markings from the master pattern.

   When you cut the paper pattern pieces apart, don't cut them out right on the cutting line; leave a little of the paper past the cutting line. Leaving the extra paper makes cutting out the paper pieces faster and easier when you get it on the fabric.

2. **Locate the lengthwise grain or place-on-fold symbols on the paper pattern pieces.**

   On a flat tabletop, before laying the pattern tissue on the fabric, mark over these symbols using a highlighter for easy reference.

3. **Fold and then lay the fabric on a table or cutting board, as shown in the pattern guide sheet instructions.**

   If the fabric is longer than your table or cutting board, prevent the excess fabric weight from stretching and pulling on your fabric by folding it and laying it on the end of the table.

4. **Following the suggested layout found on the pattern guide sheet, lay out the pattern on-grain, making sure that the grainline is parallel to the selvages as shown in Figure 4-5.**

Figure 4-5:
The grain-line of your pattern tissue should be parallel to the fabric selvages.

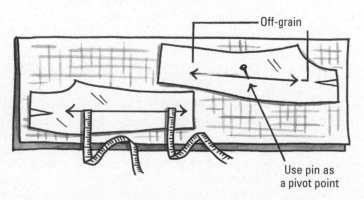

Off-grain

Use pin as a pivot point

Check that each pattern piece is placed precisely on-grain by poking a pin straight down into the grainline, measuring the distance straight across from one end of the grainline to the selvage, and then measuring the distance from the other end of the grainline straight across to the same selvage. Be sure to pivot the paper pattern so that each end of the pattern piece is equidistant from the selvage. Remember to use this technique only if a cutting board or table pad protects your tabletop.

Laying out plaids, stripes, and one-way designs

You don't often see perfectly matched plaids and stripes in ready-to-wear garments — unless you want to spend a lot of money. Garment manufacturers find it tough to match designs because they stack many layers of fabric as high as 12 inches and then cut out each pattern piece with a jigsaw. That system lets them cut 100 left sleeves at once, but it leaves little room for precision. As a home sewer, though, you cut one garment at a time, so you can more easily get a perfect match with a one-way design, stripe, or plaid.

Save yourself a major headache: If you plan to use fabric with a plaid, stripe, or one-way design, avoid patterns that say "not suitable for plaids, stripes, or one-way designs." Princess lines (seams that run from the shoulder seam, over the bust, and down to the hemline) and patterns with long vertical darts are also hard to match if you use this kind of fabric.

Because you need more fabric when working with these patterns, remember to use the *with nap* yardage requirements found on the back of the pattern envelope (see Chapter 3 for more on nap).

One-way designs

Your fabric contains a one-way design if the pattern makes sense only when you view it from one direction. For example, fabric printed with a directional floral design makes sense only if all the flowers point up. To make them right-side up all over the project, you have to lay out all the pattern pieces in the same direction, as shown in Figure 4-6.

When working with a one-way design, consider the following factors:

✔ **Size of each design in the print:** If the fabric has a small-scale, all-over print (meaning that the print has a design where it runs in all directions), you don't need to worry so much about matching the design. If the scale of the print is large — say 2½ to 3 inches in any direction — you want the design to match across the front, over to the sleeves, and to the back of the garment.

Placement is important when working with a large-scale print, so think before you cut. For example, you don't want a print with big red balloons to end up with a balloon at both bust points. You also don't want sailing ships positioned over your derriere because it may seem like some major waves toss them around when you walk.

✔ **Size of the repeat of the pattern:** This size means the distance between each repeating design on the fabric. If the repeat is ½ inch, a small example, you may not have to match it. If the repeat is 4 inches, though, the repeat is large and should be matched.

Figure 4-6:
For a one-way design, lay out pattern pieces so they run in the same direction — think "this side up."

Even and uneven stripes

Stripes have bars of color printed, knitted, or woven either horizontally or vertically in the fabric. Stripes come in two varieties:

✔ **Even stripe:** This pattern has an even number of color bars, and all the color bars are the same width. Think of a T-shirt knit with alternating 1-inch white stripes and 1-inch blue stripes. When working with an even stripe, you can lay out pattern pieces in either direction (with the top edge of the pattern at the top of the fabric or the top edge of the pattern at the bottom of the fabric), and the stripes match.

✔ **Uneven stripe:** This pattern has the same-width stripes and an odd number of color bars, or different-width stripes with an odd or even number of color bars. For example, a T-shirt knit with horizontal stripes with a 1-inch red stripe, a ½-inch white stripe, and a 1-inch blue stripe has an uneven stripe pattern. If you cut the pattern pieces in opposite directions, the stripes don't match: The color bars line up as red, white, and blue on one piece and as blue, white, and red on the other piece.

Pattern piece storage made easy

Trying to put the pattern pieces back into the envelope after using them is like putting toothpaste back into the tube. Instead, tape a gallon-sized plastic freezer bag next to your sewing machine. Put the pattern envelope, extra pattern pieces, and guide sheet into this bag — I find it much easier than using the pattern envelope, and everything fits. After you finish the project, store the bag and pattern with your other patterns.

When you finish with each pattern piece, fold it so that the pattern number, name, and company name show. This way, if you forget to mark something, you can see it through the freezer bag and locate it easily without unfolding and shuffling through multiple paper pattern pieces.

As a beginning sewer, you need to steer clear of uneven stripes. If you're unsure whether the fabric you chose is an even or uneven stripe, ask the fabric store sales associate to identify it for you. If you don't, you're asking for A.S.F.S. — Acute Sewing Frustration Syndrome.

Even and uneven plaids

Plaid fabrics have color bars printed or woven into the fabric both horizontally and vertically. As you can see in Figure 4-7, plaids come in two different flavors:

- ✔ **Even plaid:** The color bars in an even plaid match in the lengthwise and crosswise directions. To check for an even plaid, fold the fabric in half the long way (like when you lay out the pattern for cutting) and then turn back a corner, folding it on the bias (see the section "Getting to know your fabric," earlier in this chapter, for information on the bias). If the top layer of plaid forms a mirror image of the bottom layer, you have an even plaid. You can match even plaids more easily than uneven plaids.

- ✔ **Uneven plaid:** This plaid doesn't match in one or both directions and as a result is more difficult to work with. Use the test in the "Even plaid" bullet above to determine whether you have an even or uneven plaid on your hands. Until you have considerable experience in laying out and cutting fabric, avoid uneven plaids.

Uneven plaids present problems for the beginning sewer because of the matching difficulty they present. If you're unsure whether or not a fabric is an uneven plaid, ask the fabric store sales associate to identify it for you. As your skills improve, start with a small, even plaid and gain some confidence before tackling uneven plaids.

Figure 4-7:
Even plaids
have a
mirror
image when
folded back
on the bias.
Uneven
plaids don't.

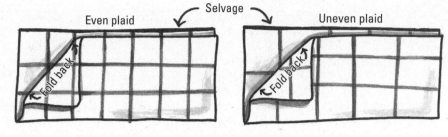

After pinning the pattern piece to the fabric (described later in "Pinning and Cutting Out the Pieces"), use an air-soluble marker to draw the design onto the pattern tissue, following the dominant color bars at or near the notches. In Figure 4-8 you can see the back and front blouse pieces and find the single and double notches at the side seams. By drawing the plaid on the pattern tissue, you can easily see how to position the pattern pieces so when the seams are sewn together, the design matches. If you need to cut each pattern piece separately on a single layer of fabric, remove the pattern tissue that you drew over, flip it over so you're cutting the other side of the pattern piece and place it on the fabric so that the color bars on the plaid or stripe you see marked on the pattern paper match those on the fabric.

Figure 4-8:
Match a
plaid by
drawing
over the
design on
the pattern
tissue at
or near the
notches.

Lay out twice and cut once

The following tips help in laying out a pattern for large, one-way designs, stripes, and even plaids:

- **Centering:** Decide what you want in the center of the project and fold the fabric there, matching the stripes, plaid, or one-way designs across the width and length of the fabric. Doing so may mean that the selvages aren't even. You may also have to pin the fabric together every few inches or so to keep the fabric from shifting when you lay it out and cut it according to the pattern.

- **Placement:** Generally, you place the dominant stripe or color bar in a project directly on, or as close as possible to, the hemline edge. This arrangement means placing the hemline marked on the pattern tissue along the dominant color bar of the fabric. Avoid placing the dominant stripe, color bar, or big red balloons across the bust or at the fullest part of the hips.

- **Crosswise matching:** Use the notches on the pattern pieces to match the fabric design from piece to piece. For example, to match the design at the shoulder seams, notice where the notches on the pattern pieces fall on a particular color bar and within the plaid itself.

  Crosswise matching is easiest when you center the first pattern piece on the fabric where you want it. After you center the pattern, take the pattern piece you want to match the fabric to and place it over the first, matching the notches.

Pinning and Cutting Out the Pieces

Pin the pattern piece to the doubled layer of fabric so that the pins go through both fabric layers and are perpendicular to and inside of the cutting line. This prevents the fabric from shifting during the cutting process. (See the section "Laying Out the Pattern," earlier in this chapter, for more information on folding your fabric to create a double layer.)

My grandmother taught me to pin parallel to the cutting line. While researching the *right* way to pin for this book, I realized I've been doing it wrong all these years but still had beautiful results. So here's the message: Whenever you find a way of doing anything in sewing that you like and that works, use it.

You don't need to pin every inch. Just pin at the notches and everywhere the pattern changes direction. On long, straight edges, such as pant legs and sleeve seams, place pins every 4 inches or so.

Cut out your pattern pieces using a pair of sharp dressmaker's shears. (See Chapter 2 for more information on choosing the right scissors for cutting.) For accuracy, cut in the middle of the solid cutting line marked on the pattern tissue, trying not to lift the fabric off the table too much when cutting.

Rather than cutting around each individual notch, save time by cutting straight across the notches on the cutting line. After you completely cut out the pattern piece, go back and, with the tips of your sharp scissors, snip into the notch about ¼ inch. A single notch gets one snip in the center of the notch; a double notch gets two snips, one in the center of each notch; a triple notch gets three snips. When you go to match up the pattern pieces at the notches, just match up the snips — a fast and accurate task.

Making Your Mark

After you cut out the pattern pieces and cut out and fuse on any necessary interfacing (see Chapter 3 for more about using fusible interfacing), you're ready for marking. Marking is important because you don't want to get half-way through a project, notice that the pattern guide sheet tells you to sew from this mark to that mark, and realize that you forgot to mark something (or thought it wasn't important). Save yourself time and frustration by marking the dots, circles, squares, or triangles, even if you think that you won't need them later. (Trust me, you will.)

Marking what matters

You need to mark the following things from your pattern pieces onto your fabric:

- Darts (see Chapter 8)
- Pleats (see Chapter 8)
- Tucks
- Dots, circles, triangles, and squares (see the section "Decoding the pattern pieces," earlier in this chapter)

When you begin constructing a project, you transfer the pattern marks indicating darts, tucks, pleats, and the other symbols to your fabric pattern pieces for a very good reason: To see and understand what the drawings and text in the pattern guide sheet mean for you to do. For example, when marking a pleat, tuck, or dart, instead of marking the entire stitching line, simply mark the dots on the stitching lines. When you put the right sides together for sewing, pin the project together by matching the dots; sew from dot to dot (pin to pin). For specific instructions on marking and sewing darts, tucks, and pleats, see your pattern guide sheet instructions.

Using the right tool at the right time

You find many marking tools on the market, but using pins, disappearing dressmaking chalk, and an air- or water-soluble marking pen is the easiest way to go. Chapter 2 gives you more information on these tools.

Use the following marking techniques, depending on the type of fabric you use in a project:

✔ **Mark light-colored fabrics by using your air- or water-soluble marker.** Place the point of the marker on the tissue pattern at the dot or circle, as shown in Figure 4-9. The ink bleeds through the pattern tissue, the first layer of fabric, and then to the second layer of fabric for an accurate mark. You can easily remove the marks from either marker with water.

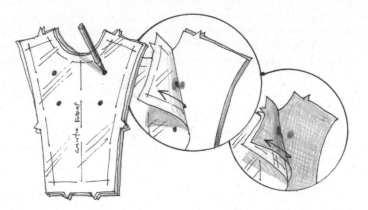

Figure 4-9: Mark light-colored fabrics with an air- or water-soluble marker.

✔ **Mark dark fabrics by using your disappearing dressmaker's chalk.** Push pins through the pattern paper and both fabric layers at the dots, as shown in Figure 4-10. Open the fabric between the layers and mark both layers where the pins enter the fabric.

When marking with chalk, I prefer marking the wrong side of the fabric. The mark is easier to see and doesn't show on the right side of the fabric. But be careful: The steam from an iron can sometimes remove the mark, which is okay when you want it to disappear and maddening when it happens accidentally.

Figure 4-10:
Mark dark
fabric with
pins and
disappearing
dress-
maker's
chalk.

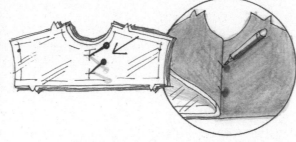

✔ **Mark hard-to-mark fabrics by pin-marking.** Two pins are inserted from opposite sides so that they remain in each piece when the pattern pieces are pulled apart. To do this, push the pin straight through both fabric layers, and then flip over the fabric and repeat the process. Carefully remove the pattern paper from one side by tearing it over the pin heads, and then pull apart the fabric layers. The pins pull right up to the heads and accurately mark the fabric, as you can see in Figure 4-11. Then adjust the pins so they go through the fabric normally, with the place where the pin enters the fabric marking the spot. Then leave them pinned into place until you complete the step that uses the mark.

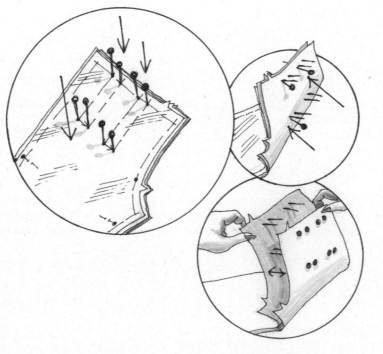

Figure 4-11:
Mark
pattern
pieces by
pushing
pins straight
through
both fabric
layers at the
dots marked
on the
pattern
tissue.

Part II
Mastering Basic Sewing Skills

The 5th Wave   By Rich Tennant

"The intruder was no match for the old woman. She took him down and hand stitched him to the carpet before he knew what was happening. Someone unzip his mouth so we can hear what he has to say."

In this part . . .

The chapters in this part focus on the fundamentals of sewing. If you're a stone-cold beginner to sewing, you'll definitely appreciate the step-by-step coverage of threading a needle, sewing many common types of hand stitches, using an iron effectively, finishing fabric edges, sewing seams, and hemming, among other fun sewing fundamentals. If you have sewn before, you may be tempted to skip over the chapters in this part — don't! Each chapter contains tips and hints that help even a more experienced sewer. Plus, this part contains some really great sewing projects that you don't want to miss.

Chapter 5

Kicking Off Your Sewing Adventure

In This Chapter

▶ Wedding needle and thread

▶ Tying knots that last

▶ Sewing stitches by hand and machine

▶ Basting projects, not turkeys

▶ Ironing and pressing for better results

▶ Creating a cozy pillow from a repurposed shirt

Whether you're a football fan or not, the most exciting part of the game is the kickoff. You never know how the game will end, and you're filled with anticipation. This is how I feel when I start a new sewing project. In my mind's eye I can see the results and anticipate the cheers and accolades from my friends and family members when they see the final product. The best news about sewing is that for the most part, you're always a winner because in a sitting or two, you can see good results right in front of your eyes.

Whether you quilt, embroider, mend, or construct a project, you need a needle, thread, fabric, and some sewing know-how. This chapter covers the important sewing fundamentals.

Threading the Needle

When a motorist *threads the needle* on the freeway, she weaves in and out of traffic, almost hitting other cars in the process. Although threading the needle in sewing is much less dangerous, it does require some skill. It's also a task that differs depending on the type of needle you're working with — hand or machine.

Hand needles

To begin threading a hand needle, reel off a strand of thread about 18 to 24 inches long. (Longer threads tend to tangle and wear out before you use them up.) Starting with the end of the thread that comes off the spool first, cut the thread cleanly and at an angle with a sharp pair of scissors. Cutting at an angle puts a little point on the thread so that it slips easily through the eye.

The cheapest sewing notion on the market is your own saliva. Moisten the thread end to help it glide right through the needle's eye.

Because some needles have very small eyes and some people have very poor eyesight, a *needle threader,* which you can find at your local sewing supply store, can help with tight threading situations. To use a needle threader, poke the fine wire loop through the eye of the needle, push the thread end through the wire loop, and then pull on the threader. The wire grabs the thread and pulls it through the needle's eye, as shown in Figure 5-1.

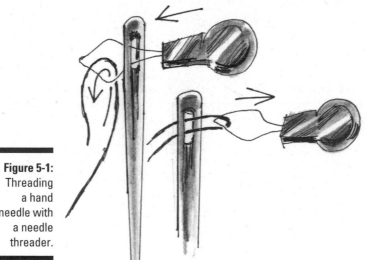

Figure 5-1:
Threading a hand needle with a needle threader.

Self-threading hand needles make threading even easier. To use a self-threading needle, hold the needle and a length of thread in one hand. Pull the thread end across the self-threading eye so that the thread lies in the notch. Snap the thread into the notch until it clips into place, as shown in Figure 5-2. If the thread keeps coming unthreaded after many uses, you've worn out the self-threading eye, so throw away the needle and use a new one. Note that the other eye below the self-threading eye can be used like a regular hand needle as well.

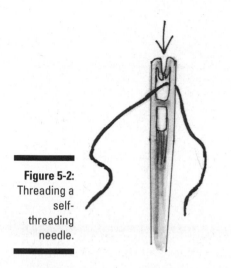

Figure 5-2:
Threading a
self-
threading
needle.

No amount of spit helps thread a tapestry needle because the embroidery
floss or yarn commonly used with these needles tends to get frizzy at the end.
Just fold over the end of the floss or yarn and poke it through the eye,
as shown in Figure 5-3.

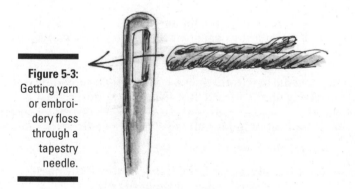

Figure 5-3:
Getting yarn
or embroi-
dery floss
through a
tapestry
needle.

Machine needles

A *machine needle,* meaning a needle for a standard sewing machine and most
sergers, has a round and a flat side, as shown in Figure 5-4. (See Chapter 2 for
more information on sewing machines and sergers.)

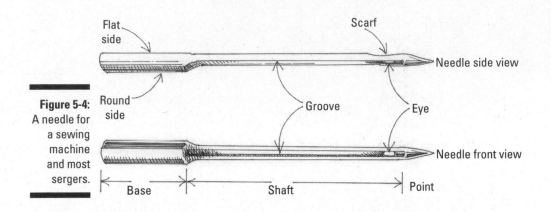

Figure 5-4:
A needle for
a sewing
machine
and most
sergers.

For sewing machines with a *side-loading bobbin* (meaning the bobbin goes in the left side of the machine), the flat side of the needle base faces to the right. For most sergers and sewing machines with *front-* and *top-loading bobbins* (meaning that the bobbin goes in the front or drops into the top of the machine's bed where the fabric rests on the machine when sewing), the flat side of the needle base faces to the back.

Make sure that you position the needle properly for your kind of machine. The long groove running the length of the shaft protects the thread as it stitches up and down through the fabric. The *scarf*, the little indentation behind the eye, creates a loop that enables the bobbin thread to lock with the top thread, making a stitch. If you put the needle in the machine backwards, nothing works right.

The anatomy of a machine needle makes threading it easier than threading a hand needle. Instead of spitting on the thread, just follow these steps:

1. **Lick your finger and then rub it behind the eye of the needle.**

2. **Cut the end of the thread cleanly and at an angle.**

3. **Starting just above the eye, run the end of the thread down the shaft in the front groove until the thread pokes through the eye.**

   When the thread hits the eye, the moisture pulls the thread through it, and you're ready to pull the thread through the eye of the needle.

4. **Pull four to five inches of thread through the needle so it won't come unthreaded as you start sewing.**

Tying a Sewing Knot

You may think that having a knot in your thread is a bad thing. That's true if you didn't put it there and the thread tangles when you don't want it to. Not to worry, however, if you tie the knot intentionally to stop the thread from pulling completely through the fabric when you sew on a button and at other times where you want to anchor the end of the thread.

When preparing to write this book, I took an unofficial poll of my sewing buddies to discover whether right-handed sewers tie a sewing knot with their right hand. (I'm right-handed, and I do.) I found out that how you tie a knot doesn't seem to have a thing to do with the dominant hand; what feels natural when it comes to knot tying depends on the way you were taught.

Using whichever hand you prefer (I show you both the left- and right-handed steps so you can try it both ways), follow these steps to tie a sewing knot:

1. **Hold the thread between your thumb and index fingers and wrap a loop of thread, about two inches from the end of the thread, around the tip of your opposite index finger, as shown in Figure 5-5.**

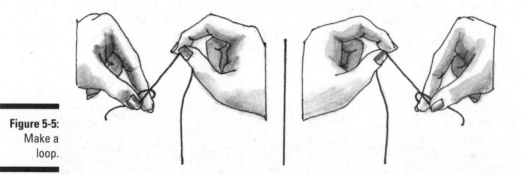

Figure 5-5:
Make a
loop.

2. **Roll the loop between your finger and against your thumb so that the loop twists, as shown in Figure 5-6.**

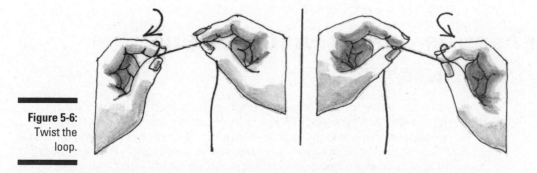

Figure 5-6:
Twist the
loop.

3. **Slide your index finger back while rolling the thread until the loop is almost off your finger, as shown in Figure 5-7.**

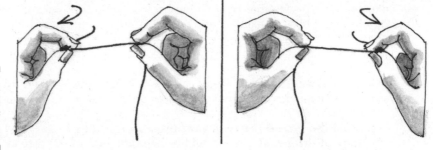

Figure 5-7:
Roll the loop to the end of your finger.

4. **Bring your middle finger to the twisted end of the loop, remove your index finger, and firmly place the middle finger in front of the twisted thread against the thumb, as shown in Figure 5-8.**

5. **Pull on the thread with the opposite hand to close the loop and form the knot.**

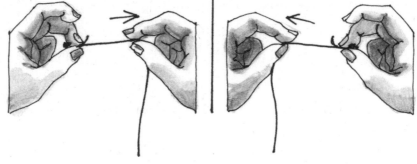

Figure 5-8:
Secure the loop end with your middle finger, and then tighten the knot.

Choosing and Using the Right Hand Stitches

Any given sewing job may entail several types of stitches, and you definitely need the right stitch for the job. For example, don't use a hand-basting stitch to permanently sew together a pair of overalls; the stitches are too far apart, and your overalls will fall apart the first time you attempt to tote that barge or lift that bale. In this section I familiarize you with the basic hand stitches and their uses.

The securing stitch

In hand sewing, you secure the end of a stitch by sewing a knot — regardless of the stitch. To sew a knot, take a small backstitch and form a loop over the point of the needle. When you pull the thread through the loop, it cinches the thread and secures a knot at the base of the fabric (see Figure 5-9). When securing a high-stress area, sew two knots.

Figure 5-9:
Use this
technique
to securely
fasten a
hand-sewn
stitch.

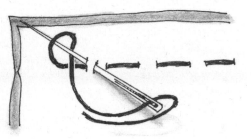

The hand-basting stitch

You use hand-basting stitches to temporarily hold two or more layers of fabric together. (See the section "Basting Project for a Better Fit," later in this chapter, for more information on its purpose.) If you use thread of a contrasting color from the fabric, the stitches are easier to see and pull out after you sew in the permanent stitches.

Working from right to left (for right-handers) or from left to right (for left-handers), weave the point of the needle in and out of the fabric for several stitches before pulling the thread through the fabric (see Figure 5-10). Make each basting stitch about ¼ inch long with less than ¼ inch in between each stitch.

Figure 5-10:
You baste
by simply
weaving the
needle in
and out of
the fabric.

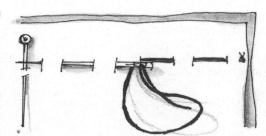

The running stitch

You use this very short, even stitch for fine seaming, mending, and gathering. The stitch is short and tight and, as a result, is usually permanent. I use it to quickly or temporarily repair a seam that comes apart.

To make a running stitch, weave the point of the needle in and out of the fabric making very short ($\frac{1}{16}$ inch), even stitches before pulling the rest of the needle through the fabric (see Figure 5-11).

Figure 5-11: Use short, even stitches when fashioning running stitches.

The even backstitch

The even backstitch is the strongest hand stitch. Because of its durability, you use this stitch more often when repairing a seam on dense, heavier fabrics than you would repair with the running stitch.

To create the even backstitch, pull the needle up through the fabric and poke the needle back into the fabric half a stitch behind where the thread first emerged. Bring the needle up half a stitch in front of where the thread first emerged (see Figure 5-12). Repeat for the length of the seam.

Figure 5-12: The even backstitch is extremely strong.

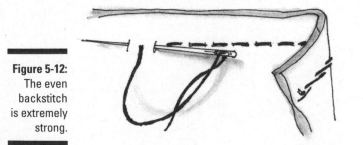

The blind hemming stitch

You sew these stitches inside the hem allowance between the hem and the garment (see Chapter 7 for more information on the fine points of hemming). With a little practice, a fine needle, and fine thread, good blind hemming stitches don't show on the right side — hence the name *blind.*

You need to turn up the hem allowance and press it into place before you use the blind hemming stitch. You should also finish the edge of the hem by pinking the edge or overcasting (see Chapter 6 for more on edge finishes).

Fold the hem allowance back ⅜ inch and take the first short stitch ¼ inch from the hem edge. Take the next short stitch by catching only a thread of the fabric. Continue with stitches spaced about ½ inch apart, catching the hem allowance in a stitch and taking as fine a stitch as possible into the garment. Stitch back and forth between the hem allowance and the garment around the hemline until you complete the blind hemming (see Figure 5-13).

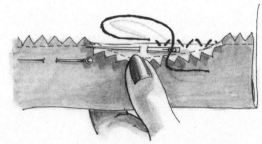

Figure 5-13: Blind hems require fine stitches about ½ inch apart.

The slant hemming or whip stitch

This stitch is the fastest — but least durable — of the hemming stitches because so much thread is on the surface of the hem edge. (If you've ever caught your heel in your hem and pulled it out, you may be the victim of a slant hemming stitch.) So use the slant hemming stitch only if you're in a hurry and you're hemming the bottom of a blouse that you tuck in. Take a stitch around the hem edge and then up through the garment, catching only a thread of the garment fabric (see Figure 5-14).

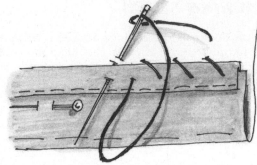

The hemming slipstitch

You use the hemming slipstitch when working with (guess what?) a folded hem edge. This stitch is very durable and almost invisible. (See Chapter 7 for more information about hemming.)

Fasten the thread to the hem allowance by poking the needle through the fold of the hem edge and bringing it up through the hem allowance. With the point of the needle, pick up one thread from the garment and work the needle back into the fold of the hem edge (see Figure 5-15). Then repeat the process.

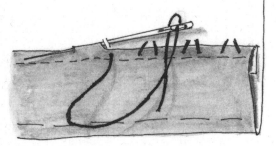

The even slipstitch

You can join two folded edges by using the even slipstitch. Most often, this stitch comes into play when you want to repair a seam from the right side because the seam is difficult to reach from the wrong side of the project.

Fasten the thread and bring it out at the edge of the fold. Taking fine stitches, slip the needle through the fold on one edge and draw the thread taut. Take another stitch, slipping the needle through the opposite folded edge (see Figure 5-16).

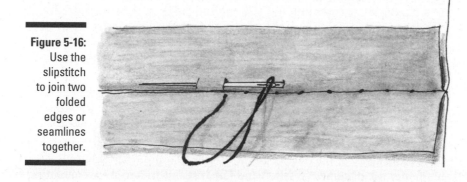

Figure 5-16:
Use the slipstitch to join two folded edges or seamlines together.

Working with Machine Stitches

My parents gave me a sewing machine for my high-school graduation. After threading the machine, the first thing I did was to try all the stitches. I had no idea what they did and thought I wouldn't use most of them. Later, after college and during my professional training as a home economist with White Sewing Machine Company, I discovered that the various stitches save time and produce more professional results.

For example, instead of sewing on buttons by hand, if I use the zigzag stitch, buttons almost never fall off. Instead of using time-consuming hand seam-finishing techniques, I can finish the raw fabric edges with my sewing machine or serger, using one of the many overcasting stitches discussed in this section and in Chapter 6. I produce beautifully machine-stitched hems in a fraction of the time it takes to hem them by hand. Finding out how to use these stitches was an epiphany, and I'm happy to share this practical knowledge with you.

Examining the basic machine stitches

Figure 5-17 shows the basic machine stitches. Of course, your machine may offer more or fewer of these stitches. Most machines have a good selection, though, so compare what's available on your sewing machine with these.

- ✔ **Straight:** You use the straight stitch for basting, seaming, and topstitching.
- ✔ **Zigzag:** Increase the stitch width to make zigzag stitches. The fabric moves under the presser foot while the needle moves from side to side. You use the zigzag stitch for stitching around appliqués, making buttonholes, sewing on buttons, and embroidering. The zigzag stitch is as practical as it is fun.

- **Three-step zigzag:** When used on the widest width, the ordinary zigzag stitch pulls the fabric into a tunnel, and the fabric rolls under the stitch — not very desirable. The three-step zigzag stitch eliminates this problem. The needle takes three stitches to one side and then three stitches to the other side, keeping the fabric flat and tunnel-free. Use the three-step zigzag for finishing raw edges, sewing on elastic, mending tears, and making decorative effects.

- **Blind hem and stretch blind hem:** The blind hem stitch is designed to hem woven fabrics so that the stitches are almost invisible when you look at the right side of the garment. The stretch blind hem stitch has an extra zigzag or two that stretches to invisibly hem knit fabrics. Both stitches have decorative applications, too.

- **Overlock:** Many of the overlock-type stitches on today's sewing machines are designed to stitch and finish seams in one step, simulating the overlock stitches that you see on ready-to-wear garments. Some of these stitches work well on woven fabrics; some work better on knits.

- **Decorative:** Decorative stitches fall into two basic categories: closed, satin-type stitches (such as the ball and diamond) and open, tracery-type stitches (such as the daisy and honeycomb). You can program many newer machines to combine these stitches with other stitches, elongate the designs for a bolder decorative effect, and even stitch someone's name.

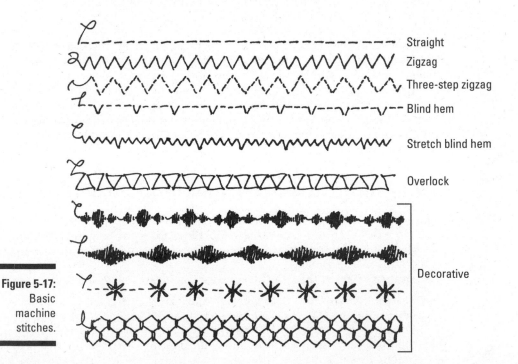

Straight

Zigzag

Three-step zigzag

Blind hem

Stretch blind hem

Overlock

Decorative

Figure 5-17: Basic machine stitches.

The newest high-end sewing machines can also create intricate embroidery designs (like the ones you see on ready-to-wear garments) by using *embroidery cards*. Embroidery cards, which are like memory cards for a digital camera, can store several large, intricate motifs. Some machines also offer scanners, which allow you to add additional patterns to the machine's stitch library. Contact machine manufacturers to find out about all the options (see the appendix).

Selecting a stitch type

If your sewing machine does more than straight stitch and zigzag, the machine must give you some way to select the stitch you want to use.

Older machines have dials, levers, buttons, or drop-in cams as *stitch selectors*. Newer, computerized models have keys or touch pads that not only select the stitch but also can automatically set the stitch length and width. Consult the operating manual that comes with your sewing machine to get the specifics on how to select a stitch type.

Choosing the length of the stitch

The length of the stitch determines the stitch's durability. Short stitches (2 to 3 mm, 9 to 13 spi) are very strong and are meant to be permanent. Longer stitches are usually temporary or used as a decorative topstitch (see the section "Topstitching" later in this chapter).

The distance the feed dogs move the fabric under the needle determines the *stitch length*. When the feed dogs move with shorter strokes, stitches are short. When they move with longer strokes, stitches are longer. (See Chapter 2 for more information on feed dogs.)

You measure stitch length two different ways — in millimeters (mm) and in stitches per inch (spi). The setting used depends on the brand and model of your machine.

Throughout this book, I give you the necessary stitch length settings both ways. Check out Table 5-1 if you want to compare stitch length in millimeters to stitch length in stitches per inch.

Table 5-1	Converting Stitch Lengths
Stitch Length in Millimeters	*Stitch Length in Stitches per Inch*
0.5	60 (fine setting)
1	24
2	13
3	9
4	6
5	5
6	4

Use the following general rules for stitch lengths:

✔ The average stitch length for mid-weight fabrics is 2.5 to 3 mm/10 to 12 spi.

✔ The average stitch length for fine fabrics is 2 mm/13 to 20 spi.

✔ For heavier fabrics, basting, or topstitching, use 4 to 5 mm/5 to 6 spi.

Setting the stitch width

The *stitch-width* control sets the distance the needle moves from side to side while creating a stitch. You don't need to worry about the stitch width when sewing straight stitches — just set it to 0 (zero).

All machines measure the stitch width in millimeters (mm). Some makes and models have a maximum stitch width of 4 to 6 mm. Others create stitches as wide as 9 mm.

Is wider better? When it comes to decorative stitches, it usually is. For the more practical stitches used in seam finishing, blind hemming, or making buttonholes, a narrower (2- to 6-mm) width works better.

Throughout this book, I give machine stitch-width settings in a range that works for most makes and models.

Stitching in the ditch

You use this simple technique to tack down facings and to tack up a quick cuff or hem. Just follow these steps:

1. **Place the crack of the seam right side up and perpendicular to the presser foot so that the needle is poised over the seamline.**

2. **Using a straight stitch, sew so that the stitches bury themselves in the crack of the seam, as shown in Figure 5-18.**

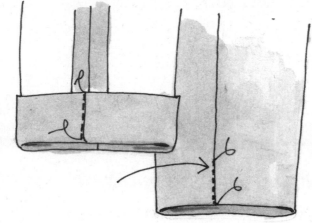

Figure 5-18: Secure cuffs and facings by stitching in the ditch.

Instead of backstitching, pull threads to the wrong side of the project and tie them off (see Chapter 6 for more on tying off threads).

Topstitching

Topstitching is an extra line of stitching sewn on the right side of the fabric that parallels a seamline or sews a hem. You see topstitching on the right side of a project like a pocket shown in Figure 5-19, so it needs to look good. Your pattern instructions tell you exactly where on the project to topstitch.

 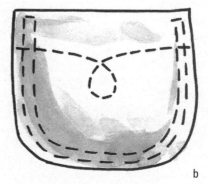

Figure 5-19: Use top-stitching to attach a pocket to a shirt (a) or pair of jeans (b).

a

b

To execute the topstitch, place the project under the needle, right side up, and stitch at the right spot. Because topstitching is usually an important part of the overall garment design, you use a longer stitch length than for seaming, and you tie off the threads (see Chapter 6) instead of backstitching at the end of each topstitched seam.

Starting and Stopping

Make sure that you properly start and stop your sewing machine and serger to prevent hurting your equipment or ruining your fabric. For smooth and easy sewing, follow these techniques for starting and stopping stitches.

. . . with your sewing machine

Pull the top and bobbin threads to the right or to the left of the needle before lowering the foot. This way, the foot pressure holds the threads firmly, and they don't tangle or jam at the beginning of a row of stitching.

Lower the presser foot onto the fabric before sewing a stitch as shown in Figure 5-20. If you don't, the fabric flops all over the place as the needle goes up and down, and you don't get anywhere. You may even jam up the machine — a real bummer. After a few seams, lowering the foot becomes second nature.

Figure 5-20:
Putting the presser foot down keeps the fabric from flopping up and down with every stitch.

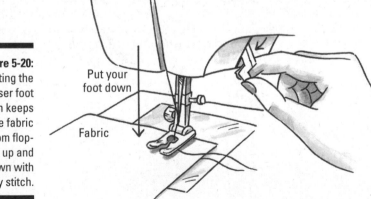

Put your foot down

Fabric

Stop sewing at the end of the fabric, stopping with the take-up lever at the highest position (see Chapter 2). If you don't, you may unthread the needle with the next stitch. Next, lift the presser foot and pull the fabric away from the machine, pulling out several inches of thread with it. Cut the threads, leaving a 6- to 8-inch thread tail on the fabric and 2 to 3 inches of thread behind the foot. Most machines have a thread cutter near the needle, or you can cut threads with a pair of scissors.

. . . with your serger

Starting and stopping with a serger is easier than with a sewing machine because a serger is designed for speed and durability. Leaving the presser foot down and with a short thread chain coming off the back of the foot, you simply butt the fabric edges under the toe of the foot and step on the foot pedal. When the serger starts, it grabs the fabric — and you're off and running.

To stop, gently pull the fabric as it comes out of the serger behind the foot, keeping constant, gentle tautness. Serge off the edge, creating a thread chain behind the foot. Stop serging and cut the thread chain, leaving enough on the fabric to tie off threads or to weave back under the stitches. See how to serge on and serge off in Figure 5-21.

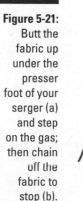

Figure 5-21: Butt the fabric up under the presser foot of your serger (a) and step on the gas; then chain off the fabric to stop (b).

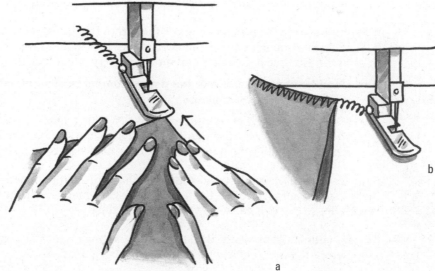

Basting Projects for a Better Fit

Basting in sewing is nothing like basting a turkey in the kitchen. In sewing, *basting* means to temporarily hold pieces of a project together. You can hold them together with your hands (called *finger-basting*), with long hand or machine stitches (called *hand-basting* or *machine-basting*), or with pins (called *pin-basting*). The long stitches and pins are easy to remove, so you can check and adjust the fit before permanently sewing the seam together.

My seventh-grade home-economics teacher made me hand-baste an entire project together before machine stitching. It took forever, and I thought it was a real waste of time. Now that I don't have to answer to my home-ec teacher, I don't baste whole projects together, but I do pin- or machine-baste in the following circumstances and suggest that you do, too:

- ✔ When you're not sure how one pattern piece fits into another
- ✔ When you need to check and adjust the fit of the project

Use a contrasting thread color to find and pull out your basting more easily. If you're machine-basting, use contrasting thread in the bobbin. (See Chapter 1 for more information on the bobbin.)

To baste two pattern pieces together, start by placing and pinning the right sides together and then use either of the following methods shown in Figure 5-22:

- ✔ **Pin-basting:** Pin parallel to and ⅜ inch from the cut edge. For small areas, such as a shoulder seam, pin every 1 to 2 inches. For larger areas, such as the side seam on a pair of pants, pin every 3 to 4 inches.
- ✔ **Hand-basting:** Thread your hand needle and run a row of hand-basting stitches along the seamline.
- ✔ **Machine-basting:** Set the stitch length to a long 4-mm/6-spi straight stitch and slightly loosen the upper thread tension. Stitch along the seamlines. Remember to put the tension back to normal when you finish basting.

Some sewing machines have an automatic machine-basting function that makes stitches from about ¼ to 1 inch long. If your machine has this function, remember to use it. It can save you time and effort.

To prevent needle breakage when machine-basting or sewing, remove the pins before the foot reaches them, as shown in Figure 5-23.

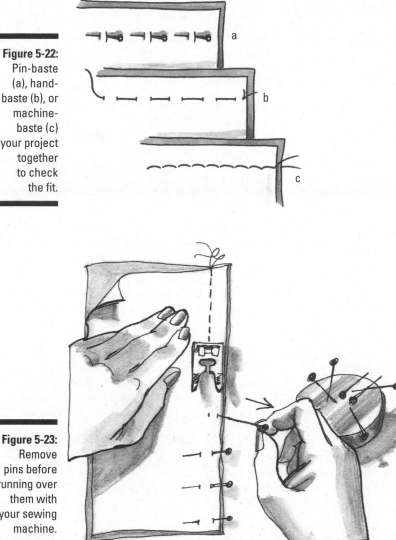

Figure 5-22:
Pin-baste
(a), hand-
baste (b), or
machine-
baste (c)
your project
together
to check
the fit.

Figure 5-23:
Remove
pins before
running over
them with
your sewing
machine.

If you're working on a fairly close-fitting project, add all elements that affect the fit of the project before basting. If you don't, your basting doesn't give you an accurate picture of what the project will look like. For example, you may work on a dress bodice that includes darts and shoulder pads. You should first sew and gently press the darts as shown in the pattern guide sheet. Next, pin in the shoulder pads and then baste the side seams together. You can then try on the bodice and get a fairly good idea of what the final product will look like.

Pressing Matters

What's the difference between ironing and pressing?

- ✔ You *iron* by pushing and pulling a hot iron across the fabric in a side-to-side motion to smooth out wrinkles in woven fabrics.

- ✔ You *press* by using an up-and-down motion as you firmly push down on an area of the fabric with an iron. Pressing is most commonly used to shape an area when sewing or when pressing out wrinkles in a knit.

When smoothing out wrinkles on knits such as t-shirts, use the up-and-down pressing motion. Ironing knits distorts and stretches the fabric out of shape, sometimes permanently.

Why press and iron as you sew?

Sewing changes the texture of the fabric wherever stitching occurs. Seams pucker a bit due to the thread, the fabric, the stitch used, or the shape of the pattern pieces, so for the seam to look good after sewing you must smooth it out by pressing.

Pressing up and down with the iron sets the stitches so that they become part of the fabric. Ironing back and forth smoothes the seam and puts the fabric back as close to its prestitched state as possible. If you don't press and iron while constructing a project, the seams stay as they come out of the sewing machine or serger and the project has a rough, puckered, unfinished look.

A Seam Stick is a handy tool made of a very smooth, hard wood and curved like a seam roll (see Chapter 2 for more on pressing tools). The stick is much longer and narrower than a seam roll so you can easily slip it into a sleeve or pant leg and press these longer seams without repositioning the tool 4 to 6 times.

When and where to press

Press every seam right after you sew it and every time the pattern guide sheet tells you to.

Use a hotter steam setting for natural fibers, such as silk, cotton, wool, and linen. Use lower synthetic-temperature settings for man-made and synthetic fiber fabrics. Depending on your iron, you may or may not be able to use steam at these cooler settings. If you're in doubt about what works best on your fabric, do a test-press on a fabric scrap using the iron with and without steam.

Be careful to set your iron for the appropriate temperature for the fiber content of your fabric (see Chapter 3 to read about fiber content). An iron that's too hot melts the fiber and creates unwanted shine that never presses out.

Follow these steps to properly press a seam. Since the seam is inside, be sure the ironing and pressing takes place on the wrong side of the fabric:

1. **Iron the seam flat and together, setting or "blending" the stitches into the fabric.**

2. **Position one long edge of the iron at the stitching line and press the seam allowance together and then out toward the edge (see Figure 5-24a).**

3. **Press a ⅝-inch seam open over a seam roll (see Figure 5-24b), and press a ¼-inch seam to one side.**

Your pattern guide sheet may instruct you to press other items throughout the course of a project. Don't try to cut corners by skipping these instructions.

Make pressing easy on yourself by setting up your pressing area close to your sewing area. If your chair is on wheels, lower the ironing board to a comfortable height so that you can use your iron and ironing board from a seated position.

Figure 5-24: Press along the seam-line to set the stitches (a). Press seams open over a seam roll or to one side (b).

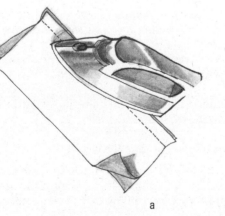

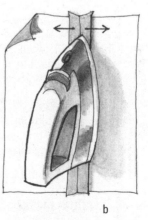

a   b

Pressing napped fabrics

Napped fabrics like velvet, velour, corduroy, and Polarfleece all have a fuzzy texture that can crush under iron pressure. Follow these tips when pressing napped fabrics:

- ✔ **Corduroy:** Press and iron corduroy from the wrong side of the fabric.

- ✔ **Polarfleece:** Don't press Polarfleece.

- ✔ **Upholstery velvet:** Upholstery velvet is designed for sitting, so the nap doesn't crush as easily as it does with dressmaking velvet and cotton velveteen. Nonetheless, you should also press upholstery velvet from the wrong side using a press cloth.

- ✔ **Velour:** Lightly press velour using a good deal of steam and pressing from the wrong side using a press cloth.

- ✔ **Velvet:** Velvet practically crushes when you look at it. Lay a large scrap of velvet or a terry cloth towel on the ironing board, nap side up. Lay the napped side of the velvet you're pressing against the napped side of the towel and lightly press it from the wrong side.

If you sew a lot of napped fabrics, invest in a press cloth designed for pressing napped fabrics. It has a very thick, dense texture so when you put the right side of the napped fabric against it, you won't damage the fabric when applying iron pressure.

Repurposed Shirt Pillow

When our son grew out of his favorite flannel cowboy shirt it was still good enough for someone to wear, but I couldn't bring myself to give it away, so I made a pillow like the ones you see in the color section. You can help preserve the little kid in all of us or turn that lucky shirt into something that the recipient really treasures when you present it as a gift.

To make this project, you need the following materials in addition to your sewing survival kit (see Chapter 2):

- ✔ A flannel shirt, cotton blouse, or team jersey.

- ✔ A throw pillow that coordinates with and fits inside the shirt. (Fold the shirt into a square until it looks the way you want it to show on the final pillow, measure it, and then use a pillow that measures the closest to that size.)

- ✔ Thread that matches the fabric.

Follow these steps to transform a shirt into a personalized pillow cover:

1. **Button up the front of the shirt.**

   If the shirt isn't a button-up style, skip to Step 4.

2. **Set your machine like this:**

   - Stitch: Straight

   - Length: 3 mm/9 spi

   - Width: 0 mm

   - Foot: All-purpose

3. **Sew the front opening of the shirt closed, sewing next to the buttons as you see in Figure 5-25.**

   If the shirt already has a row of topstitching, just sew over it, and if the foot keeps running into the buttons, reposition the needle to the far right or far left, if you can. This way, just a skinny part of the foot rides next to and not over the buttons.

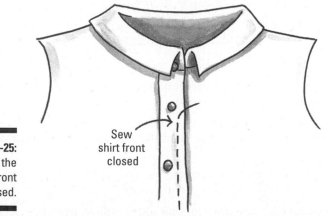

Figure 5-25: Stitch the shirt front closed.

Sew shirt front closed

4. **Turn the sleeves inside out, pushing them back through the armholes, up to the shoulder seams, and out of the way. Pin them to the back of the shirt.**

   Although you can cut off the sleeves and shirttails to square up the shirt to fit the pillow cover, I keep them intact, turn them inside the shirt, and tuck them at the back of the pillow. The sleeves make wonderful hiding places for action figures, toy cars, special rocks, and the remote control.

5. **Turn the shirt inside out and pop in the fabric-covered pillow through the open, shirttail end.**

   Snug the pillow up to the neck and into the shoulders to see where to pin the shirt tail closed so it fits the pillow.

6. **Pin the shirttail shut, pinning next to the bottom of the pillow from side seam to side seam.**

   This pinning marks the stitching line for the bottom of the pillow cover.

7. **Using a fabric marker or dressmaker's chalk, mark the stitching line on both the front and the back of the shirt as shown in Figure 5-26. Remove all the pins and the pillow form.**

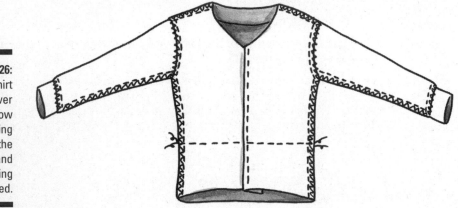

Figure 5-26: Fit the shirt pillow cover to the pillow by marking across the shirt tail and then sewing it closed.

8. **Pin the shirt together at the shirttail, pinning perpendicular to the marks from side seam to side seam.**

9. **Using the machine settings from Step 2 sew the shirttail closed, pulling out the pins as you get to them. Backstitch at the beginning and end of the seam.**

   Depending on how much of a shirttail your shirt has, you may want to trim it off, leaving about a ⅝-inch seam allowance.

10. **Turn the shirt right-side out and pop in the pillow from the neckline end. Smooth the sleeves into the back side of the pillow cover (see Figure 5-27).**

Figure 5-27:
Turn the
shirt right-
side out,
pop in
the pillow
through the
neck hole;
then stuff
the sleeves
smoothly
behind the
back of
the pillow
cover.

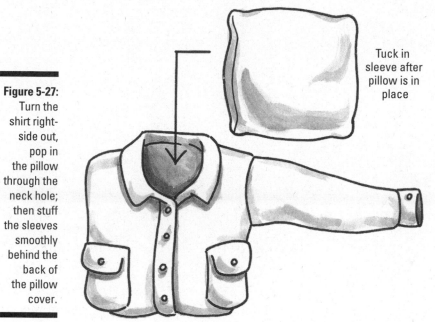

Tuck in
sleeve after
pillow is in
place

Chapter 6

Securing Sensational Seams

In This Chapter

▶ Finishing the seams before you begin

▶ Keeping your seams in place

▶ Practicing skills with a no-sew fleece throw

▶ Sewing seams in straight lines and around corners

▶ Unsewing when things go wrong

▶ Smoothing seams with shaping shortcuts

Simply put, you form a seam every time you sew two pieces of fabric together. You need straight seams, curved seams, and corner seams to build a project. After you sew a seam, you beat it into submission with the iron, scissors, and the sewing machine so it keeps its shape.

Before you sew two pieces of fabric together, though, you must do a little preparation work. Strangely enough, you finish a seam before you begin it!

Finishing the Edges First

You *finish* the raw edges on a fabric so that the seam allowance (the fabric from the seam to the cut edge) doesn't ravel up to the *seamline* — the line of stitching that joins the fabric pieces together to make a seam.

The seam finishes in this section are for woven fabrics. If you're working on a knit, skip ahead to the section "Seaming Fabrics" later in the chapter. There you see how you can simultaneously stitch and finish the seams of knit fabrics. Before putting those steps to practical use, be sure to review the information on knit fabrics in Chapter 3.

Pinking your edges

Pinking the raw fabric edges is a quick way to finish a seam. You pink the edges by trimming the raw edge of a single layer of fabric with a pair of *pinking shears,* which are shears with a zigzag pattern on the blades. Pinking shears work best on woven fabrics because the blades cut clean little zigzags into the fabric, thereby preventing the raw edges from raveling.

Don't use pinking shears on a knit fabric. The blades chew up and snag the fabric beyond recognition. Skip ahead to the section "Seaming Fabrics" for information on sewing seams on knits.

Don't cut out a project with pinking shears and think that you're saving a step — a pinked cutting line isn't accurate, which means your project won't fit correctly. Instead, cut out your pattern pieces using your dressmaker's shears. Then remove the paper pattern and pink the raw edges of each pattern piece, pinking one layer of fabric at a time. Even though you're cutting away some fabric with this finish, you still use a standard seam allowance, so be sure you pink on the very edge of the fabric.

Using your sewing machine or serger

Woven fabrics ravel, so you can finish the edges by *overcasting* with stitches on your sewing machine or your serger. Knits don't ravel, but the edges on a knit sometimes curl and are hard to press flat, so you handle the seams a bit differently (see "Seaming Fabrics" later in this chapter).

Follow these steps to finish woven fabric edges as shown in Figure 6-1:

1. **Set your sewing machine like this:**

   - Stitch: Three-step zigzag
   - Length: 1 to 1.5 mm/20 spi or fine
   - Width: 5 to 6 mm
   - Foot: All-purpose

   If you're using a serger, set your serger like this:

   - Stitch: Three-thread overlock
   - Length: 3 mm
   - Width: 5 mm
   - Foot: Standard

2. **With either the right or the wrong side up, start sewing or serging the raw edge, guiding the fabric so that the stitches catch the fabric on the left and sew just off the raw edge at the right.**

   Because you use these stitches to finish the edge of the fabric rather than to construct a seam, you don't need to backstitch (see the "Securing Your Seams" section to find out more about backstitching).

Figure 6-1:
Better than pinking a raw edge (a), the three-step zigzag stitch (b) and three-thread overlock stitch (c) are available on most sewing machines.

a   b   c

Securing Your Seams

When sewing a seam with a straight stitch, you want to secure the stitches at the beginning and end so that the stitches don't pull out during construction. You can prevent stitches from coming unstitched in two ways:

- ✔ By backstitching at the beginning and end of the seam
- ✔ By tying off the threads

The standard seam allowances

A pattern piece indicates the seam allowance by a line that shows you where to stitch the pattern pieces together. As a rule, you can count on the following seam allowances as industry standards:

✔ ⅝ inch for woven garments

✔ ½ inch for home-decorating projects

✔ ¼ inch for knit fabrics

Look on your project's pattern guide sheet if you're unsure about the seam allowances for your project.

Backstitching or not

Most machines have a backstitch or reverse button, lever, or function (see Chapter 2). To secure a seam with backstitching, simply sew the first two or three stitches and then touch the reverse button while stepping on the foot pedal. The machine automatically sews backward until you release it. Backstitch at the beginning and at the end of a seamline (see Figure 6-2), and you have all the stitch security you need!

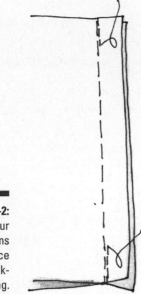

Figure 6-2: Keep your seams in place with back-stitching.

Only backstitch when using a straight stitch. Backstitching with a zigzag or more complex stitch globs up the thread, creates knots that you can never rip out if you make a mistake, and may damage your sewing machine.

Removing stitches that haven't been backstitched is easier, so when you aren't sure that you want a seam to be permanent, just sew the seam without backstitching and leave the thread tails free at both ends of the seam.

Tying off threads

You may want to tie off threads rather than backstitching at the point of a dart or at the beginning and end of a line of topstitching. Tying off the threads is less bulky — important at the point of a dart — and it just plain looks better than backstitching.

Rather than tying an overhand knot that often comes untied, I prefer the method in this section because the knot won't come out. It takes a little practice, but after you get it down, it will take you about a millisecond to tie off thread ends.

First you need to get both top and bobbin threads to the same side of the fabric. Lift the presser foot and remove the fabric, pulling off and cutting a length of thread at least 8 inches long. Then, from the wrong side of the stitching line, pull up on the bobbin thread. The pulled thread brings a loop to the wrong side. Now grab the loop and pull it through until both threads are on the same side of the fabric. Tie off the threads as follows:

1. **Starting with thread tails at least 8 inches long, hold the threads together and form a loop as shown in Figure 6-3a.**

2. **Bring both threads around and through the loop, working the loop to the base of the stitch as shown in Figure 6-3b.**

3. **Holding the threads with your thumb against a flat surface, pull them taut so that the loop forms a knot at the base of the fabric at the stitching line as shown in Figure 6-3c.**

Figure 6-3:
Tie off
threads so
they don't
unravel.

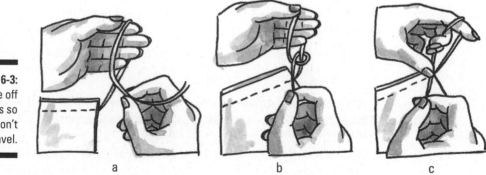

a   b   c

Fleece Throw with Colorful Fringe

My son is a college student and he asked for a fleece throw made in his school colors for Christmas this year — so how could I refuse? And why should you care? Well, besides making a cool project for yourself or someone else, this project gives you a lot of practice in tying secure knots. Once you master this knotting technique by tying on bulky fringe strips, knotting off thread ends will be a piece of cake.

For information on the care and feeding of Polarfleece, read more about it in Chapter 3.

To make this project, you need the following materials in addition to your sewing survival kit (see Chapter 2):

- ✔ 1⅔ yards fleece (54 to 60 inches wide), which makes one square throw
- ✔ Four to five contrasting colors of fleece, each ¼ yard, to create the fringe

Follow these steps to make the fleece throw:

1. **Carefully trim off the selvages from both sides of the large fleece square and the contrasting-colored fringe fleeces, making sure the edges are straight and have a clean cut (see Chapter 4 for more on cutting fabric).**

    These clean-cut edges are what I refer to as the *side edges* of the throw.

2. **Carefully cut the top and bottom edges of the throw, making them clean cut and perpendicular to the side edges.**

    My rotary cutter, rotary cutting board, and large see-through ruler really come in handy for cutting fleece edges straight and true (see Chapter 2 for more on these great tools). Because the straight edges are part of the overall design of the throw (and because fleece doesn't ravel) no edge finishing is needed here.

3. **Fold the fleece in half so that the fold is perpendicular with the side edges of the throw.**

    Folding the throw this way makes it easy to pin-mark the fringe placement on both ends of the throw at the same time. (See Chapter 3 for more on pin-marking.)

4. **Using your straight pins and ruler, pin-mark the hole placement 1 inch from the raw edges on both ends of the throw (or mark holes on both edges with a fabric marker; see Figure 6-4).**

    Push one pin straight through both layers of fabric so the pin head is snug against the fleece. Repeat for the opposite side of the fleece. When you pull the fabric layers apart, the pins mark where the fringe holes are cut.

5. **Using the tips of a sharp pair of sharp embroidery scissors, cut a ¼-inch slit from the mark made in Step 4, up into the body of the fleece.**

    When cutting the slits, use your scissor tips. If you use any other part of the scissors, you may end up cutting too big a hole and the fringe may tear off the edge of the throw.

6. **Cut 30 strips of fringe ⅜ inch wide and 20 inches long from each of the other four fleece colors.**

7. **Alternating fringe colors, thread a fringe strip through each slit and tie in a secure knot at the edge of the fleece, as shown in Figure 6-5.**

    See the earlier section "Tying off threads" to find out how to tie a secure knot.

8. **Even up the fringe by cutting the loose ends to the same length.**

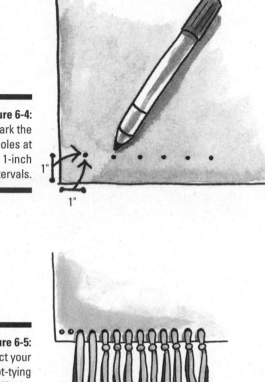

Figure 6-4:
Mark the holes at 1-inch intervals.

1"

1"

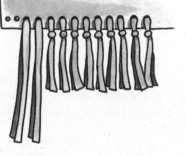

Figure 6-5:
Perfect your knot-tying ability by knotting off the fringe at the edges of the throw.

You can add a personal accent to the fleece throw with an *appliqué,* a second piece of smaller, cut fabric that is applied to a base or background fabric. Rather than cutting out the appliqué and then stitching it onto the fabric, do it the easy way. This is an optional step but easy to do because fleece doesn't ravel.

1. **Copy the appliqué pattern onto a piece of paper.**

   For my appliqué pattern, I took in a t-shirt with the school logo on it and had the copy center enlarge it to the size I wanted it.

2. **Cut a piece of appliqué fabric at least 1-inch larger all the way around than the design itself.**

   Cutting it larger than the appliqué design makes it easier to work with and ensures your success.

3. **Sandwich the appliqué fabric between the top of the throw and the paper appliqué pattern as shown in Figure 6-6.**

Blanket ⟶

Figure 6-6:
Sandwich the contrasting appliqué fabric between the paper pattern and the base fabric.

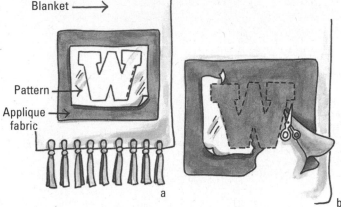

Pattern ⟶

Applique fabric ⟶

a

b

4. **Set your machine like this:**
   - Stitch: Slight zigzag
   - Length: 3 mm/8 to 10 spi
   - Width: 1 mm
   - Foot: Embroidery

5. **Starting on a straight side of the appliqué, sew around the edge of the design and stop sewing when you get all the way around; don't backstitch.**

6. **Tie off thread ends.**

   For a neater finish that won't pull out, remove the project from under the presser foot, cut the thread, and pull the loose threads to the wrong side of the fabric (the backside of the fleece throw) to tie them off.

7. **Remove the paper pattern by carefully tearing it against and away from the stitches.**

   Taking a little extra time with this step ensures a clean, paperless appliqué.

8. **Using a sharp pair of scissors, carefully trim the appliqué fabric close to the stitching line.**

Seaming Fabrics

Sewing a seam is kind of like driving a car. In fact, I passed my driver's test on the sewing machine before I could sew a stitch (or drive a car). I had to prove that I could control the sewing machine — that I could start, stop, maneuver both inside and outside curves, and turn corners safely. Thank goodness I didn't have to parallel park!

Consider this next section your driving test and put the pedal to the metal and sew some seams.

Sewing straight seams

For straight seams every time, follow these steps:

1. **Set your machine like this for woven fabrics:**

   - Stitch: Straight
   - Length: 2.5 to 3 mm/10 to 12 spi
   - Width: 0 mm
   - Foot: All-purpose

   This traditional seaming technique is used mostly on woven fabrics when applying a ⅝-inch seam allowance. Knit fabrics usually are constructed using ¼-inch seams as I show you in the upcoming section "Sewing ¼-inch seams."

2. **Place and pin your pattern pieces so that the right sides of the fabric are together.**

   In instructions, this is what *place the right sides together* means. Use as many pins as it takes to hold the edges together so that they don't slide around. The more you sew, the closer you can estimate how many pins you need for a particular job.

   For easy pin removal, pin perpendicular to the seamline so that the pin heads are toward your dominant hand and the pins either enter or exit the fabric about ¼ inch from the edge of the fabric as shown in Figure 6-7.

3. **Place the seam under the presser foot and line up the edge of the fabric with the appropriate seamline marked on the needle plate.**

   On the needle plate, look for a set of lines to the right of the needle. Depending on your machine, the lines may be marked as ⅝, ½, and so on; sometimes you find just plain old lines. Placing the bulk of the fabric to the left, line up the raw edges of your fabric along the ⅝-inch line. If you have everything lined up properly, the needle should be poised to hit the fabric right on the ⅝-inch seamline.

If your needle plate has unmarked lines, place your sewing tape measure under the needle so that the long length of the tape is to the left. Poke the needle into the tape at the ⅝-inch mark and lower the foot. Make sure the short end of the tape lines up with the ⅝-inch line in the needle plate. Note which line is needed for the ⅝-inch seamline, or place a strip of tape along the ⅝-inch line.

4. **Lower the presser foot onto the fabric and stitch, backstitching at the beginning and end of the seam. (See "Backstitching or not," earlier in this chapter, for more information.)**

Figure 6-7:
Place the right sides of the fabric together and pin so the pin heads are perpendicular to the seamline and toward your dominant hand.

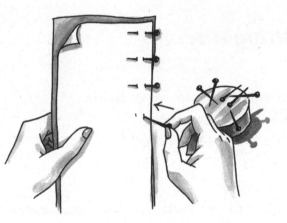

If the needle hits a pin, both can break, sending shards all over the place. Unless you plan on wearing safety goggles when you sew, pull out the pins before sewing over them.

Slow down when you seam a curve. Using the line in your needle plate, guide the edges along the appropriate line for an even sewing distance along the length of the curve.

5. **Press the seam flat and together. From the wrong side, press the seam open. (See Chapter 5 for more information on pressing.)**

To match a plaid perfectly when seaming, put one pin on every other color bar so one pin goes in from *east to west* and the next goes in from *west to east,* like in Figure 6-8. (Check out Chapter 4 for more about matching plaids.) As with any other seam, remember to pull out the pins before sewing over them.

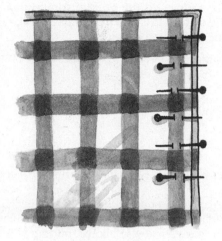

Figure 6-8:
Pin plaids or stripes on color bars with pins alternating *east to west* the *west to east* for a perfect match.

Turning corners

When turning a corner in the car, you slow down and stop, look both ways, and then turn. You do the same when turning a corner in sewing. Follow these steps for good-looking corners every time:

1. **Using a fabric marker, mark the corner on the wrong side of the fabric with a dot so that you know exactly where to stop and pivot.**

   After you stitch several corners, you have a good idea of where to stop sewing to turn a corner without marking the corner first.

2. **As you approach the corner, slow down and stop with the needle all the way into the fabric as shown in Figure 6-9.**

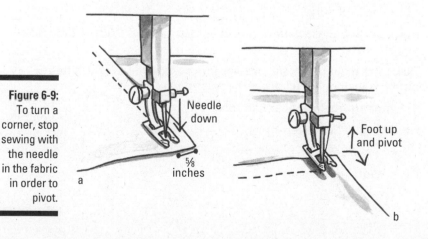

Figure 6-9:
To turn a corner, stop sewing with the needle in the fabric in order to pivot.

Needle down

⅝ inches

a

Foot up and pivot

b

3. **Leaving the needle in the fabric, lift the presser foot and pivot the fabric around the needle so that the other edge of the fabric lines up with the appropriate line in the needle plate.**

4. **Lower the presser foot and start sewing again. Easy, isn't it?**

Sewing ¼-inch seams

When seaming a T-shirt, sweatshirt, and other active knit sportswear fabrics, you usually stitch and press a ¼-inch seam to one side. Why? Knit fabrics stretch and many curl, so you want the seam to be both secure and smooth.

Some patterns call for ¼-inch seam allowances; others call for ⅝-inch seam allowances. If the pattern you're working with calls for the wider seam allowance, instead of trimming it to ¼ inch, leave it wider to allow for fitting and then trim it off later. Exceptions are those areas where you apply ribbing at the neck edge and cuffs — trim those to ¼ inch before sewing. You can make ¼-inch seams in one or two steps, depending on your sewing machine's capabilities.

This technique for seaming knits is called the two-step method because you sew the seam with two separate passes through the sewing machine. It also works better on most fabrics when using ⅝-inch seam allowances and then trimming them to ¼-inch after sewing.

Follow these steps to make ¼-inch seams:

1. **Set your sewing machine like this:**

   • Stitch: Zigzag

   • Length: 1.5 to 2 mm/13 to 20 spi

   • Width: 1 to 1.5 mm

   • Foot: All-purpose

2. **Place and pin your pattern pieces so that the right sides of the fabric are together.**

3. **Place the seam under the presser foot so that the needle stitches either ¼ inch or ⅝ inch from the raw edge and sew.**

4. **Set your sewing machine like this:**

   • Stitch: Three-step zigzag

   • Length: 1 to 1.5 mm/13 to 24 spi

   • Width: 4 to 5 mm

   • Foot: All-purpose

5. **Guiding to the immediate right of the tiny zigzag stitches, sew the second row of stitching with the three-step zigzag stitch, as shown in Figure 6-10.**

    If you used a ⅝-inch seam allowance, trim the excess fabric up to, but not through, the stitches.

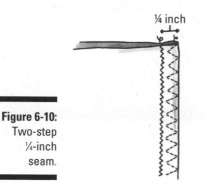

Figure 6-10:
Two-step
¼-inch
seam.

6. **Press the seam to one side.**

    See Chapter 5 for details about pressing a seam.

Serging ¼-inch seams

You can serge ¼-inch seams in one step on your serger by using a four-thread overlock stitch. The four-thread overlock has an extra stitch within the seam allowance as an insurance policy: If you pop a seam, the extra row of stitching prevents the seam from coming completely unraveled.

I always check my serger settings on a scrap first to make sure the seam will look the way I want it to. Using scraps of the project fabric I duplicate the scenario — if the seam is sewn on the lengthwise grain, cut two fabric scraps on the lengthwise grain, place right sides together then serge a few inches. If the fabric waves or puckers, I adjust the stitch length appropriately until I get the results I'm looking for.

1. **Set your serger like this:**

    • Stitch: Four-thread overlock

    • Length: 3.0 to 3.5 mm/8 to 10 spi

    • Width: 4 to 5 mm

    • Foot: Standard

2. **Place and pin the seam, right sides together, so the pins are parallel to the seamline and about 1 inch from the cut edge.**

    This way you don't accidentally serge over pins and ruin your serger.

3. **Serge the seam, guiding the raw edge along either the ¼-inch or ⅝-inch line on the needle plate of your serger.**

    The serger automatically trims off the excess seam allowance, giving a nice, ¼-inch finished seam (see Figure 6-11).

¼ inch

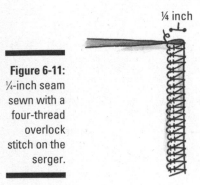

Figure 6-11: ¼-inch seam sewn with a four-thread overlock stitch on the serger.

Differential feed, abbreviated D.F., is a feature on many sergers that prevents the unnecessary stretching out of stretchy fabrics. Without D.F., serged knit seams can distort, ending up longer than they should. These distorted seams throw off the look and fit of a garment. If you're in the market for a new serger, buy a model that has this feature. Check out your operating manual to find out how it works.

Ripping into Seam Mistakes

You may think that if you're a careful sewer you won't make mistakes that you need to rip out. *Wrong*. Ripping is part of sewing, no matter how experienced you are. But I do have a rule: Don't rip it out if you can live with it. The mistake may actually look worse after you fix it than it did before you ripped it out. So sleep on it, look at your project with new eyes in the morning, and then decide if doing it over is worth the extra effort.

My two favorite methods for ripping out stitches are using a seam ripper (see Chapter 2 to read more about a seam ripper) and pulling the needle and bobbin threads.

A *seam ripper* has a very sharp point that lifts a stitch away from the fabric and a knife-edge that cuts the thread in one smooth motion. Work the point of the ripper under the stitch and cut through the thread. After you cut the stitch, gently tug open the seam until another stitch holds the seam closed. Cut this stitch with the ripper and pull the seam open as before until you have *unsewn* the distance you want to open (see Figure 6-12).

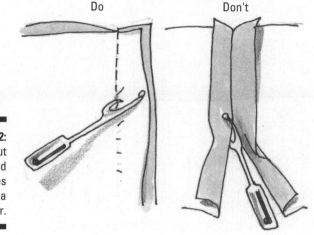

Figure 6-12:
Rip out
unwanted
stitches
using a
seam ripper.

A seam ripper is sharp enough to cut fabric. So don't push the ripper and cut through a whole line of stitching at once or you may cut a slit in the fabric, right next to the seamline — an almost impossible place to fix (refer to Figure 6-12).

If you prefer to rip out stitches without the aid of a seam ripper, follow these steps:

1. **Loosen the stitches enough to have about a 2-inch thread tail.**

2. **Holding the project in one hand, jerk the thread tail back toward the stitching line, against the stitches, with your other hand as shown in Figure 6-13.**

   This action breaks four to six stitches at once.

3. **Turn the project over and pull out the bobbin thread tail.**

4. **Jerk on that bobbin thread tail, pulling against the stitches and breaking another four to six stitches.**

5. **Keep pulling the top thread and then the bobbin thread until you have unsewn as much stitching as needed.**

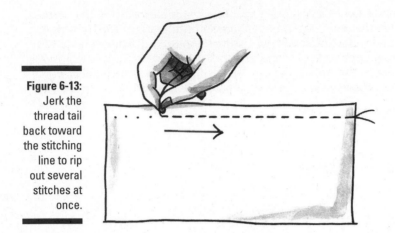

Figure 6-13: Jerk the thread tail back toward the stitching line to rip out several stitches at once.

Shaping Up the Seams

When it comes to sewing, the devil is most certainly in the details. Sewing would be wonderful (but very boring) if all the seams were straight. No such luck. In this section you see how to take curved seams and whip them into shape by using your sewing machine and scissors. You use these techniques time and time again in many aspects of sewing, so mark this spot in the book with a sticky note and refer to it often.

Starting by stitching the seam on your sewing machine

The three stitching techniques in this section help you smooth and shape seams into doing what you need them to do. Their purposes are fairly self-explanatory. Staystitching "stays," or keeps a piece of fabric from misbehaving (such as keeping a collar from flipping up). Understitching is done under or inside a seam allowance to keep a neckline or armhole facing from coming out of its hole. Edgestitching is a line of stitching on the very edge of something like a collar or cuff.

Staystitching

Staystitching is a technique that you can use on a single layer of fabric inside the seam allowance to *stay* or prevent curved fabric edges from stretching out of shape while you work on a project. You only need to staystitch woven fabrics, because knit fabrics recover their normal shape after being stretched. Staystitch neckline curves, armhole curves, and edges cut on the bias (see Chapter 5 to read more about the bias).

To staystitch an edge, use a regular straight stitch and sew a row of stitching ½ inch from the raw edge, as shown in Figure 6-14. If you're not sure whether to staystitch an area, see your pattern guide sheet for a recommendation.

If you're inclined *not* to staystitch an area recommended in the pattern instructions (like I was when I was learning the craft), subdue the urge and save yourself some time. If you skip it, the pattern pieces won't fit together the way they should and you'll struggle unnecessarily.

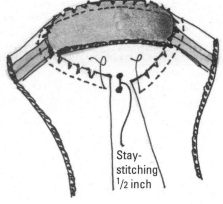

Figure 6-14:
Staystitch
curves to
keep the
fabric from
stretching
out as you
handle the
project.

Stay-
stitching
¹/₂ inch

Understitching

Understitching is a line of stitching found under or on the inside of a project close to the seamline. You understitch collars and facings so that they stay in shape and conform to the opening you sew them into. You can't see understitching, but without it, armhole and neckline facings pull out of their openings and collar seams roll and look . . . well . . . tacky and homemade.

You finish curved seams, like those on an armhole or neckline, with another piece of fabric called a *facing.* After you sew the facing to the neckline or armhole, you press the seam allowance to one side, toward the facing. After you press, understitch the seam allowance to compress the bulk created by the extra thickness of the seam allowance and to conform to the curve's shape.

You can understitch with a straight stitch, but on mid-weight to heavy fabrics, the stitch doesn't really compress all that bulk. Using the three-step zigzag stitch really flattens the seam allowance and gives you beautifully finished edges.

To understitch, do the following:

1. **After sewing the seam in question, press the entire seam allowance to one side.**

For a neckline or armhole that has a facing stitched to the opening, press the seam allowance toward the facing.

2. **Set your machine like this:**

   - Stitch: Three-step zigzag
   - Length: 1 to 1.5 mm/20 to 24 spi
   - Width: 4 to 5 mm
   - Foot: All-purpose

3. **Place the fabric right-side up under the presser foot so that the crack of the seam allowance is to one side of the needle or the other, as shown in Figure 6-15.**

   Which side? The side where you pressed the seam allowance. When the right side of the project is up and you press the seam to the right, the needle should be to the right side of the seamline. When you press to the left, the needle should be to the left side of the seamline.

4. **Sew, guiding the needle so that when it travels over to the left side of the stitch it comes to within ¹⁄₁₆ inch of the seamline.**

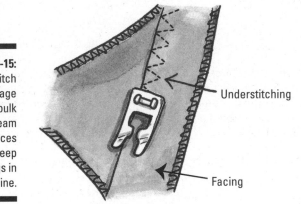

Figure 6-15: Understitch to manage the bulk in seam allowances and keep facings in line.

Understitching

Facing

As you sew, grasp the facing and seam allowance in your right hand with your thumb under the facing. By periodically peeking under the fabric, check that you're pushing the seam allowance toward the facing side of the seam. This way, you catch all the bulk of the seam allowance in the understitching.

Edgestitching

Edgestitching is *topstitching* (stitching sewn on the top or right side of the fabric) that is very close to the finished edge. You find edgestitching on the edge of collars, cuffs, pockets, waistbands, front shirt plackets, and other edges where you want a crisp, tailored look as shown in Figure 6-16. Even though you can edgestitch with an all-purpose presser foot, sewing in a straight line is tricky because you sew so close to the fabric's edge.

Figure 6-16:
Edgestitch
the edge
of shirt
pockets,
collars, and
cuffs to
create a
crisp,
tailored
look.

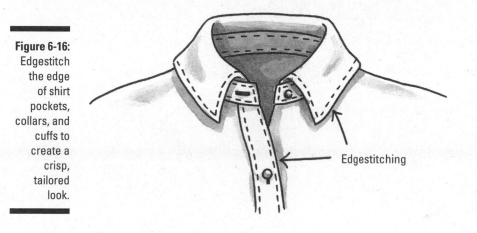

Edgestitching

This technique uses the blind hem or edgestitch foot (see Chapter 2) as a guide, enabling you to edgestitch quickly, accurately, and professionally:

1. **Set your machine like this:**

   • Stitch: Straight

   • Length: 2 to 3 mm/9 to 13 spi

   • Width: 0 mm

   • Foot: Blind hem or edgestitch

   • Optional: Near left needle position (check your operating manual)

2. **Place the guide in the foot along the finished edge and sew, as shown in Figure 6-17.**

   Instead of backstitching, pull the threads to the underside of the project and tie them off (see "Tying off threads" in this chapter for more information).

   If you don't have a blind hem foot and a variable needle position, place the fabric under the foot so that when the needle is in the fabric, the edge of the fabric is about $\frac{1}{16}$ inch from the needle. Notice where the edge of the fabric is in relationship to the foot (this spot could be at the edge of the needle hole, where you see a line in the foot, or where the foot changes direction). Sewing slowly, guide the edge of the fabric by that spot on the foot.

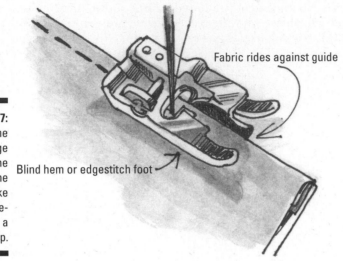

Fabric rides against guide

Blind hem or edgestitch foot

Figure 6-17:
Snug the fabric edge against the guide in the foot to make even edge-stitching a snap.

Clipping the curve with your scissors

Clipping a seam to the staystitching or seamline releases the seam allowance on an inside curve, making it flexible enough to spread open. This way, after you stitch the armhole or neckline facing, for example, the facing turns smoothly to the inside of the garment. If you didn't clip the seam, when you turn the facing to the inside of the armhole or neck edge, the seam would be stiff and bunchy and the facings would pop out of the opening and bind.

When clipping, use very sharp scissor tips. Cut clips in the fabric perpendicular to the seamline and to within ⅛ inch to a ¹⁄₁₆ inch of the staystitching or seamline, as shown in Figure 6-18. Rather than holding the seam allowance closed and clipping both seam allowances simultaneously, clip each seam allowance separately, alternating the clips across the seamline from one another. This surefire clipping technique pads the seam allowance, creating the smoothest curved seam ever.

Notching a seam to the staystitching or seamline is just the opposite of clipping. You notch a seam to reduce the bulk in the seam allowance of an outside curve, such as the outside edge of a collar, or an inside curve, such as a princess seamline (refer to Figure 6-18).

Notch a seam allowance by cutting away little triangular-shaped pieces of fabric. Rather than holding the seam allowance closed and notching both seam allowances simultaneously, use your scissor tips to cut one notch out of a seam allowance separately, alternating notches across the seamline from one another. Cut away each notch to within ⅛ inch of the seamline.

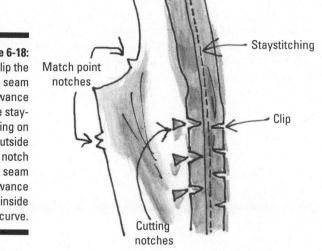

Figure 6-18:
Clip the seam allowance to the staystitching on an outside curve; notch the seam allowance on an inside curve.

Cut away small notches from small curves that are spaced about ¼ to ½ inch apart. Cut away larger notches from larger curves spaced from about ½ to ¾ inch apart.

After some experience, you find that cutting away more notches is usually better than cutting fewer, bigger ones. This way, when you stitch, notch, turn, and press an affected area, the seam allowance fits and presses smoothly — no unwanted lumps or bumps.

When notching an edge, don't cut through the stitching at the seamline or you'll end up with a hole that's very tough to repair.

My favorite way to notch an edge on light- to mid-weight woven fabric is by using my pinking shears. I trim or grade the seam with the pinking shears, cutting to within ⅛ inch of the stitching line. Pinking automatically notches the edge, so I'm on to the next step in no time.

Don't confuse notches that are match points marked on the pattern paper with notches that you cut out of the seam allowance at a curve. (See Chapter 4 for more on notches and match points.) Even though the word is the same, it represents two different sewing concepts.

Trimming seams eliminates bulk from the seam allowances that you stitch and then turn right side out so that the seamline is on the edge — like on the edge of a collar or cuff. When do you trim these seams? Only when your pattern instructions tell you to! To do this, trim about ⅛ inch from the stitching line, leaving enough seam allowance that the stitches don't pull off the fabric (see Figure 6-19).

Trimming corners is another use for your scissors in shaping a piece of fabric. After you have sewn a corner, like at a pocket corner or collar point, you turn your project right-side out and press it into submission. But if you leave all the fabric created by the seam allowance in the corners, you often end up with an unsightly wad in the corner. You can prevent this by clipping away a little triangle at the corner.

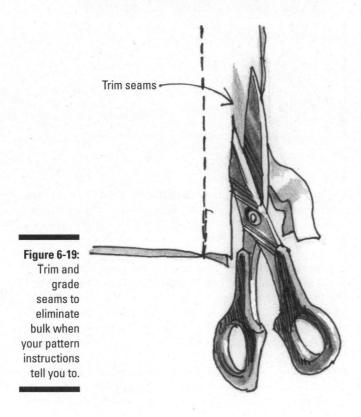

Trim seams

Figure 6-19:
Trim and grade seams to eliminate bulk when your pattern instructions tell you to.

Chapter 7

Fast and Easy Hems by Hand and Machine

In This Chapter

▶ Indicating where the hem should go

▶ Determining how much hem allowance to leave

▶ Cleaning up the raw edges of a hem

▶ Taking a look at invisible hemming by hand or machine

▶ Discovering hemming tricks for pant legs and knit fabrics

*H*ave you ever bought a pair of pants and left them hanging in the closet until the dust settled on the hanger before shortening them? Have your kids outgrown their clothes before you could get to the hemming? If this sounds familiar, this chapter's for you. A hem is a turned-up edge that you stitch in place at the bottom of skirts, pants, shorts, sleeves, and drapery panels. Besides making the edges neat, hems add weight to an edge, so the garment or drapery hangs better with a hem than without one. You can see several types of hems in Figure 7-1.

The following tips, tricks, and techniques are my favorites for hemming and may keep you from procrastinating the next time a new outfit needs hemming or rehemming.

Figure 7-1:
Hems can be narrow, wide, top-stitched, cuffed, tapered, flared, straight, or doubled.

Marking the Hem's Placement

Before you can sew a hem, you need to mark it. When you're hemming clothing, to get a hem an even distance from the floor, you also need a helper. (My husband, although reluctant, became a really good helper after he understood what he had to do.) You and your helper take the roles of hem-ee and hemmer.

If you're the hem-ee

As the hem-ee, you wear the garment, so the hemmer marks the hem to fit you. Here's what you do:

1. **Try on the garment, right-side out, wearing the same underwear and shoes that you'll normally wear with the garment.**

   There's nothing more frustrating than hemming a project and finding out afterward that it's too long or short because you didn't wear the correct shoes. As far as the underwear issue . . . this applies more to women. If you plan on wearing control undergarments or control-top pantyhose, for example, these undergarments can smooth over curves that may lift or drop a hem up to ½ inch.

2. **Stand on a hard floor, table, or stool.**

   Carpet can distort the measurements.

3. **Stand up straight with your hands down at your sides and don't lock your knees.**

   When I was a kid, I locked my knees once when my mom was the hemmer, and I passed out. Quite a shock for both of us!

If you're the hemmer

As the hemmer, your job is to measure and mark the hem of the garment worn by the hem-ee. Here's what you do:

1. **Find a pleasing hem length by temporarily pinning up the hemline.**

   By temporarily pinning up a section of the garment at the proper length, you create a *hem fold.* This fold allows you to measure the hem for the rest of the garment more accurately.

   When hemming a skirt or dress, you don't have to pin all the way around, just about 12 inches or so in the front to make sure you have the right length. For slacks, pin both pant-leg hems all the way around, making them even with each other at the heel and creases. Typically, the standard length has the leg creases break slightly at the top of the shoe, but if you prefer a different length, simply compare to a pair of pants with the hem length you want.

2. **Using a yardstick, measure the distance from the floor to the hem fold and tightly wrap a thin rubber band around the yardstick the proper distance from the floor.**

If you find yourself doing a lot of hemming, you'll save time with a wonderful hemming tool that looks like a yard stick in a stand. The hem marker has a little tripod on the bottom that rests on the floor and a guide that adjusts up and down along the yardstick. The guide is a scissor-type clamp that has a horizontal slot where a pin slides through to easily to mark the hem fold perfectly parallel to the floor. Adjust this cool tool to the correct height and hem marking goes a lot faster.

3. **Pin through a single thickness at the hem fold by using two pins and pinning parallel to the floor. Remove the rest of the pins so that the hemline hangs free.**

The pins mark the hem fold like drawing a straight line.

4. **Using the rubber band on the yardstick as a guide, pin-mark the hemline even with the rubber band, pinning all the way around the garment.**

Place pins about every 2 to 3 inches, pinning parallel to the floor. Pin-mark a few inches, move, and then measure and pin-mark again until you mark the entire hemline.

Move around the hem-ee rather than the other way around. This way, the hem-ee doesn't shift weight and distort the hemline.

Deciding on the Hem Allowance

After you measure and mark the hemline, decide how deep you want the *hem allowance* — the distance from the folded hemline to the finished edge of the hem. Hem allowances for clothing range from ¼ to 3 inches depending on the type of garment and the fabric. Drapery and curtain hems range from about 2 to 3 inches in the lining to 4 to 6 inches for longer drapes. Drapery hems are made by turning up the hem twice, called *double hemming*. So for a 4-inch hem, you turn up the hem 4 inches and then turn it up again another 4 inches. The extra weight in the hem helps keep the bottom of the drapery straight and even.

When you sew a project, look for the hem allowance marked on the pattern. If you're preparing to alter a ready-made garment and are clueless about the best hem allowance for your project, refer to Table 7-1 for some general guidelines.

Table 7-1	Recommended Hem Allowances
Garment or Item	*Recommended Finished Hem Allowance*
T-shirts, sleeves	⅝ to 1¼ inches
Shorts, slacks	1¼ to 1½ inches
Jackets	1½ to 2 inches
Straight skirts and coats	2 to 3 inches
Curtains and drapery linings	2- to 3-inch double hems
Drapery hems	4- to 6-inch double hems

Finishing the Raw Edges of the Hem

After you measure and mark the hemline and determine the proper hem allowance, you even up the hem allowance and finish the hem edge.

Even up the hem allowance by measuring from the hemline to the raw edge. Say that you need the hem allowance to be 2½ inches. On your project, the hem depth varies from 2½ to 3 inches, so measure down from the hemline 2½ inches and mark around the hem edge by using a fabric marker. Trim off the excess fabric so that the hem allowance measures an even 2½ inches all the way around.

You finish the hem edge of each fabric type differently:

✔ Knits that don't ravel don't need finished hem edges, although a finished hem may look better. If you choose not to finish the hem edge, skip ahead to the section "Securing the Hem" later in this chapter.

✔ You hem knits that curl, such as T-shirt knits and fleeces, with twin needles; skip to the section "Hemming Knits with Twin Needles" later in this chapter for instructions.

✔ Finish the raw hem edges on woven fabrics so that they don't ravel by using one of the methods in the following sections.

Using a straight stitch

If your sewing machine has only a straight and zigzag stitch, finish the hem edge by sewing on hem tape or hem lace, as follows:

1. **Pin the hem tape to the hem edge.**

   Place the hem tape or lace on the right side of the fabric, overlapping the raw hem edge about ¼ inch. Pin-baste the tape to the hem edge. (After you really know what you're doing, you can sew on the tape or lace without pin-basting.)

2. **Set your machine like this:**

   - Stitch: Straight
   - Length: Appropriate for the fabric (see Chapter 5)
   - Width: 0 mm
   - Foot: All-purpose

3. **Sewing with the right side of the fabric up, stitch the hem tape or lace in place without stretching it, as shown in Figures 7-2 and 7-3.**

Figure 7-2:
Overlap the raw hem edge with hem tape, and then pin and topstitch it to the hem edge.

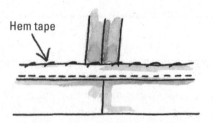

Hem tape

Figure 7-3:
Overlap the raw edge with hem lace, and then pin and topstitch ¼ inch from the hem edge.

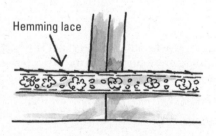

Hemming lace

Quick-fix hemming with Res-Q-Tape

You're getting ready for work and reach in the closet for the only suit that isn't at the cleaners. With one leg in the trousers, you slip and catch your big toe in the hem and rip it out. You really don't know one end of the needle from the other, so you grab the Res-Q-Tape. You fix the hem and walk out the door in five minutes.

Res-Q-Tape is a very sticky, double-faced tape that doesn't harm fabric. Find it on the notions wall of your local fabric store or through your favorite sewing mail-order source.

Why is it called Res-Q-Tape? Because it's the quick-fix superhero: It holds up strapless dresses, fixes gaps, keeps shoulder pads in place, and holds spaghetti straps on padded hangers. It also holds ties and scarves in place, secures bra straps, keeps leather belt ends from flapping, and tapes up loose lining.

Don't iron over Res-Q-Tape or it melts. Res-Q-Tape isn't washable or dry-cleanable, so remove it before cleaning your garment, and unless you want to reapply the tape every time, use one of the hemming techniques found in this chapter to repair a loose hem.

Using a three-step zigzag or overlock stitch

If your sewing machine has a three-step zigzag or an overlock stitch, finish the hem edge by following these steps:

1. **Set your machine like this:**

   • Stitch: Three-step zigzag or overlock

   • Length: 1 mm/24 spi (three-step zigzag) or longest (overlock)

   • Width: 4 to 5 mm

   • Foot: All-purpose

2. **Sewing with the right side of the fabric up, overcast the edge by guiding the needle so the stitch catches the fabric on the left and stitches just over the raw edge on the right.**

   Figure 7-4 shows the three-step zigzag finish.

Using a serger

If you have a serger, finish the hem edge by following these steps:

1. **Set your serger like this:**
   - Stitch: Three-thread overlock
   - Length: 2 to 2.5 mm/10 to 12 spi
   - Width: 3 to 5 mm
   - Foot: Standard

2. **Sewing with the right side of the fabric up, serge-finish the edge by guiding the needle so the stitch catches the fabric on the left and stitches just over the raw edge on the right as shown in Figure 7-5.**

Figure 7-4: Finish hem edges with a three-step zigzag stitch on a sewing machine.

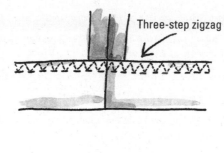

Three-step zigzag

Figure 7-5: Finish a hem edge with your serger by using a three-thread overlock stitch.

Serged

Securing the Hem

TIP

After you mark the hem, even up the hem allowance, and finish the raw edge, you're ready to pin up the hem and either fuse or sew it in place.

If you're not following pattern instructions or are re-hemming, refer to Table 7-1 to find the right hem depth for your project.

No-sew hemming

Fuse up a quick, permanent hem using paper-backed fusible web (available through your local fabric store or sewing mail-order sources).

A fused hem is almost impossible to change because adhesive residue sticks all over the place when you try to unfuse it. If you foresee a hem change later on, skip ahead to the sections "Hand blind hemming" and "Machine blind hemming" later in this chapter.

1. **Measure, mark, and finish the hem as described in the previous sections of this chapter.**

2. **Fold up and pin the hem, placing the pins at the hemline.**

3. **Press the hem edge without pressing over the pins, pressing firmly enough so that you see the hem fold when you're done.**

4. **Place the project on the ironing board with the inside facing you.**

5. **Remove the pins and open up the hem.**

6. **Fuse the paper-backed fusible web to the wrong side of the hem edge following the manufacturer's instructions.**

   You place the exposed fusible side against the fabric and the paper-side up against the iron.

7. **Let the release paper cool and remove it.**

8. **Fuse up the hem as shown in Figure 7-6, following the manufacturer's instructions.**

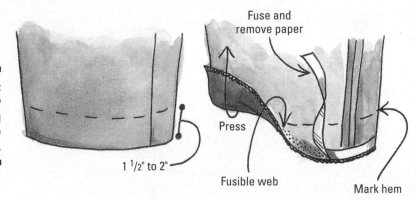

Figure 7-6:
No-sew hemming with fusible web.

Pinning up the hem for hand or machine hemming

For an almost invisibly stitched hand or machine blind hem, the stitches end up between the hem allowance and the inside of the project itself — tricky to do unless you pin your hem this way. What's cool is that you pin the same way for both hand and machine blind hemming.

The trick is to pin through both fabric layers, ¼ to ⅜ inch from and *perpendicular* to the finished edge, as shown in Figure 7-7. This way, when you fold the hem allowance back for stitching, the fold naturally stops where the pins enter the fabric.

Figure 7-7:
Pin the hem the same way, whether blind hemming by hand or machine.

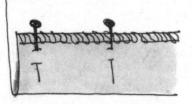

Hand blind hemming

If you don't have a blind hem stitch on your machine, or until you master blind hemming by machine, stitch your hems this way by hand:

1. **Thread the needle with a 15- to 18-inch length of thread one shade darker than the fabric.**

   If the thread is much longer, it tangles and wears out before you use it all.

2. **Lay the hem across your lap wrong-side up so that the inside of the garment is up and the hem fold is away from and perpendicular to your body. Fold the hem allowance back to where the pins enter the fabric so the finished edge is away from you (see Figure 7-8).**

   Approximately ¼ to ⅜ inch of the hem allowance is showing.

3. **Take the first stitch on the single layer of the hem allowance, poking the point of the needle down into the fabric and then bringing it up no farther than ⅛ inch from where it entered (see Figure 7-8).**

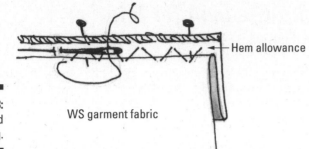

Figure 7-8:
Hand blind
hemming.

Hem allowance

WS garment fabric

4. **Stitching from right to left (if you're right-handed) or left to right (if you're left-handed), take another stitch, picking up one fine thread (at the edge of the fold and where the pins enter the fabric) from the garment fabric.**

   You want to make the stitches as invisible as possible on the right side of the project, so take the finest stitch you can on the wrong side of the garment fabric.

5. **Continue stitching all the way around the hem, taking one stitch on the hem allowance and then taking the next stitch on the garment fabric where the hem is folded back to the pins.**

Take shorter stitches on finer fabrics, sewing a stitch ¼-inch on the project, ¼-inch on the hem edge. Take longer stitches on heavier fabrics, spacing them about ½-inch apart.

Machine blind hemming

After you use your sewing machine to blind hem, I bet you don't go back to doing it by hand. Here's how you do it by machine:

1. **Set your machine like this:**

   • Stitch: Blind hem

   • Length: 2 to 2.5 mm/10 to 12 spi

   • Width: 2 to 2.5 mm

   • Foot: Blind hem

2. **Fold the hem allowance back to where the pins enter the fabric and place it under the blind hem foot.**

   The right side of the project is against the feed dogs (the teeth that grip and feed the underside of the fabric through the machine; see Chapter 2), the wrong side is up, and the hem fold snuggles up against the guide in the foot.

3. **Make the first few stitches on the hem allowance; the zigzag bites into the fold as shown in Figure 7-9.**

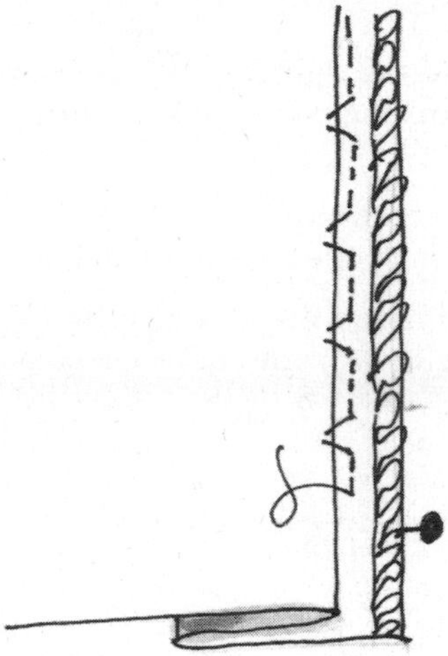

Figure 7-9: Machine blind hem, letting the stitch bite barely into the hem fold.

You want to create invisible stitches here (just like with hand blind hemming), so if the stitch grabs too much of the hem fold, you've made it too wide. Use a narrower stitch width. Using the blind hem foot made to fit your machine helps you guide the fabric more uniformly so the needle bites into the hem fold the same amount with every stitch.

4. **Remove the project, pull the threads to one side of the fabric, and tie them off.**

5. **Gently press the hem allowance from the wrong side of the project in an up-and-down motion and applying more iron pressure on the hem fold than on the top of the hem allowance.**

Overpressing the hem causes the finished edge of the hem to shadow through to the right side of the project, so use a press cloth to prevent this (see Chapter 2 for more on using a press cloth).

Sewing Tapered Hems

Whether making pants or rehemming ready-made pants, you taper the hem allowance so that it conforms to the shape of the pant leg. If you don't taper the hem allowance, the hem edge is narrower than the leg circumference. What happens? The hemming stitches pull at the fabric, so the pant leg puckers at the top of the hem allowance. Yuck. This is how you taper a hem allowance:

1. **Measure, mark, and finish the hem edge, leaving about a 1½- to 2-inch hem allowance.**

2. **Starting at the bottom, rip out each inseam (the seam on the inside of the legs) and each outseam (the seam on the outside of the legs)** *only* **up to the hem fold.**

3. **Restitch the inseam and the outseam, sewing from the new hemline fold out to the finished edge, tapering each seam as shown in Figure 7-10.**

   Tapering these seams from the hemline fold out to the finished edge ensures that they fit comfortably into the circumference of the opening.

4. **So the hem allowance fits smoothly all the way around each leg, cut a notch at the hem fold at both the inseam and outseam (see Figure 7-10).**

Figure 7-10: Taper the side seams to match the tapered seam allowance for a comfortably-fitting pant hem.

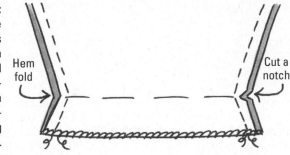

Hemming Knits with Twin Needles

Knits stretch. Because of this tendency, traditional hand and machine blind hemming techniques often don't hold up to a lot of wear. Commercial hemming techniques keep your knits looking good for a long time. You can duplicate these techniques by hemming knits using your twin needles. So how does this work? Twin needles have one shank that fits up into the sewing machine and a bar that holds two needles. To use them, thread each needle separately, lower the presser foot and sew. If you turn over the fabric and look at the wrong side of the stitch, you see that the bobbin thread shares itself between the two top threads creating a zigzag stitch that stretches with the fabric so you don't pop stitches. You can see a twin needle in Figure 7-11.

Twin needles are sized in two ways: By the distance the needles are from one another and by the needle size and point type. You use twin needles with narrower widths on lightweight fabrics and wider widths on heavier fabric. A *4.0 80/12 Universal twin needle* tells you the following information:

✔ You have two needles that are 4 millimeters apart.

✔ Each needle is a size 80 (European sizing) or 12 (American sizing).

✔ Each needle has a Universal point.

When shopping for twin needles, take your machine's all-purpose presser foot to the store with you. Some needles are too wide for the opening in some feet, so check before you buy.

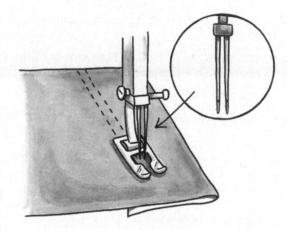

Figure 7-11:
Use twin needles for durable hems on knit fabric.

Only sewing machines with top- or front-loading bobbins (a category that includes most machines) can use twin needles. If your bobbin goes in the side, the needles sit in the machine sideways and don't work. If you can't use twin needles in your machine, fuse the hem by using fusible web (see "No-sew hemming" earlier in this chapter).

Follow these steps to make a twin-needle hem:

1. **Mark, press, and pin up the hem as I describe in previous sections.**

   When pressing a knit hem, use an up-and-down pressing motion rather than sliding the iron from side to side. If you slide, you may stretch out the hem permanently.

2. **Set your machine like this:**

   • Stitch: Straight

   • Length: 3 to 4 mm/6 to 9 spi

   • Width: 0 mm

   • Foot: Embroidery

   • Needle: 4.0 mm 80/12 Universal twin

If you notice that your hem has some skipped stitches (several normal-length stitches and then an occasional long one), try using a *Stretch* twin needle. The tips on the needles are specially designed to slip through the loops of knit fabrics, preventing skipped stitches.

3. **Thread your twin needle by following the instructions in your operating manual.**

4. **With the right side of the project up, place the hem so that the presser foot rests completely on a double layer of fabric (the hem allowance and the garment) and sew.**

   Sewing straight and even is easier when the foot rests completely on a double layer of fabric.

5. **After sewing around the hem, pull all of the threads to the wrong side and tie them off securely (see Chapter 6).**

6. **Press the hem using an up-and-down pressing motion.**

7. **Carefully trim away the excess hem allowance above the stitch as shown in Figure 7-12.**

The scissors shown in Figure 7-12 are called appliqué scissors. They come in handy when trimming one layer of fabric away from another (like you do when you're appliquéing or trimming away excess fabric from hem allowances) because the wider "duck bill" blade prevents you from cutting an unwanted hole in the fabric. Simply place the blade against the back of garment, and then trim the excess hem allowance away. If you're doing a lot of knit hems or appliqué work, these babies are a super investment.

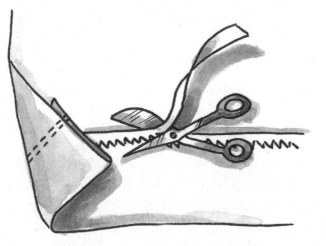

Figure 7-12: Trim off the excess hem allowance.

Part III
Fashion Sewing Fun-damentals

The 5th Wave   By Rich Tennant

"I usually use a buttonhole maker."

In this part . . .

When the pattern guide sheet of your fashion project tells you to "Sew in the zipper," you may be left scratching your head. How in the world are you supposed to do that? Your first step is to turn to Chapter 9 in this part, where you find step-by-step instructions on how to sew in a zipper. This part also gives you the skinny on sewing darts, pleats, sleeves, pockets, attaching elastic, and other sewing necessities. And to help you firm up your fashion fundamentals, I include stylish projects that show you step-by-step how to sew a computer sleeve, a clutch purse, a sweet ruffled apron, and the ultimate pair of pajama pants.

Chapter 8

Shaping Things Up

• •

In This Chapter

▶ Adding shape with darts and gathers

▶ Making a ruffled apron

▶ Taking on fabric pleats

▶ Stretching your skills with elastic

▶ Putting together pajama pants with cuffs

• •

Darts, gathering, pleats, and elastic enable you to give form to otherwise lifeless pieces of fabric. You can use these structural elements separately or together to turn a potato sack into a creation that conforms to all sorts of contours, not only in clothing, but also in almost anything made of fabric. In this chapter you find out how to fit and shape fabric with these elements, and then to practice your newfound fabric-shaping skills, you can make a cute little apron or a pair of pretty and practical pajama pants.

Darting Around

Darts are little wedges of fabric that you pinch out and stitch to shape pattern pieces at the waistline, back waist, shoulder, bustline, and hips, as shown in Figure 8-1.

Paper patterns mark darts with stitching lines and sometimes a foldline that converges to the point of the dart. (See Chapter 4 for more information on how to decipher the markings on patterns.)

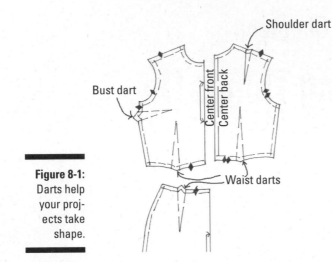

Figure 8-1: Darts help your projects take shape.

You may come across two dart types depending on the project. If the project has a horizontal waistline seam as you see in Figure 8-1, fabric needs to be "nipped in" to follow the natural curve at the waistline. So the darts on the bodice and the skirt have a wider amount of fabric taken out of the fabric at one end of the dart and then taper off at the point. This type is called a *straight dart*.

If you need to nip in the waistline on a garment without a horizontal waistline seam, such as a blouse with a contoured waistline or a drop-waist or one-piece dress, then you make a dart that's wide in the middle and is stitched to points at either end. This type is called a *contoured dart*.

Sewing the straight dart

To construct perfect straight darts every time, just follow these steps:

1. **Mark the dart with pins or a fabric marker. (See Chapter 4 for more about marking elements from a pattern.)**

2. **Fold the dart, right sides together, matching at the foldline and pinning perpendicular to the stitching line at the dots marked on the pattern piece.**

3. **Place a strip of invisible tape the length of the dart, next to the stitching line, as shown in Figure 8-2.**

   The tape forms a stitching template that helps to keep your sewing straight.

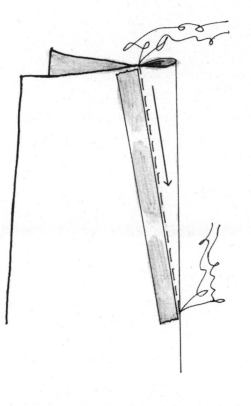

Figure 8-2:
Use tape as
a stitching
template
and sew
from the
wide end to
the point of
the dart.

4. **Set your machine like this:**

   - Stitch: Straight

   - Length: 2.5 to 3 mm/10 to 12 spi

   - Width: 0 mm

   - Foot: All-purpose

5. **Starting at the wide end of the dart, lower the presser foot and sew next to the tape for a perfectly straight dart, pulling out the pins as you sew.**

   Don't make a dart by starting at the point and sewing to the wide end or by backstitching at the point. If you do, it won't be shaped properly and will probably bulge at the point.

6. **Tie off the threads at the point (see more about tying off threads in Chapter 6).**

Sewing the contour dart

Without bust and back waist darts, your project hangs on you like a flour sack. Follow these steps to turn those flat, lifeless pieces of fabric into parts of a shapely dress you love to wear:

1. **Mark the contour darts using your dressmaker's chalk and/or pins.**

   Check out the information in Chapter 4 for all the marking details. Review the information above on "Making straight darts" for more on sewing the perfect dart.

2. **Set your machine like this:**
   - Stitch: Straight
   - Length: 2.5 to 3 mm/10 to 12 spi
   - Width: 0 mm
   - Foot: All-purpose

3. **Starting at the widest part of the dart, sew to the point in one direction, and then turn the dart around and repeat for the other end of the dart, as shown in Figure 8-3.**

   This two-step method makes the dart smooth and perfectly tapered at both ends.

4. **Tie off threads at both ends and in the middle of the dart (see Chapter 6 for more on tying off threads).**

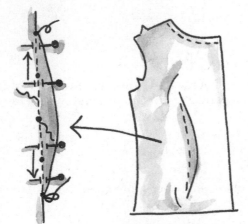

Figure 8-3:
Mark and sew the contour dart in two steps.

Finishing the dart

After sewing your dart, press it so that the dart forms a clean, smooth line in the fabric. Just follow these easy steps:

1. **Remove the tape and press the dart flat and together.**

   Place the dart on the ironing board with the wrong side of the fabric up. Place one edge of the iron over the stitching line with the rest of the iron over the fold of the dart; press the dart flat from the stitching line out to the fold. Sewers refer to this procedure as *pressing the dart flat and together.* By pressing over the seamline, you set the stitches so that they blend well into the fabric.

2. **Press the dart to one side of the inside of the garment.**

   Press horizontal darts so that the bulk of the dart is down. Press vertical darts so that the bulk of the dart is toward the center of the garment. If you have a tailor's ham, press the darts over a ham so when the dart is pressed it mimics the body curves. Check out Chapters 2 and 5 to learn more about pressing with a ham.

Don't use a too-hot iron for your fabric. *Do* use a press cloth. Some fabric is tricky to work with because, if pressed with a too-hot iron and/ or without a press cloth, it can shine and the seam allowances create *shadows* on either side of the seamline. If you're not sure about the iron's heat setting and what it does to your fabric, use a press cloth and test-press a fabric scrap.

Gathering Fabric from One Piece into Another

Gathering adds softness and shape to a project. Picture a gently gathered waistline and puffed sleeve in a child's dress, soft gathers above a shirt cuff, or a skirt gathered onto a waistband. All these examples use gathers as a way to fit a larger fabric piece, such as a skirt, into another, smaller fabric piece like a waistband or dress bodice. In this section I show you two methods for gathering fabric. The method you use depends on the type of fabric you're working with.

Gathering with two threads

The two-thread method works best for creating fine, controlled gathers on lightweight fabrics, such as batiste, challis, charmeuse, gauze, gingham, georgette, lace, silk broadcloth, and voile. (See Chapter 3 for more information on these fabrics.) Just follow these steps:

1. **Set your machine like this:**

   - Stitch: Straight

   - Length: 2.5 to 3 mm/9 to 13 spi

   - Width: 0 mm

   - Foot: All-purpose or embroidery

   - Upper tension: Loosen slightly

2. **Thread your needle with the thread you used for sewing your project together; thread your bobbin with a contrasting thread color.**

   Using a different thread color in the bobbin makes these stitches easier to find when you're ready to pull up the gathers.

3. **Sew a row of gathering stitches ½ inch from the raw edge, leaving at least a 2-inch thread tail at the beginning and end.**

   Do not backstitch at the beginning or end.

   The gathering stitches for a seam sewn together at the ⅝-inch seamline are just inside the seam allowance and don't show on the outside of the project.

4. **Sew a second row of gathering stitches ⅜ inch from the raw edge, leaving at least a 2-inch thread tail at the beginning and end, as shown in Figure 8-4.**

   Be careful not to cross the stitching lines.

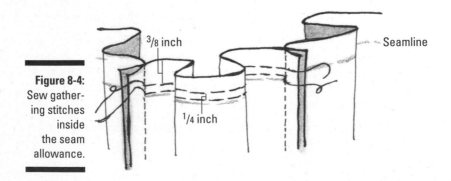

Figure 8-4: Sew gathering stitches inside the seam allowance.

3/8 inch

1/4 inch

Seamline

5. **Pin-mark the gathering strip into quarters and repeat for the flat piece the gathering strip will be attached to.**

6. **Pin the seam allowances of the gathered piece and the flat piece of fabric together, matching the quartered pin marks.**

7. **Pull up the gathers by pulling on the contrasting bobbin threads adjusting the gathering evenly from pin to pin as shown in Figure 8-5.**

   Working from the ends toward the center, hold the bobbin threads taut in one hand while sliding the fabric along the stitches with the other. Adjust the gathers as needed for the fullness you desire. Not only are the gathers even, but using two threads also gives you a back-up thread if the first one breaks. Remember to put your upper tension back to the normal setting before you sew the gathered and straight pieces together.

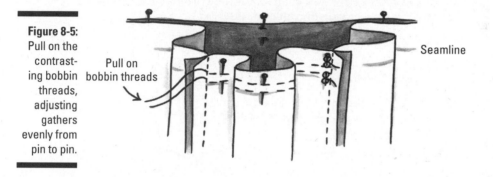

Figure 8-5: Pull on the contrasting bobbin threads, adjusting gathers evenly from pin to pin.

Pull on bobbin threads

Seamline

Gathering over a cord

You can use gathering over a cord as a terrific way to gather mid- to heavy-weight fabrics, such as chambray, chintz, corduroy, lightweight denim, linen and wool suiting, oxford, pique, poplin, and seersucker. (See Chapter 3 for more information on these fabrics.) The cord technique also works well when you gather yards of fabric all at once when sewing ruffles. Just follow these steps:

1. **Set your machine like this:**

   • Stitch: Zigzag

   • Length: 2.5 to 3 mm/9 to 13 spi

   • Width: 3 to 4 mm

   • Foot: Embroidery

2. **Cut a strand of *pearl cotton* twisted embroidery floss, dental floss, or three or four strands of any thread long enough to accommodate the area you want to gather.**

   For example, if you're gathering 10 inches, the cord should be 12 to 14 inches long. If you're using thread, slightly twist the strands together — making a sort of cord.

3. **Place the fabric under the needle with the wrong side up.**

4. **Leaving the foot up, pierce the fabric with the needle ½ inch from the raw edge.**

5. **Center the cord lengthwise under the foot and lower the presser foot.**

6. **Zigzag over the cord, as shown in Figure 8-6.**

   Be careful not to sew through the cord when zigzagging over it. The zigzag stitches create a channel for the cord to slide through, and if you sew the cord, it won't be able to slide.

Figure 8-6: Zigzag over the cord for fast, strong, and easy gathering.

7. **Pull up the gathers by sliding the fabric down the cord.**

   You can easily adjust the gathers, and the cord doesn't break when working the stitches up and down for dense gathering.

Ruffled Apron

Aprons are all the rage, with some cute numbers showing up in fashion magazines, retail stores, and on Etsy (www.etsy.com), the eBay for crafters and independent designers worldwide. This stylish, quick-to-make apron gives you an opportunity to practice your gathering skills. By starting with a short denim skirt, which has a finished waistband, belt loops, and pockets, your project is half done before you start. I found several wonderful apron candidates at my local Goodwill and Salvation Army stores for about $3 each — simply add some ruffles and a tie belt, and voilà! A very cute apron that's a snap to make. Check out a photo of the finished project in the color section.

To make this project, you need the following materials in addition to your sewing survival kit (see Chapter 2):

- A short denim skirt with belt loops at the waistline. (Choose a skirt that when laid flat is the width you want your final apron to be. Don't worry about whether it fits you.)

- 1 yard each of three or four woven prints that complement each other. (After making the ruffles for this project you'll have enough of each of the prints left over to make matching napkins — see Chapter 13 for more on making napkins.)

- Thread that matches the fabric.

Cutting out the apron parts

Follow these steps to get the parts of your apron ready for sewing:

1. **Lay the skirt flat on a table top, smoothing it from the center to the side seams.**

2. **Cut the front and back of the skirt apart where it folds at the sides, usually slightly behind of the seams (see Figure 8-7).**

   You don't need the back half of the skirt for this project, but if you like its looks, you may be able to make another apron out of it.

Figure 8-7: Cut the skirt apart at the side fold (not necessarily on the side seams).

3. **Open one of the print fabrics so it's flat. Find the bias (the diagonal grain) by folding one selvage down so it's even with one cut edge, and press the fold.**

   When you unfold the fabric, the bias makes a perfect diagonal as shown in Figure 8-8. The pressed fold becomes one of your cutting lines.

4. **Open up the fabric so it's flat again and cut one strip 4-inches wide by the length of the pressed bias crease. (See Figure 8-8.)**

5. **Repeat Steps 3 and 4 for the other print fabrics.**

   By cutting out the ruffles on the bias, you won't have to finish any of the raw edges because they won't ravel (see Chapter 4 for more on finding true bias). The raw edges also give the apron a cool handmade look you'll love.

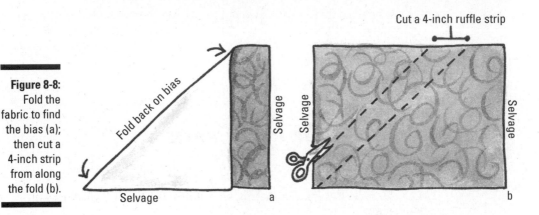

Figure 8-8:
Fold the fabric to find the bias (a); then cut a 4-inch strip from along the fold (b).

6. **Choose one of your prints for the apron sash. Cut two additional strips across the grain that are four times the width of the skirt waistband and as long as the fabric allows.**

   For example, if the skirt's waistband is 1½ inches, make these sash strips 6 inches wide.

Finishing the apron side seams

To cut down on the excess bulk at the edges of the apron, the edges are pinked and stitched. Here's how:

1. **Pink the side edges of the denim apron front by cutting with pinking shears to prevent unraveling.**

2. **Set your machine this way:**
   - Stitch: Straight
   - Length: 4 mm/6 spi
   - Width: 0 mm
   - Foot: All-purpose

3. **Straight stitch just inside the pinked edges as shown in Figure 8-9.**

   Instead of backstitching at the top and bottom of the edge, pull the threads to the back of the project and tie them off (for more on tying off threads, see Chapter 6).

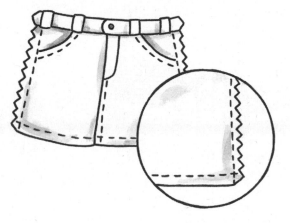

Figure 8-9:
Pink and stitch the side edges of the apron for a smooth, finished look.

Gathering and attaching the ruffle strip

Gather each ruffle and sew it to the apron front. Here's how:

1. **Run two rows of gathering stitches at the top of each ruffle strip as described in "Gathering with two threads" above.**

2. **Pin-mark the bottom of the skirt and the first ruffle strip into fourths.**

3. **Match the pin marks of the ruffle strip to the pin marks on the skirt front, pinning the ruffle so it lays on top of and overlaps the denim by about 1 inch, as shown in Figure 8-10.**

4. **Start gathering from pin to pin by pulling on the two bobbin threads and evenly adjusting the fullness along the gathering stitches.**

Figure 8-10:
Gather the ruffle to fit the front of the apron by adjusting fullness from pin to pin.

5. **Set your machine like this:**
   - Stitch: Straight
   - Length: 2.5 to 3 mm/6 to 8 spi
   - Width: 0 mm
   - Foot: All-purpose

6. **Stitch on the ruffle strip, guiding the presser foot so you're sewing *between* the two rows of gathering stitches.**

   Remember to backstitch at the beginning and end of each ruffle.

7. **Pull out the two rows of gathering stitches sewn in Step 1 by pulling out the bobbin threads.**

8. **Repeat this section for each subsequent ruffle, placing the bottom of the ruffle slightly over the gathered stitches of the one below it.**

Tying up the apron strings

This method is not only great for making the apron tie for this project, but works well for making straps for a tote bag or sundress.

1. **Set your machine like this:**
   - Stitch: Straight
   - Length: 2.5 to 3 mm/6 to 8 spi
   - Width: 0 mm
   - Foot: All-purpose

2. Using the two sash strips cut in "Cutting out the apron parts," lay the strips short end to short end and seam together with a ⅝-inch seam allowance.

3. Trim the unsewn ends so that the sash is two and a half times your waist measurement.

   For example, if your waist measurement is 30 inches, the sash needs to be 75 inches.

4. Fold the apron sash strip in half the short way, pressing a crease down the length of the long strip (see Figure 8-11a).

5. Open up your fabric strip at the ironing board and with the wrong side up, fold and press the two long edges to the center crease and refold along the center as shown in Figure 8-11b.

Figure 8-11:
The two-step process of folding and pressing the apron tie makes it strong and stable.

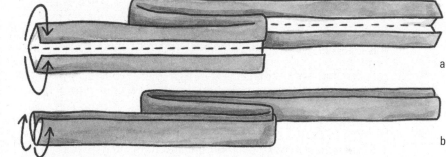

a

b

6. Stitch around all four sides of the apron tie, guiding the foot ¼ inch from the edge.

7. Pink the two short edges of the apron tie as shown in Figure 8-12.

Figure 8-12:
After sewing around all four edges of the apron string, pink the short edges for a quick, easy finish.

8. **Thread the apron tie through the belt loops on the apron skirt and put it on.**

If you have only two belt loops on the front of your apron, stitch the tie at each end of the waistband to secure it.

Completing Pleats

Pleats are folds in the fabric that control fullness. You find pleats in all sorts of places, including the following:

- Around a whole garment, like on a pleated skirt
- In sections, such as at the waistline of a pair of trousers
- As a single pleat, like a kick pleat in the back of a skirt

You make most pleats by folding a continuous piece of fabric and then stitching the folds to hold them in place. Beginner and easy sewing projects don't often have pleats, but many intermediate and advanced patterns do. The pattern guide sheet explains how to fold and construct pleats for a particular project; refer to the pattern often as you sew your pleats.

To make a pleat, mark it as you would a dart or other symbol found on the pattern tissue (see marking instructions in Chapter 4). Fold the pleat on the foldline and stitch the pleat on the stitching line.

Defining the types of pleats

When you look through pattern catalogs and fashion magazines (and probably your own closet), you see a variety of pleats. Become familiar with the different types of pleats (see Figure 8-13) and where you find them on clothing:

- **Knife pleats:** These pleats have one foldline and one placement line and are pleated in one direction. You often find several knife pleats clustered together on each side of a garment, where one cluster faces one direction and the other cluster faces the opposite direction — like at the top of a pair of trousers.

- **Box pleats:** These pleats have two foldlines and two placement lines. The folds of each pleat face away from each other, and the backside of the folds may or may not meet. You most commonly see box pleats down the center front of a dress or skirt and in bed skirts.

✔ **Inverted pleats:** You find two foldlines in these pleats, but they come together at a common placement line. Like box pleats, you most commonly find inverted pleats down the center front of a dress or skirt and in bed skirts.

✔ **Kick pleats:** These pleats have one foldline and one placement line, and you usually find them at the hem edge at center back of a slim skirt. Besides adding style, kick pleats give the skirt enough room for comfortable walking.

✔ **Accordion pleats:** Sorry — you can't make these pleats at home. Accordion pleats look like the bellows of an accordion, providing a kicky, flared effect. Commercial pleaters permanently set these pleats into the fabric using a combination of heat and steam. You can purchase accordion pleated fabric by the yard.

Figure 8-13:
Look for knife pleats (a), box pleats (b), inverted pleats (c), kick pleats (d), and accordion pleats (e) in garments.

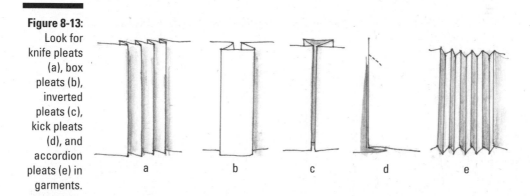

a   b   c   d   e

Making a pleat

Regardless of the type of pleat you make, with the exception of the accordion pleat, you make all pleats just about the same. After you know how to make a knife pleat, you have the basic skills you need to make the others. Follow these steps:

1. **Mark the pleats at the dots as directed on your project's pattern guide sheet. Check out Figure 8-14 for an illustration.**

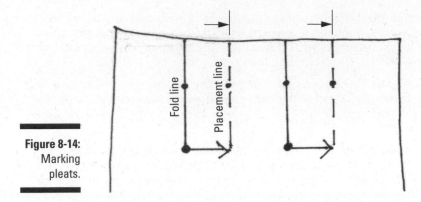

Figure 8-14:
Marking
pleats.

2. **Fold and pin the pleat, bringing the foldline over to meet the placement line.**

3. **Stitch the pleat on the stitching line, as shown in Figure 8-15.**

Figure 8-15:
Folding and
stitching
to create
pleats.

Adding Stretch and Comfort with Elastic

Besides adding shape and form to a project, elastic usually makes a garment more comfortable to wear. Elastic comes in a variety of configurations, each of which may be appropriate for a different use. Refer to Chapter 3 for more information on the different types of elastic and which type may be appropriate for your project.

In this section you discover the easy way to put elastic through a casing. And if you want to know how to sew elastic to an edge, I show you two techniques — one using a sewing machine and one using a serger.

Inserting elastic in a casing

A *casing* is a fabric tunnel that holds a drawstring or elastic at waistlines, wrists, and ankles to shape a garment. Traditionally, you create a casing in one of the two following ways:

↙ By folding down and stitching a casing, using fabric at the top of a waist-line. You often see and use this method for the waistband on pull-on pants or shorts.

↙ By sewing another strip of fabric to the wrong side of the fabric. This method is popular at the waistlines of dresses and at the back of jackets.

In this section you make a casing by using the fold-down method. Pattern instructions often tell you to create the casing and then thread the elastic through the casing with a large safety pin or *bodkin* (a little tool that pinches together over the end of the elastic like a pair of tweezers with teeth).

I've made hundreds of casings, and I can't tell you how many times I've gotten to within 2 inches of the end and given the elastic one last tug, just to have the safety pin or bodkin pull off the end before the elastic was all the way through the casing. If that didn't happen, the safety pin or bodkin got hung up in the seam allowances. By the time the elastic was through the casing, I felt like I had acute arthritis in both hands. Painful and frustrating!

So my friend Karyl Garbow devised the following technique for creating elastic casings. This technique takes about as long as the conventional method, but you don't lose the elastic or stress out your hands in the process. The trick is to start with a length of elastic that's longer than the circumference it's going into. Manufacturers often package elastic in multiple-yard lengths, so you get enough elastic for several treatments.

Try this fold-down method at the wrist of a sleeve or ankle of a pair of pants. You can also use this method for the waistline of pull-on shorts, pants, and skirts:

1. **Set your machine like this:**

   • Stitch: Three-step zigzag

   • Length: 1 to 1.5 mm/25 spi or fine

   • Width: 4 to 5 mm

   • Foot: All-purpose

If you're using a serger, use the following settings:

- Stitch: Three-thread overlock

- Length: 3 mm

- Width: 5 mm

- Foot: Standard

2. **Overcast the raw edge of the casing so the fabric doesn't ravel.**

   To *overcast,* guide the fabric so that the stitches catch the fabric on the left and sew just off the edge at the right.

3. **To form the casing, fold down the top of the fabric toward the inside of the project the width of the elastic plus ⅝ inch. Press the casing into place.**

4. **Set your machine like this:**

   - Stitch: Straight

   - Length: 2.5 to 3 mm/10 to 12 spi

   - Width: 0 mm

   - Foot: All-purpose or edgestitch

   - Needle position: Left (optional)

5. **Edgestitch around the top of the casing, sewing ⅛ inch from the folded edge. (See Chapter 6 for more on edgestitching.)**

   The edgestitch foot has a guide in it that keeps your sewing straight. It's not a standard foot, so ask your dealer whether they make one for your machine.

6. **Leaving the elastic in one long strip, place and pin the elastic into the casing, snuggling it up against the edgestitched fold, as shown in Figure 8-16.**

   Pin parallel to and just under the elastic. A lot of elastic hangs off either end of the casing, which you cut to fit later.

7. **Anchor one loose end of the elastic with a pin. Using your all-purpose foot, stitch under (but not through!) the elastic, as shown in Figure 8-17.**

   Instead of stitching the casing down all the way around, leave a 2-inch opening in the casing for the elastic ends to pull through.

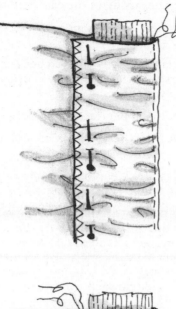

Figure 8-16:
Pin the casing close to the elastic.

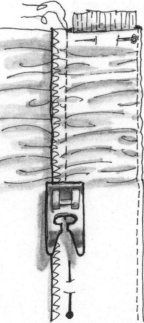

Figure 8-17:
Be careful not to stitch through the elastic when you sew the casing.

8. **Pull the elastic taut through the opening in the casing until it fits comfortably around your waist.**

9. **Pin the elastic ends together.**

   Don't cut off the elastic until you check that it stretches enough to fit over your hips. Nothing is worse than sewing in the elastic and then discovering that you can't pull up your pants.

10. **Cut the elastic to fit, adding a 1-inch overlap at the ends.**

11. **Overlap one end of the elastic over the other 1 inch and sew a square to really secure the ends.**

   Join the elastic at the overlap by straight stitching across the top, down the side, across the bottom, and then up.

   When you work with a shorter piece of elastic or replace worn out elastic, thread the elastic through the casing. Instead of using a safety pin or bodkin, which can sometimes pull off the end or get hung up on the seam allowances, cut a small slit in the elastic at least ½-inch from the end and thread a bobby pin through it. The bobby pin has smooth ends and is narrow enough to easily slide through almost any casing.

Attaching elastic on an edge

Elastic sewn into ready-made clothing is stitched on an edge of an opening and then flipped over and topstitched. You can very easily duplicate this factory technique with your sewing machine or serger. The trick is using elastic thread in the bobbin.

Use the following technique to apply elastic to just about any edge where you need it, including waistbands, sleeves, and pant legs:

1. **Set your machine like this:**

   • Stitch: Overlock

   • Length: Longest (see operating manual)

   • Width: 5 mm

   • Foot: All-purpose

   If you're using a serger, use these settings:

   • Stitch: Three-thread overlock

   • Length: 3 to 3.5 mm

   • Width: 5 mm

   • Foot: Standard

2. **Using your fabric marker, mark off the edge of the fabric at the garment opening into eight equal parts.**

   Eighths, rather than quarters, are easier to work with. (See Chapter 2 for more about markers.)

3. **Stretch the elastic around your waist (or wherever you plan to sew the elastic) until it fits comfortably and cut it to the correct size.**

   Remember to add about one inch extra at the ends of the elastic for overlap.

4. **Using your fabric marker, mark off the elastic into eighths.**

5. **Pin the elastic into the opening, matching the marks on the elastic with the marks on the garment opening.**

   When you put elastic into a waistband or leg opening, leave one of the side seams open. This way you can easily sew in the elastic and adjust the fit at the open seam.

6. **Sew the first couple of stitches to anchor the elastic to the edge of the fabric.**

7. **Stop and reposition your hands, grabbing the fabric and elastic in front of and behind the presser foot. Stretch the elastic to fit the fabric, sewing from pin to pin so that the fabric and the elastic edges match up.**

   Stitches should catch with the fabric and elastic on the left side of the stitch and then swing just off the edges on the right side of the stitch, as shown in Figure 8-18.

   Remove the pins as you get to them so that you don't sew over them and break a needle.

   When serging, serge from pin to pin, removing pins before getting to them and guiding the elastic so that the knife slightly trims away the excess fabric and does not cut into the elastic.

8. **Wind the bobbin with good quality elastic thread.**

   Quality elastic thread is available at your local sewing machine dealer. This type has a stretchy core wrapped in cotton and is beefier and more resilient than what you typically find on the fabric store notions wall.

   Place the bobbin on the bobbin winder and the tube of elastic thread on your lap. Loosely tie the elastic thread onto the bobbin and then wind the bobbin slowly, guiding the elastic thread evenly and *without stretching the thread as you go*. If you do, the elastic thread stretches out and loses its oomph and resiliency.

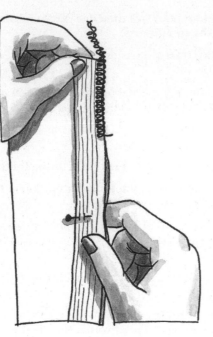

Figure 8-18:
Stretch the
elastic as
you sew
from pin
to pin.

If your machine has a self-winding bobbin, wind the bobbin by hand. Self-winding bobbins only work when the thread is threaded through the eye of the needle and the needle moves up and down while the bobbin winds. This up-and-down needle action tears up the elastic thread (and would probably put your machine into the hospital, too).

9. **Change the settings on your machine as follows:**

- Stitch: Straight

- Length: 3 to 3.5 mm/8 to 9 spi

- Width: 0 mm

- Foot: Embroidery

- Bobbin: Thread with elastic thread snapped securely into the bobbin tension (the part of the bobbin where the thread snaps into place and doesn't come unthreaded).

Because elastic thread is stretchy, it's easy to mistakenly think you threaded it in the bobbin case correctly when it's not snapped into the bobbin tension. Double check that you thread your bobbin correctly by tugging on the elastic thread tail. It shouldn't come out of the bobbin case.

10. **Flip the elastic over so that the *overcasting stitches* (those stitches that you used to sew the elastic to the edge) are to the wrong side of the project and then topstitch the elastic.**

    With the right side up, guide the edge of the casing, following a line on your needle plate so that the topstitching just catches the bottom edge of the elastic, as shown in Figure 8-19. You may have to gently stretch the elastic in front of and behind the presser foot as you sew to get a nice smooth line of stitching.

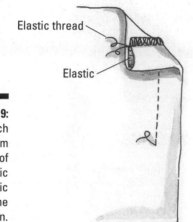

Figure 8-19: Topstitch the bottom edge of the elastic using elastic thread in the bobbin.

11. **Now that you've stitched the elastic into place, sew up the side seam, catching the elastic ends in the seamline.**

    Trim away excess elastic to the edge of the seam allowance.

Most sergers have a special elastic applicator foot that you purchase separately that makes quick work of elastic application. Thread the elastic through the slot in the foot and then adjust the tautness of the elastic by tightening or loosening the adjustment screw on the foot.

Cuffed Pajama Pants

Pajamas have been elevated from something you sleep in to a fashion necessity. My friends at DIY Style teamed up two fashion-forward prints and created the pretty pair of practically perfect pajamas, pictured in the color section.

To make this project, you need the following materials in addition to your sewing survival kit (see Chapter 2):

- An elastic-waist pajama or pant pattern.

- 2 to 2½ yards of woven cotton or cotton/poly blend fabric such as poplin or flannel for pj's (check the back of your pattern envelope for yardage requirements); if you're new to sewing, ask the sales associate at the fabric store if they sell special pj prints. There are some very fun and creative choices available for all ages.

- ½ yard of a coordinating print for the cuff (optional).

- One package of 1-inch-wide soft waistband elastic.

- All-purpose sewing thread.

- Tube of quality elastic thread.

- Thread that matches the fabric.

Laying and cutting out your pj's

Follow these steps to make the pj's. This method eliminates the outside leg seam for a quick and comfy fit. Make these pants with or without the cuff for just about anyone in the family.

1. **Find and cut out the front leg and back leg pattern pieces (see Figure 8-20a).**

   Many commercial patterns come with several sizes printed on one piece of pattern tissue, but when cutting out pattern pieces, leave some extra space outside your size's cutting line. It makes cutting out the fabric easier.

2. **Lay out the front and back pant pattern pieces on a large surface and tape them together, overlapping the outseams (the seams sewn on the outside of each leg) of each pattern piece the width of the seam allowance as shown in Figure 8-20b.**

   Check your pattern instructions to see whether your pattern calls for ⅝- or ¼-inch seam allowances. Overlap the pattern pieces by that much.

3. **Cut off the leg pattern at the finished hemline.**

   A decorative cuff is added at the bottom of these pj's, so if you want the pj's to come down to your ankles, adjust the pattern so the finished length is to your ankles. If you want the pj's to be capri length, adjust the finished length so it is between your knee and ankle.

Figure 8-20:
Overlap
and tape
the front
and back
leg patterns
together
at the out-
seams to
make one
leg pattern,
cut off the
hem allow-
ances, and
then make
your cuff
pattern.

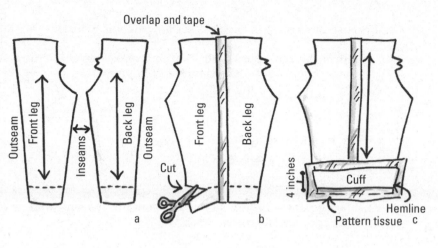

4. **To make the cuff pattern, use an extra piece of pattern tissue and place it on the leg pattern as shown in Figure 8-20c. Draw a rectangle with its top edge four inches above and parallel to the finished edge of the leg pattern, its bottom edge at the bottom of the leg pattern, and each of its sides parallel to and ¼-inch wider than the leg pattern.**

5. **Fold the coordinating cuff fabric in half the short way so the fold is at the bottom (see Figure 8-21).**

6. **Cut out two cuffs from the coordinating fabric, placing the bottom of the cuff on the fold as shown in Figure 8-21.**

Figure 8-21:
Cut out
two cuffs
from the
coordinat-
ing print for
very sassy
loungers.

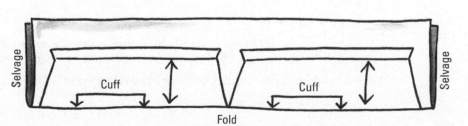

Sewing your pj's together

After just a few runs through the sewing machine, your pj's take shape.

1. **Finish the raw edges of the inseams, outseams, and crotch seams using one of the seam finishes found in Chapter 6.**

2. **Set your machine like this:**

    • Stitch: Straight

    • Length: 2.5 to 3 mm/10 to 12 spi

    • Width: 0 mm

    • Foot: All-purpose

3. **Starting at the bottom of one leg, sew a ⅝- inseam as shown in Figure 8-22 and press the seam open.**

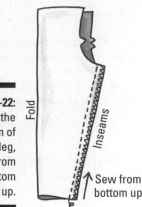

Figure 8-22:
Sew the inseam of each leg, sewing from the bottom up.

4. **Repeat Step 3 for the other leg.**

5. **Turn one leg right-side out and slip it inside the other (inside out) leg, matching the front and back notches as shown in Figure 8-23.**

6. **Pin and stitch the crotch seam as shown in Figure 8-23.**

7. **Set your machine as follows:**

    • Stitch: Three-step zigzag

    • Length: 1 to 1.5 mm/Fine setting

    • Width: 4 to 5 mm

    • Foot: All-purpose

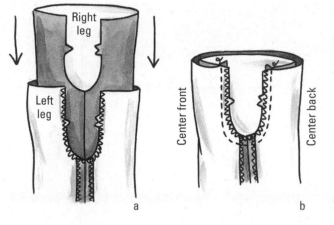

Figure 8-23:
Slip one leg inside the other then stitch the legs together at the crotch.

8. **So your pj's are comfortable in the crotch, trim the seam allowance to ¼-inch from notch to notch and overcast the raw edges together.**

9. **Press the center front and center back seams open.**

Sewing elastic at the waist

You're almost done! Just the elastic and cuffs to go and you'll be sipping tea and watching your favorite movie at home in your new lounge wear.

1. **Measure the waistline elastic and mark it at the length where it comfortably fits around your waist plus 1 inch for overlap.**

   You want to be able to pull these pj's up over your hips so be sure that the length of elastic is long enough with a little extra left over for seam allowance.

2. **Seam the elastic into a circle, overlapping the ends 1 inch and stitching the join in a square to secure it.**

3. **Pin-mark the elastic and the pj waistline into eighths as shown in Figure 8-24.**

4. **Starting at the center back, follow the instructions in "Attaching elastic on an edge" earlier in this chapter.**

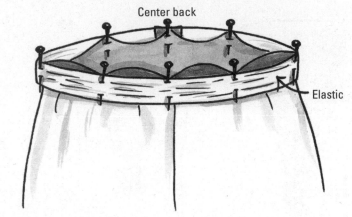

Center back

Elastic

Figure 8-24:
Mark the elastic and waistline into eights then pin them together.

Cuffing each leg

Adding the cuffs really sets these pj's apart from others, and it's so easy!

1. **Set your machine like this:**

   • Stitch: Straight

   • Length: 2.5 to 3 mm/10 to 12 spi

   • Width: 0 mm

   • Foot: All-purpose

2. **Fold the cuff into a circle and sew the right sides together (see Figure 8-25a).**

3. **At the center of the seam, where the fabric was folded when you cut it out, clip the seam allowance to within ⅛ inch of the stitching line (see Figure 8-25a), then press the seam open.**

4. **Turn the cuff right-side out and fold it in half so that it's half as wide (see Figure 8-25b); then pin and stitch it to the wrong side of the bottom of one pant leg.**

5. **Set your machine as follows:**

   • Stitch: Three-step zigzag or overlock stitch

   • Length: 1 to 1.5 mm (three-step zigzag) or longest (overlock)

   • Width: 4 to 5 mm

   • Foot: All-purpose

If you're using a serger, use these settings:

- Stitch: Three-thread overlock
- Length: 3 mm
- Width: 4 mm
- Foot: Standard

6. **Overcast the cuff seam, trimming it to ¼-inch seam as shown in Figure 8-25c.**

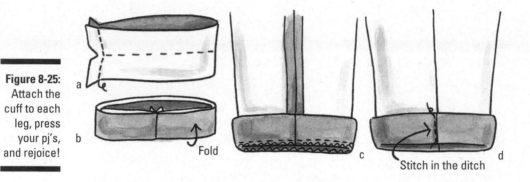

Figure 8-25: Attach the cuff to each leg, press your pj's, and rejoice!

a

b

Fold

c

d

Stitch in the ditch

7. **Turn the cuff up and to the right side of the pant leg. To keep the cuff in place, stitch in the ditch (see Figure 8-25d and Chapter 5 for tips on stitching in the ditch) and press.**

8. **Repeat for the other leg.**

Chapter 9

Zippers, Buttons, and Other Closure Company

In This Chapter

▶ Installing a zipper in minutes

▶ Exploring easy ways to make buttonholes and attach buttons

▶ Taking a look at other types of fasteners

▶ Making an easy fold-over clutch with a button or embellishment

I remember searching through catalogs for patterns without zippers or buttonholes early in my sewing career. After a while, though, I didn't have many choices, and I was bored by the styles that fit the bill. I realized I had to overcome my fear if I wanted to make anything with pizzazz. I took a deep breath and took on patterns with zippers and buttonholes, and in the process I picked up some cool shortcuts.

In this chapter I start with the wonderful world of zippers and tell you how to sew in two different types. Then I move on to all you need to know about making buttonholes and sewing on buttons. I touch on a few other types of fasteners that you may come across in your sewing adventures before closing with a fun (and fast!) project: a fold-over clutch.

Welcoming Easy Ways to Put in Zippers

Pattern guide sheet instructions often assume that you have some knowledge of sewing, and they've been recommending the same zipper application techniques for decades. In my search for an easier way, I ran across some great factory methods that I share with you in this section, along with information on using invisible zippers.

At first glance, these techniques may look complicated, but they overcome the typical roadblocks most folks have when sewing in zippers. So follow along with me step by step and you can have a really professional-looking project with a zipper you love to use.

You can use several methods to sew in zippers. The two most common methods are:

- **Centered application:** Center the zipper teeth at the seamline, such as down the center back of a dress.

- **Invisible application:** When sewn in a seam, this fabulous zipper invention looks just like the seam itself. Use invisible zippers at side seams, center back seams, and to close up a simple pillow cover.

Putting in a centered zipper

The following tips can save you a lot of frustration when sewing a centered zipper — take my word for it:

- **Use a longer zipper than necessary.** How much longer doesn't really matter — just go longer. This way, the *zipper pull* (the part you tug on to open and close the zipper) is out of the presser foot's way when you sew the top of the zipper. The result? Nice, even stitching at the top of the zipper. After you finish sewing on the waistband or facing, you simply cut the zipper tape to fit.

- **Use ½-inch tape — like Scotch Magic Mending Tape — and baste in the zipper across the back without using pins.** The tape holds everything flat and in place, and sewing through it doesn't damage the needle or the fabric.

- **Use ½-inch tape on the right side of the project as a topstitching guide when sewing in the zipper.** This way, the stitching lines are parallel, and the zipper application looks as good as in ready-made clothing. (Who cares whether the zipper looks good from the wrong side, anyway?)

Sewing in a centered zipper is as easy as following these steps:

1. **Before taking the paper pattern off the fabric, use the points of your scissors to clip into both layers of the seam allowance ¼ inch to mark the bottom of the zipper placement.**

2. **Remove the pattern paper from the fabric and then place and pin the seam, right sides together.**

Put two pins parallel and close together in the seamline at the zipper placement marks you clipped in Step 1 as reminders to stop sewing when you get to them.

3. **Starting from the bottom of the seamline and using a 2½ to 3 mm (10 to 12 spi) stitch length, sew the ⅝-inch seam.**

   Stop and securely backstitch at the bottom of the zipper placement clip and double pins.

4. **Remove the project from the sewing machine, cutting the threads off at the fabric.**

5. **Set your machine like this:**
   - Stitch: Straight
   - Length: 4 to 6 mm/4 spi
   - Width: 0 mm
   - Foot: All-purpose
   - Upper tension: Loosen slightly

6. **Starting at the backstitching, baste the remainder of the seam together at the ⅝-inch seamline, leaving generous thread tails (see Figure 9-1).**

7. **Remove the pins, press the seam flat and together, and then press the seam open (see Chapter 5 for the best way to press seams open).**

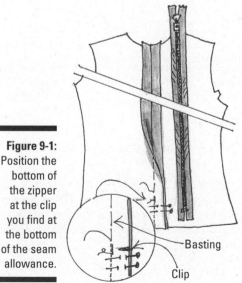

Figure 9-1:
Position the bottom of the zipper at the clip you find at the bottom of the seam allowance.

Basting

Clip

8. **Match the bottom of the zipper with the clips in the seam allowance, centering the zipper teeth over the seamline.**

9. **Using ½-inch tape, tape across the zipper every inch or so.**

   The zipper pull should be up on the zipper tape, out of the way (see Figure 9-2).

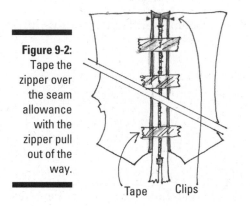

Figure 9-2:
Tape the zipper over the seam allowance with the zipper pull out of the way.

Tape   Clips

10. **On the right side of the fabric, place a strip of ½-inch tape over the basted seamline, centering the seamline under the tape.**

    This tape is your stitching guide or template.

11. **Set your machine like this:**

    - Stitch: Straight
    - Length: Appropriate for the fabric (see Chapter 5)
    - Width: 0 mm
    - Foot: Zipper
    - Upper tension: Return to normal

12. **Move your zipper foot so that the toe of the foot is to one side of the needle.**

    A zipper foot has one toe (rather than two toes like the all-purpose foot) so that you can move it from one side of the needle to the other for easy zipper application. Moving the toe in this step prevents the foot from riding over the zipper teeth (see your operating manual and Figure 9-3).

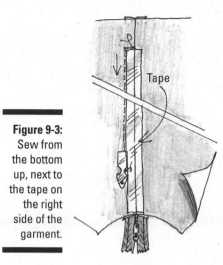

Figure 9-3:
Sew from the bottom up, next to the tape on the right side of the garment.

13. **Starting from the bottom of the zipper, stitch next to the tape, sewing across the bottom and then up one side of the zipper on the right side of the fabric (refer to Figure 9-3).**

   Don't backstitch; you pull the threads through to the wrong side and tie them off later.

14. **Move the toe of the foot to the other side of the needle. Starting at the bottom of the zipper again, sew in the other side of the zipper, guiding next to the tape template.**

   Sew next to the tape, starting back at the bottom and sewing up the other side of the zipper.

15. **Pull off the tape from both sides of the project and remove the basting stitches by pulling on the bobbin thread.**

   Because you loosened the upper thread tension, the stitches should pull out easily.

16. **Tug the zipper pull to the bottom of the zipper.**

17. **Place, pin, and stitch the facing or waistband, intersecting the seam at the ⅝-inch seamline, and securely backstitch over the zipper coil at the top of the zipper (see Figure 9-4).**

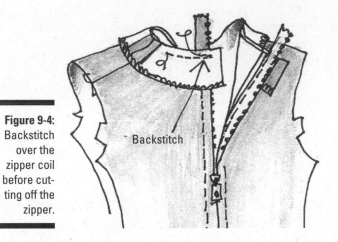

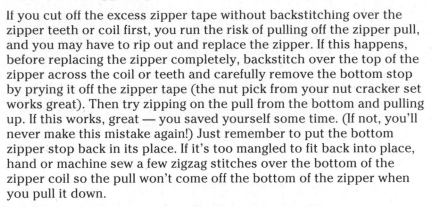

Figure 9-4:
Backstitch
over the
zipper coil
before cut-
ting off the
zipper.

Backstitch

Backstitching prevents the zipper pull from coming off the track so
that you can safely cut off the zipper tape. When you sew the rest of
the project together, the intersecting seam at the top of the zipper
tape that crosses over the teeth or coil prevents the pull from coming
off the track.

18. Cut off excess zipper tape.

If you cut off the excess zipper tape without backstitching over the
zipper teeth or coil first, you run the risk of pulling off the zipper pull,
and you may have to rip out and replace the zipper. If this happens,
before replacing the zipper completely, backstitch over the top of the
zipper across the coil or teeth and carefully remove the bottom stop
by prying it off the zipper tape (the nut pick from your nut cracker set
works great). Then try zipping on the pull from the bottom and pulling
up. If this works, great — you saved yourself some time. (If not, you'll
never make this mistake again!) Just remember to put the bottom
zipper stop back in its place. If it's too mangled to fit back into place,
hand or machine sew a few zigzag stitches over the bottom of the
zipper coil so the pull won't come off the bottom of the zipper when
you pull it down.

Putting in an invisible zipper

Invisible zippers are very easy to apply once you have one under your belt —
so to speak. The cool thing about the invisible zipper is that it looks like a
seam and only the small pull is visible from the right side of the project. You

do need a special invisible zipper foot, so make sure you purchase one for your machine at your local fabric store or sewing machine dealer. Unlike conventional zipper applications, you sew an invisible zipper in an open seam, before any of the seam has been sewn together, and you use a zipper that's the same length as the opening.

1. **Before taking the paper pattern off the fabric, use the points of your scissors to clip into both layers of the seam allowance ¼ inch to mark the bottom of the zipper placement. Remove the pattern paper.**

2. **Lay the invisible zipper wrong-side up on your ironing board, place the tip of your iron against the coil, and press the zipper tape smoothly on both sides of the coils.**

   This helps the coils stand away from the zipper tape and makes it easier for the foot to sew as close to the zipper coils as possible and so you get a very good-looking seam.

3. **Place and pin the open zipper to one side of the seam, right sides together and so the coil is along the seamline (where the seam will be sewn).**

   Match the bottom of the zipper with the clips in the seam allowance.

4. **Set your machine like this:**

   - Stitch: Straight

   - Length: Appropriate for the fabric (see Chapter 5)

   - Width: 0 mm

   - Foot: Invisible zipper

5. **Sliding the foot over to avoid sewing over the zipper coil, sew the first side of the zipper, starting from the top stop and sewing as close to the pull as you can, as shown in Figure 9-5.**

   To prevent the zipper tape from flopping around while you sew, gently grasp the seam allowance and zipper in front of and behind the presser foot. Remember to backstitch at the bottom of the zipper.

6. **Pin and sew the unstitched side of the zipper to the right side of the other seam allowance as shown in Figure 9-6.**

   Remember to slide the foot over to avoid sewing through the zipper coil and then sew from the top stop to the zipper pull as you did in Step 5.

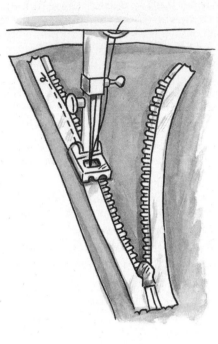

Figure 9-5:
Sew along
the left side
of the
zipper coils
from the
top to the
zipper pull.

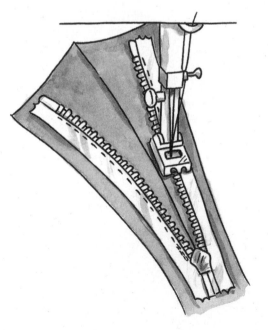

Figure 9-6:
Move the
foot over
to the right
and sew the
second side
of the zipper,
sewing
from the top
down to
the pull.

7. **Change the presser foot from the invisible zipper to the zipper foot that fits your machine, moving the one toe to the left of the needle.**

8. **Close the zipper and pin the seam allowance together.**

9. **Starting where you backstitched at the bottom of the zipper, sew the rest of the seam closed as shown in Figure 9-7.**

   Rather than backstitching, securely tie off thread ends where the seam and the bottom of the zipper come together.

10. **With the zipper open, stitch across the top end of each side of the zipper tape so the coil is in the "rolled back" position as shown in Figure 9-8.**

    This stitch keeps the zipper tape smooth and flat and the coil rolled back into its original position for easy sliding.

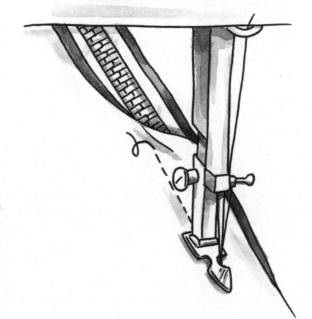

Figure 9-7:
Sew the rest of the seam using the conventional zipper foot.

Figure 9-8:
Stitch over
the ends
of the
zipper tape
so the coil is
in the
"rolled back"
position.

Mastering Buttonhole Basics

Buttons (and their corresponding buttonholes) close a garment, and they may have a decorative function as well. When shopping for buttons, decide whether you want a bold statement or a subtle one to guide your color choices. Keep in mind that contrasting buttons draw the eye vertically or horizontally, and tone-on-tone buttons usually don't draw the eye anywhere, which may be exactly what you want for a particular project.

Many folks think buttonholes are difficult to make, but modern sewing machines make them easier than ever. As long as you buy the correct sized buttons for the project (found on the back you're your pattern envelope), mark the buttonhole placement (shown on the pattern paper), and follow my directions for marking, making, and cutting open your buttonholes, you can't go wrong. It may sound like a lot of steps, but after you make a few button-holes you'll never avoid them again.

Sizing buttonholes

What comes first, the button or buttonhole? To make the buttonholes, you need to know the size of the buttons, so you have to have the buttons for your project before you can make the buttonholes.

Buy buttons the size that the back of the pattern envelope recommends. Following the pattern instruction ensures that the buttons are in the best proportion to the garment and give you the best fit and look.

Even two buttons that measure ½ inch may not fit through the same-sized buttonhole. The difference is in the shape: Thicker buttons need longer buttonholes than flatter ones. For example, a ½-inch, half-round, ball button needs a longer buttonhole than a ½-inch, flat, four-hole button. The fastest and easiest way to determine how long to make buttonholes is to do the following:

1. **Cut a strip of paper ¼-inch wide by about 5 to 8 inches long.**

   Cut a longer strip when working with larger buttons.

2. **Fold the paper strip in half and snug one edge of the button, at its widest diameter, against the fold in the paper strip.**

3. **Pin-mark the edge of the button on the other end of the paper strip.**

4. **Pull the button out of the paper strip, flatten the paper strip, and then measure the length from the fold to the pin as shown in Figure 9-9.**

   The buttonhole must be this length for the button to easily slip through it.

Figure 9-9:
Use a folded paper strip to determine the correct buttonhole size.

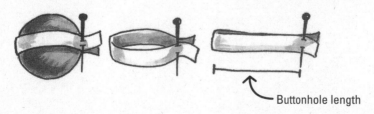

Buttonhole length

Marking buttonholes

Buttonholes have become easier to make because sewing machine companies are manufacturing sewing machines that have easy-to-sew built-in buttonhole functions. Some models even have several buttonhole styles to choose from based on the fabric you're working with. So the only tricky part about making buttonholes these days is measuring and marking them correctly.

For most projects, position buttonholes ½ inch from the finished edge. The exception is buttons larger than an inch — sew these buttonholes as directed by your pattern guide sheet. To prevent sewing a buttonhole too close to the edge, stick a strip of ½-inch-wide tape the length of the opening, placing one straight edge even with the finished edge as shown in Figure 9-10. This marks the starting and ending point of the buttonhole.

When making your first few buttonholes, you may want to place a second piece of tape perpendicular to the first. This keeps you on track so all your buttonholes are straight and parallel.

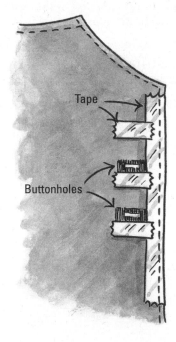

Tape

Buttonholes

Figure 9-10:
Use tape to mark your buttonhole placement.

Sewing beautiful buttonholes

You can probably make buttonholes by hand, but unless you have the practiced hand of a master tailor, your buttonholes just don't look right. The sewing machine companies have done a wonderful job of making buttonholes easier to create, and each brand and model has a special way of making them.

Buttonholes consist of two long sides made with short, narrow zigzag stitches called *satin stitches,* and with wider zigzag stitches, called *bartacks,* on the ends. Even basic sewing machines have some kind of an automatic buttonhole function (meaning that you make the buttonhole without turning the fabric), so read your operating manual to determine how the process works with your make and model.

On a scrap of your fabric, mark and stitch a test buttonhole or two, using your buttonhole foot and the same thread and interfacing that you use in the project. Make sure the scrap is large enough to make a couple of buttonholes, because you may not get the length right on the first pass. Then cut open the buttonhole and check to see that the button slides smoothly through the hole. This way, you know that the buttonhole is long enough to fit the button.

When making a buttonhole, don't backstitch at the beginning and end like you do when sewing a seam. Instead, pull all the threads to the wrong side of the fabric and tie them off (see Chapter 6 for more on tying off threads).

Cutting open buttonholes

Buttonholes are cut open after they're sewn. I open buttonholes two ways: By using the seam ripper or by using a buttonhole cutter and block. If you plan on making a lot of buttonholes, buy a cutter and block. This tool saves you time and cuts open buttonholes very accurately.

Prevent your buttonholes from coming undone before their time. Put a drop of seam sealant, such as FrayCheck, on the knot on the backside of the buttonhole by dotting it on the thread. Before cutting the buttonhole open, dribble a thin bead of sealant on the cutting space between the two sides of the buttonhole. Let it dry and then cut open the buttonholes.

Using a ripper

Carefully cut open your buttonholes with a ripper by following these steps:

1. **Score the cutting space between the two rows of stitching by running the backside of the ripper blade between the two rows of buttonhole stitches.**

   Doing so separates the threads, allowing you to more easily cut the buttonhole open without cutting the buttonhole stitches.

2. **Place a pin at the inside edge of one of the bartacks.**

   The pin acts like a brake and prevents you from cutting open the buttonhole past the bartack.

3. **Starting at the inside edge of the opposite bartack, push the point of the ripper down through the fabric, bringing the point up and through the cutting space in front of the pin, using the same motion you use when pinning.**

4. **With the point of the ripper up through the cutting space, push hard, cutting the fabric between the sides of the buttonhole as shown in Figure 9-11.**

When cutting open a buttonhole with a seam ripper, make sure it is sharp. A dull ripper can pull and snag the threads between the zigzag stitches, and if you're impatient, you may even cut too hard and ruin your project.

Figure 9-11: Cut open buttonholes carefully using a seam ripper.

Using a cutter and block

These little tools are really great. You can find them through your local sewing machine dealer or mail-order source.

Follow these steps to cut open your buttonholes using a cutter and block:

1. **Center the buttonhole over the little wood block.**

2. **Center the cutter blade over the cutting space in the buttonhole, as shown in Figure 9-12.**

3. **Push down firmly on the cutter, cutting through the fabric to the wood block. For heavier fabrics, use one hand to position the cutter and the other to press down firmly on the top for a clean cut.**

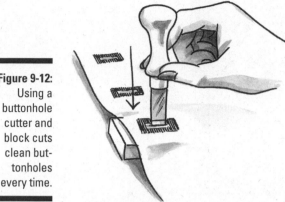

Figure 9-12:
Using a buttonhole cutter and block cuts clean buttonholes every time.

Figuring out button placement

TIP

You can mark the button placement before removing the paper pattern piece, but I like marking the button placement after I make and cut open the buttonholes because the mark is more accurate.

Follow these steps to mark the button placement:

1. **Hold the project so that the buttonholes and button opening are wrong sides together.**

   If the project has an overlapping front placket (like the front of a dress shirt), hold it as though the front placket is buttoned.

2. **Mark the end of the cutting space at the bartack.**

   From the button side of the opening, push a pin straight through the project so that it goes in at the buttonhole opening, right next to the bartack. Using a fabric marker, mark the button placement at the pin (see Figure 9-13).

   • For horizontal buttonholes, mark button placement just before the bartack (see Figure 9-13).

   • For vertical buttonholes, mark button placement so that all the buttons are placed at the top of the bartack or are centered between the top and bottom bartacks.

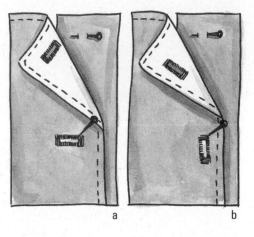

a   b

Figure 9-13:
Mark button
placement
for horizon-
tal (a) and
vertical (b)
buttonholes
using a pin.

3. **Before sewing on the button by hand or machine (which I cover in the next section), double-check that the button is three-fourths to a full button-diameter's distance from the finished edge and then adjust the placement as needed.**

Attaching buttons

For many people, sewing on a button is an introduction into the world of sewing. It's a great way to get started because it shows you the importance of technique when doing anything with a needle and thread — even something small.

You can avoid a mishap by correctly sewing on a button, which you can do either by hand or using the sewing machine. If I replace or move one button, I sew it on by hand. If I make something that requires sewing on several buttons at once (the front of a shirt or along the top of the button strip used on a duvet cover you see in Chapter 16), I use my machine.

By hand

Follow these steps to sew on a button of any size by hand:

1. **Using a fabric marker or dressmaker's chalk, mark the spot on the project where you want the button to go.**

2. **Pull off a strand of thread 18 to 24 inches long.**

   A thread that's longer than 24 inches may tangle and break before you finish sewing on the button.

3. **Thread the needle (as described in Chapter 5), pulling one end of the thread to meet the other so that you have a double thread.**

4. **Knot the ends of the thread as described in Chapter 5.**

5. **From the top right side of the project, stab the needle all the way through the fabric so that the knot ends up on the mark.**

6. **Bring the needle back up and all the way through the fabric, a short stitch (not more than ⅛ inch) away from the knot.**

7. **Thread the needle through the button's left hole, pushing the button firmly against the surface of the fabric, and then pull the thread up as shown in Figure 9-14a.**

8. **Create a *spacer* by placing a toothpick, matchstick, or hand-tapestry needle on top of the button between the holes.**

    This technique gives you enough thread to raise the button off the fabric's surface so that you have room to button the buttonhole. The extra room the spacer creates is called a *thread shank*.

    If you're sewing on a button with a shank (a little loop on the underside of a blazer button, for example), the shank of the button acts as an automatic spacer, raising the button off the surface of the garment for easy buttoning, so you don't need the toothpick.

9. **Push the needle down through the hole on the right (the one directly opposite the hole you started with — see Figure 9-14b). Pull the thread tight.**

    Repeat this process, stitching up through the left hole and down through the right hole one more time for each set of holes so that you secure the button with two passes of the needle.

Figure 9-14:
Thread the
button on
the needle
(a), use
a spacer
to make
a thread
shank (b),
and create
a thread
shank (c).

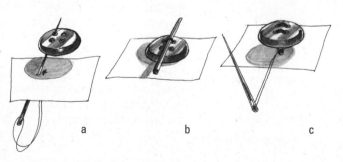

a   b   c

10. **After you stitch the button on, remove the spacer.**

11. **Poke the needle through a hole in the button (it doesn't matter which one) so that the needle comes out between the button and the fabric.**

    Take a look at what's going on between the button and the fabric: Those connecting threads running out the back of the button into the fabric make the base of the thread shank.

12. **Wrap the thread around these connecting threads three times or so to secure the thread shank, as shown in Figure 9-14c.**

13. **Tie a knot by pushing the needle through a thread loop as it goes around the shank and pulling the thread tight.**

14. **Repeat Step 13 to make another knot and clip the thread close to the shank.**

By machine

If you have several buttons to sew on at one time, consider using your machine to help you with the job. To use this technique, you need a glue stick, a button-sewing foot for your machine, or a presser foot shank with a removable presser foot sole (check your operating manual to see if your model has this feature).

Sport snaps (the button alternative)

Sport snaps, which hold up to a good deal of wear and tear, were available only to clothing manufacturers — until now. Several companies make and sell commercial-grade sport snaps. These snaps are quite tailored and often make a wonderful alternative to buttons and buttonholes.

Snaps have two sides — a ball and a socket. Instead of sewing them onto a project as you do with traditional snaps, you attach sport snaps to the fabric in two ways:

✔ By poking a hole for post-style snaps

✔ By pushing prongs through the fabric for prong-style snaps

Sport snaps range from about ¼ inch (size 12) to about ¾ inch (size 27). When shopping for snaps, consider the project and where you plan to place the snaps before buying the first thing you see. For instance, you probably don't want a big and bulky size 27 snap at the crotch of a pair of toddler's overalls.

Don't mix snap parts from different brands. Manufacturers make snap parts to function in harmony and don't guarantee their product if you use a wrong part or tool.

Each brand of sport snap has its own method of application, so make sure that you have the proper snap-setter tool(s) for the brand. For successful application, read the instructions thoroughly before putting them on your project. As with buttonholes, apply a test snap, using the same fabric, number of layers, and interfacing before putting sport snaps on your finished project.

Just follow these steps:

1. **Using a fabric marker or dressmaker's chalk, mark the spot on the project where you want the button to go.**

2. **Dab the back of the button with a glue stick and place the button over your mark.**

3. **Set your machine like this:**

   - Stitch: Zigzag

   - Length: 0 mm/0 spi

   - Width: 4 mm

   - Foot: Button-sewing, all-purpose, or foot shank without the sole

   - Feed dogs: Down

   - Needle position: Left (see Chapter 2)

4. **With the presser foot up, turn the flywheel by hand, stabbing the needle through the left hole in the button; lower the presser foot or the foot shank.**

   For a four-hole button, start with the holes farthest away from you.

5. **Slide a toothpick, matchstick, or tapestry needle over the button, between the holes and perpendicular to the foot or the foot shank.**

   Adding this spacer raises the button off the fabric's surface so that the buttonhole doesn't gap and lies smoothly under the button.

   Sometimes, the foot has a helpful little groove that holds the spacer in place.

6. **Check that the needle clears each of the holes in the button by taking a couple of zigzag stitches, moving the flywheel by hand, as shown in Figure 9-15.**

   Adjust the stitch width, if necessary.

7. **Slowly step on the foot control and stitch, counting five stitches — zig left, zag right, zig left, zag right, zig left.**

   For a four-hole button, lift the foot and move the project so that the needle is over the front two holes, and then sew five more zigzags to secure the front of the button.

8. **Move the stitch width to 0 (zero), place the needle over one of the holes, and step on the foot control again, taking 4 to 5 stitches in the same hole.**

   This step helps to secure and knot the stitches.

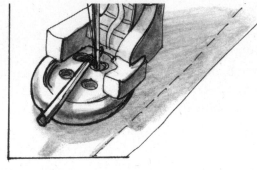

Figure 9-15:
Make sure
that the
needle
clears the
buttonholes.

9. **Lift the foot and remove the project, reeling off a 7 to 8-inch tail of thread.**

10. **Remove the spacer and save it for reuse.**

11. **Proceed to the rest of the buttons, repeating Steps 1 through 10 until you've sewn on all the buttons.**

12. **Pull the needle and bobbin threads between the button and the fabric so that you're ready to create a thread shank, as follows:**

    1. Thread a large-eye tapestry needle with the long thread tail from the needle and, between the button and the fabric, pull the tail through any hole in the button.

    2. Thread a large-eye tapestry needle with the long thread tail from the bobbin and pull the tail through the fabric between the button and the fabric.

    3. Thread both tails through the needle's eye and wrap the thread tails around the connecting threads three times, creating a thread shank to secure the button.

13. **Push the needle through a thread loop as it goes around the shank, pulling the thread tight.**

    This action ties a knot.

14. **Repeat Step 13 and then clip the thread close to the connecting threads.**

Three ways to sew on a button

I collect buttons and as a result have a lot of one or two of a kind. So before shopping for buttons, I look through my collection to see if I can create something unique for my project from it. My favorite types of buttons are those with two or four holes. This way I can stack them together and sew them on using floss, pearl cotton, silk ribbon, or yarn.

Four-hole buttons can also be sewn on by hand or machine in the traditional "x" or "bartack" style, but they can also be sewn on in an "arrow" or "z." Check out Figure 9-16 for some interesting ways to sew on buttons.

Figure 9-16:
Three ways to sew on a button.

Checking Out Other Fasteners

Without the fasteners described in this section (and shown in Figure 9-17), you couldn't keep your pants up or your shirt closed! In this section, I give you a brief introduction to these closers. You find the specific use and application of many of the fasteners I list here in the projects throughout the book.

The following fasteners all come in a variety of sizes, shapes, and colors. The back of your pattern envelope tells you which (if any) of these fasteners you need and exactly which type and size of fastener to use.

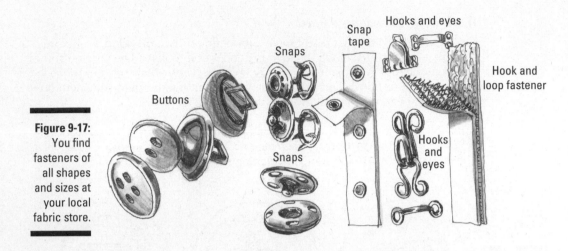

Figure 9-17: You find fasteners of all shapes and sizes at your local fabric store.

Without further ado, I give you some fabulous fasteners:

- **Snaps:** You use sew-on snaps to close necklines on dresses, blouses, and baby clothes, among other uses. You use the *gripper-type* sport snaps on active sportswear and outerwear. (See the sidebar "Sport snaps (the buttonhole alternative)" for more on these.)

- **Snap tape:** Snap tape is a soft twill tape with a row of snaps running the length of it. Snap tape is as fast to undo as hook and loop fastener and much more flexible. You use snap tape on baby clothes and home décor projects.

- **Hooks and eyes:** You use hooks and eyes at the top of a zipper to keep the neckline closed and in shape. You can also use a specially designed hook and eye at the waistband of skirts and pants.

- **Hook and loop fastener:** Better known by the trade name Velcro, hook and loop fastener comes in many weights, colors, and widths. Some types of this fastener are sew-on, some are fusible; others even have a peel-and-stick backing.

Fold-Over Clutch with Button Closure

Every now and then you need a fashion accessory to pull an outfit together, and one of the fastest and easiest ways to do this is by making a fold-over clutch. Make yours from a winter-type fabric such as fleece-backed suede you see in the color section, or from a ready-made place mat. All it takes is a shopping adventure to your local Pier 1, Target, or Bed, Bath and Beyond. I got carried away on one trip and bought three mats and coordinating napkin rings for under $20. So each clutch ran me a little over $6 each — and that's only because the napkin rings were as expensive as the mats! All you need is 15 minutes to make each one. It's as easy as sew . . . sew . . . and go!

Choosing the materials

If you choose to make your clutch from a ready-made place mat, here are the features to look for when shopping:

- ✔ Look for a mat made with the same materials as a ready-made clutch such as straw or heavier quilted fabric.

- ✔ Find a mat that looks nice on both sides. This way you can use either side as the outside and have a fully lined clutch.

- ✔ Some mats have extra adornment. This beading, braid, embroidery, or appliqué can be a real plus so you don't need to add a button or other adornment.

- ✔ For a fastener or embellishment, use an interesting button or look for a coordinating napkin ring that you can take apart and attach to your clutch.

If you make your clutch from something other than a place mat, find a fabric that's good-looking on both the right and wrong sides. I chose to use fleece-backed suede because it doesn't ravel or require extra seam finishing (and because I had it leftover from making the computer slipcover project in Chapter 17). Here's what you need to make your clutch:

- ✔ Sewing survival kit (see Chapter 2)

- ✔ Thread to match or coordinate with your fabric

- ✔ One place mat or thick double-sided fabric cut approximately 12 inches wide by 18 inches tall.

- ✔ Large (2-inch) button or napkin ring embellishment

- ✔ Heavy button-sewing thread, floss, or yarn

- ✔ Wire cutters if needed for removing adornment from the napkin ring

Sewing the clutch

Just a couple of quick seams and your clutch is done. Here's how:

1. **Place the mat or fabric on a table top with the wrong side up and the shorter ends at the top and bottom.**

2. **Fold the bottom up 6 inches and pin the sides of the clutch.**

3. **Fold over the top flap and mark where you want the buttonhole or adornment to be placed.**

   Choose a spot that's horizontally centered, parallel to the bottom edge of the flap, and at least 1 inch away from the finished edge, as shown in Figure 9-18.

   If your place mat or fabric is very stiff and you don't need a closure to keep your stuff from falling out, you may still want to add an embellishment. If you plan to carry the clutch under your arm, position the embellishment on one end or the other so it doesn't rub against your arm.

Figure 9-18:
Fold up the bottom of the clutch, then fold over the top to see where you want to place the button closure.

Selvage

4. **Determine and mark the buttonhole length using the steps from "Mastering Buttonhole Basics" earlier in this chapter.**

   If the adornment is too bulky to fit through a buttonhole, you simply hand sew it to the top edge of the clutch, so skip ahead to Step 7.

5. **Set your machine this way:**

   - Stitch: Straight

   - Length: 3 to 4 mm/6 to 9 spi

   - Width: 0 mm

   - Foot: All-purpose or embroidery

6. **Sew a narrow rectangle as shown in Figure 9-19a.**

   The fleece-backed microfiber used in this project (shown in the color section) doesn't ravel, so rather than sewing a traditional buttonhole, you make a small rectangle as the opening. If you choose to make your clutch out of a placemat and want to use a button closure, make the buttonhole the traditional way (see "Mastering Buttonhole Basics").

7. **Open the buttonhole rectangle using one of the buttonhole cutting techniques described earlier in the chapter.**

8. **Sew on the button or adornment using one of the methods described in "Sewing on buttons."**

   For my suede clutch, I cut a ⅛- x- 8-inch strip of the suede, stacked two buttons together, and sewed the buttons on using this suede strip through a large-eyed tapestry needle. Notice that rather than knotting the suede strip on the back of the project, I used the knot as a design detail (see Figure 9-19b and c).

   For the place mat clutch, I used a hand whip stitch (see Chapter 5) and a heavy doubled thread; then hand sewed the napkin ring adornment to the top flap of the clutch.

Figure 9-19:
Make a long narrow rectangle large enough for the button(s) to fit through (a), and then sew on the button using a decorative cord or thread (b and c).

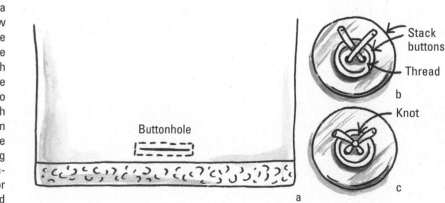

9. **Sew up both sides of the clutch, backstitching at the top and bottom of each side as shown in Figure 9-20.**

Figure 9-20:
Stitch up
the sides of
your clutch.

Chapter 10

Sleeves: The Long and the Short of It

In This Chapter

▶ Figuring out armhole facings

▶ Wrangling with raglan sleeves

▶ Discovering the secrets to set-in sleeves

▶ Making a sleeve cover for a laptop computer

Sleeves are easy to put in when you know how. In this chapter I show you the easiest methods for dealing with them, first by not putting in a sleeve at all but by facing a sleeveless armhole. Facing the armhole gives you practice staystitching, seaming, trimming, notching, pressing, and under-stitching — all skills you use elsewhere in garment construction. (If these terms are new to you, read Chapters 5 and 6.)

Next I tackle sleeves, starting with the raglan sleeve. Raglan is not the best style for perfectly fitting sloping shoulders, but you can appreciate how easy it is to sew and how good it looks when you use the right shoulder pad underneath. I save set-in sleeves for last, showing you a factory technique for setting in sleeves. After a little practice, you get perfect results every time.

Finally in this chapter, you make a computer sleeve. While it's not a sleeve in the conventional garment sense, it lets you practice some of the skills in this chapter, and you'll love how it fits and protects your laptop.

Finishing Sleeveless Armholes

Have you ever cut off the sleeves of a T-shirt or sweatshirt to make it sleeveless? Cutting off the sleeves does give you extra room and ventilation, but after a while the armhole stretches out, never to be the same size again. Because your only sacrifice is a T-shirt or a sweatshirt, it's no big deal. But for your other clothes, you want to finish the armholes with either a facing or binding that keeps those armholes in shape and looking good for the life of the garment.

Facing sleeveless armholes

This section focuses on the most common method of finishing off an armhole by facing it for a clean, smooth finish. By the way, if you want to make that sleeveless T-shirt or sweatshirt last longer, you can use the following technique to give your old favorites staying power.

A *facing* is a piece of fabric that you reinforce with an extra piece of interfacing. Interfacing is lighter weight and may be woven or knitted and fusible or not. Its job is to stabilize and reinforce so an opening won't stretch out of shape (see Chapter 3 for more on interfacings and how to use them). You attach an interfacing to a facing; then stitch the facing to the opening and turn it back toward the inside of the project to finish off the opening. You can attach facings not only to armholes but also to other areas such as necklines and some hem edges.

Follow these easy steps for the best-finished armholes in town:

1. **Cut out and interface the armhole facing using fusible interfacing as shown on your pattern guide sheet instructions and in Figure 10-1.**

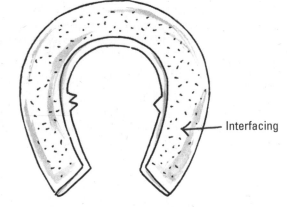

Figure 10-1: Interfacing added to the wrong side of the armhole facing provides stability.

Interfacing

2. **Staystitch the facing and the armhole as described in your pattern guide sheet (for more on staystitching, see Chapter 6).**

3. **After placing the right sides together and matching the notches, pin and sew the facing together as shown in Figure 10-2, backstitching at the top and bottom of the seam.**

4. **Overcast the outside edges of your facing using one of the seam finishes described in Chapter 6.**

5. **Place the facing in the armhole, right sides together and matching the notches.**

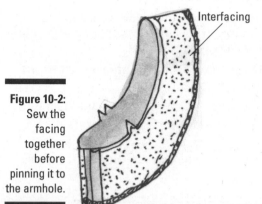

Interfacing

Figure 10-2:
Sew the
facing
together
before
pinning it to
the armhole.

REMEMBER

Double notches are at the back of the armhole; single notches are at the front of the armhole. The seam allowances have different curves, so if you mistakenly place the left facing into the right armhole, the pieces don't match.

6. **Starting at the underarm seam, sew the facing on the armhole at the ⅝-inch seamline.**

7. **Clip the seam allowance at the inside curves to the staystitching within ⅛-inch of the seamline, as shown in Figure 10-3.**

   Use your scissor tips to clip almost to the stitching line at the front and back of the armhole (see your pattern guide sheet and Chapter 6 for info on clipping seams). Armholes and armhole facings are inside curves, so clipping releases the seam allowance so that it doesn't bunch up when you turn and press the facing to the inside of the garment.

Clip

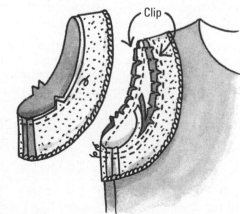

Figure 10-3:
Clip into
the seam
allowance
around the
armhole and
facing.

8. **Trim the facing seam allowance to ½ inch.**

   Trimming one seam allowance narrower than another is called *grading the seam*. The facing falls automatically toward the narrower seam allowance, making it easier to turn and press the facing.

9. **From the wrong side of the fabric, press the seam allowance toward the facing.**

10. **Understitch the facing seam, sewing ¹⁄₁₆ inch away from the seamline on the facing side of the seam allowance, as shown in Figure 10-4.**

    Understitching helps the facing turn toward the inside of the garment and stay there. (See Chapter 6 for more information on understitching.)

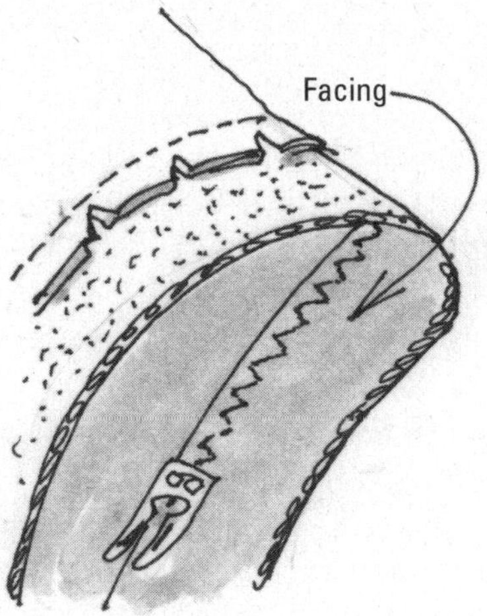

Facing

Figure 10-4: Understitch the facing seam.

11. **Press the facing toward the inside of the garment and tack down the facing by stitching in the ditch (see Figure 10-5 for an illustration and check out Chapter 5 for more stitching in the ditch info).**

    Sewing from the right side of the garment, center the crack of the seam under the needle. Sew, guiding the stitches so that they bury themselves in the crack of the seam. Don't backstitch; simply pull the threads to the facing side and tie them off (see Chapter 6 for the best way to tie off threads).

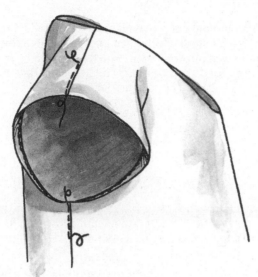

Figure 10-5:
Secure the armhole facing by stitching in the ditch.

Binding sleeveless armholes

You can use binding as a particularly clean way to finish an edge on an armhole, neckline, or other hem edge. You sew a doubled band of fabric to the wrong side of the garment, bring the folded edge of the binding over the seam allowance toward the right side of the garment, and edgestitch it in place. This commercial binding method ensures a sensational ready-to-wear look on any bound edge.

This technique works best on light- to mid-weight fabrics.

Choosing the binding fabric

The best type of binding to use is a bias-cut woven fabric, preferably the same fabric as the project or slightly lighter in weight.

Which type of fabric should you choose? Look at the fabric you're working with and match the trim with the fabric by color, fiber content (see Chapter 2 for more on fibers), and *hand* (how well it drapes after you put it on the edge of the project). Also read the back of the pattern envelope to see what the pattern company recommends. Bias-cut woven fabric stretches a little bit, so it shapes smoothly to a curved edge such as an armhole or neckline. (Check out Chapter 4 to find out more about bias and grainlines.)

Cutting the binding

When cutting your own binding, cut woven fabric on the bias. Cut the fabric into a strip four times the finished width, plus another ½ inch for the seam allowances (two ¼-inch seam allowances = ½ inch). So for a ½-inch finished binding width, you start with a strip that's 2½ inches wide. I always cut the binding a little longer than I need so I don't run out.

Sewing the binding

Follow these steps to construct the binding that goes around the edge of the armhole:

1. **Trim the garment armhole seam allowance to ¼ inch.**

   When working with a woven fabric, use pinking shears for trimming because pinkers automatically notch the seam allowance for you, making the seam allowance easier to work with (see Chapter 6 for more information on notching seams).

2. **Staystitch around the trimmed armhole under the arm from notch to notch. (Chapter 6 tells you more about staystitching.)**

3. **Fold and press the binding in half the long way so that the *wrong* sides of the fabric are together.**

4. **Open the binding strip, fold down one short end ½ inch, and press.**

   This end overlaps the binding at the other end, giving the opening a clean, finished look.

5. **Fold and press the binding strip in half the long way again, as done in Step 3.**

6. **Starting slightly to the backside of the underarm seam (and with the folded end first), pin the binding to the *wrong side* of the garment so that all the raw edges are even.**

7. **When you get back to where you started pinning on the binding, overlap the free end over the folded end of the binding by about ½ inch, and cut off the excess from the free end of the binding strip.**

8. **Tuck the cut end into the folded end of the binding to create a clean finish.**

9. **Set your machine like this:**
   - Stitch: Straight
   - Length: 2.5 to 3.5mm/10 to 12 spi
   - Width: 0 mm
   - Foot: All-purpose

10. **Sew the binding to the armhole using a 1/4-inch seam allowance, backstitching at the end of the seam.**

11. **With the wrong side of the garment up, press the seam allowance toward the binding side.**

12. **Fold, pin, and press the band in shape around the armhole opening.**

    Fold the edge of the band over the opening, toward the right side of the project, so that the edge of the band covers the seam allowance and the previous stitching line.

13. **Edgestitch the band to the opening, guiding ⅛ inch from the folded edge of the band. (See Chapter 6 for more on edgestitching.)**

Rarin' to Sew Raglan Sleeves

You find raglan sleeves on garment tops from sweatshirts to cashmere sweater sets. What makes them different from traditional set-in sleeves? The seams on the front run from the neck edge diagonally across to the underarm and up the back to the neckline, making them a lot easier to sew than set-in sleeves. Check out the shirt with finished raglan sleeves in Figure 10-6.

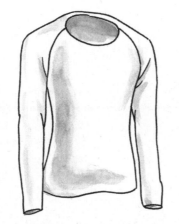

Figure 10-6:
The raglan sleeve is easy to sew and very comfy.

Because the raglan sleeve covers the shoulder, either a seam or dart shapes the top of the sleeve so that it fits smoothly at the shoulder line. The pattern piece for a raglan sleeve in Figure 10-7 shows a dart sewn at the top, the most common way of shaping it to your shoulder.

Neck edge ⟍   ⟋ Shoulder dart

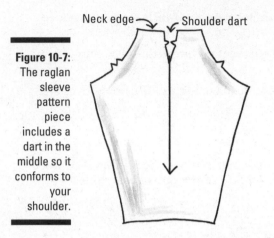

Figure 10-7:
The raglan
sleeve
pattern
piece
includes a
dart in the
middle so it
conforms to
your
shoulder.

Just follow these steps to sew in a raglan sleeve:

1. **Sew the shoulder dart and press it open so it looks like Figure 10-8.**

   Placing the right sides together, pin the shoulder dart as shown in your pattern guide sheet. Sew the dart, starting from the wide end and stitching to the point (see Chapter 8 for more information on sewing darts).

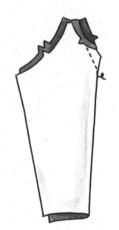

Figure 10-8:
Sew the
dart and
press it
open for a
smooth fit.

2. **Pin the sleeve to the garment by matching the notches and pinning right sides together.**

When pinning the raglan sleeves to the front and back pattern pieces, the project can get very large and unwieldy. Make it easier on yourself and pin it together on a large table top.

3. **Sew the sleeve to the garment at the recommended seam allowance, as shown in Figure 10-9.**

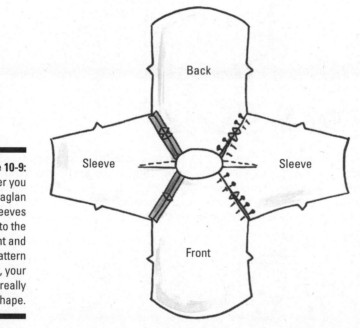

Figure 10-9:
After you sew raglan sleeves onto the front and back pattern pieces, your top really takes shape.

4. **Starting at the bottom, sew the garment side seams, right sides together, at the recommended seam allowance. Backstitch on both ends of the seam as shown in Figure 10-10.**

By sewing the sideseams after putting in the sleeve, the underarm seam won't bunch up and cut off the circulation under your arm.

5. **Press the front and back shoulder seams open, from the notches up to the neckline.**

See Chapter 5 for tips and tricks for perfect pressing.

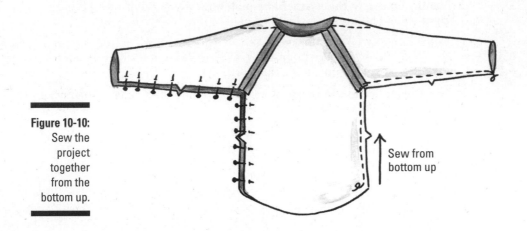

Figure 10-10:
Sew the
project
together
from the
bottom up.

Sew from
bottom up

Taking On Set-In Sleeves

Set-in sleeves have a seam that goes all the way around your arm where your
arm connects to your torso. Instead of going diagonally across your body
from the neckline, as with raglan sleeves, a set-in sleeve starts at the underarm (or armpit), travels up, runs over your shoulder, and then goes straight
back down again to the underarm. Figure 10-11 shows a typical set-in sleeve.

Figure 10-11:
The seam of
a set-in
sleeve
circles
around the
top of
your arm.

Here's the big news: Set-in sleeves are bigger than the armholes they go into
so you can comfortably move your arms around. This extra fabric in the
sleeves causes a lot of sewers major sleeve-setting difficulties. So how do you
get the sleeve in there — shrink it? Yes and no. In this section I share some

tricks with you to help make set-in sleeves less mysterious. The following easestitch-plus is one of my favorite tried-and-true methods of getting a set-in sleeve ready for the armhole.

Using easestitch-plus to prepare traditional set-in sleeves

Traditional set-in sleeves are the most challenging because you have to make the circumference of the sleeve smaller to fit into the armhole opening *without* gathering the sleeve to fit. You can accomplish this feat by a type of *easestitching.* In this section, I show you a more extreme version called *easestitch-plus,* in which you manipulate the fabric to get it to shrink enough so that the sleeve fits the armhole.

Easestitching-plus varies from gathering because instead of seeing a visible line of gathering, you see a line of stitching that slightly cinches in the sleeve cap — looking like a little pucker — without the pinched-in look of gathers. This way when the sleeve is set in the armhole it stands slightly away from the sleeve seam, providing the necessary room for your arm to move comfortably in the garment. Here's how to use the easiest technique to get your sleeves ready to set into the armholes:

1. **Using a fabric marker, transfer the dots on the armhole and sleeve seamlines from the paper pattern pieces to the fabric. Also mark the top of the sleeve cap.**

   These dots are additional match points. If you don't find a dot at the top of the sleeve cap pattern, just mark one there or make a tiny clip into the seam allowance. This way, when you put in the sleeve, the mark at the top of the sleeve cap matches up with the shoulder seam.

2. **Set your machine like this:**

   - Stitch: Straight
   - Length: 2.5 mm/12 spi for fine fabrics; 3.5 mm/10 spi for mid-weight to heavy fabrics
   - Width: 0 mm
   - Foot: All-purpose
   - Upper tension: Tighten slightly
   - Needle position (optional): Far right

3. **Position the sleeve under the needle so that the wrong side faces up and the needle starts at one of the notches on the sleeve.**

   You do easestitching-plus inside the seam allowance, so guide the sleeve so that you sew ½ inch from the raw edge.

4. **Lower the presser foot, and as you begin sewing, hold your index finger firmly behind the foot so that the fabric bunches and piles up behind it, as shown in Figure 10-12.**

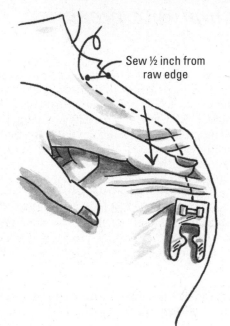

Sew ½ inch from raw edge

Figure 10-12:
Hold your finger firmly behind the presser foot so the fabric bunches up.

5. **When the fabric piles up to the point you can't hold it any longer, release the fabric, and then repeat the process until you easestitch-plus the sleeve cap from notch to notch.**

This technique eases in the fabric automatically without stitching in unwanted tucks or gathers. Your sleeve will look like Figure 10-13.

Now that your sleeve is ready to sew into the armhole, you have a choice of whether you want to sew the sleeve in flat or sew it in the round. There are advantages and disadvantages to both.

✓ It is easier to sew a set-in sleeve flat.

✓ The project generally fits better and is easier to alter when the sleeve is set in the round.

See the following sections for the best way to do both.

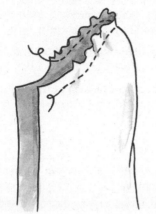

Figure 10-13:
Your set-in sleeve cap is eased in so it fits into the smaller armhole opening.

Setting sleeves in flat

Setting sleeves in flat means that the side seams of the shirt or bodice are open (not sewn yet) and the sleeves are not sewn into a tube. Even if the pattern says to sew the underarm sleeve seam first, try this simple flat method. By sewing with the sleeve against the feed dogs of your sewing machine (rather than the other way around), the excess sleeve fabric works itself into the armhole seam almost automatically. Follow these steps to relieve your sleeve-sewing worries:

1. **Sew and press the shoulder seam of the shirt as the pattern instructs you and then open the shirt flat so that the right side of the fabric is up.**

2. **Pin the sleeve to the shirt, right sides together, matching the front and back notches and centering the sleeve cap at the shoulder seam.**

   You may want to use a lot of pins until you have sewn a few sleeves.

   Double notches are at the back of the armhole and sleeve; single notches are at the front of the armhole and sleeve. The seam allowances have different curves, so if you get the left sleeve into the right armhole, the pieces don't match, and the garment really feels funny when you wear it (ask me how I know this).

3. **Sewing with the sleeve side down against the feed dogs, stitch the sleeve into the shirt at the ⅝-inch seamline.**

   The feed dogs, which are directly under the presser foot, feed the under-layer of fabric a little faster than the top layer of fabric. So by sewing with the sleeve side down, the feed dogs ease in just enough fullness so the sleeve fits perfectly into the armhole.

4. **Trim the seam allowance to ⅜ inch under the arm from notch to the underarm seam only. Repeat for the second sleeve.**

5. **Overcast the edges of both trimmed seam allowances together by using the three-step zigzag on your sewing machine or serging them together (see Chapter 6 for the details of overcasting).**

   Overcasting this narrow seam allowance together gives the underarm more strength and overall comfort.

6. **Pin and sew the garment side seam and underarm at the ¼-inch or ⅝-inch seamline, sewing the entire side seam and underarm sleeve seam in one step.**

   Start sewing the seam from the project's hem edge and up through the underarm seam, as shown in Figure 10-14. At the intersection of the two seams under the arm, for light to mid-weight fabrics, pin the seam allowance toward the sleeve; for heavier fabrics, pin the intersecting seam open.

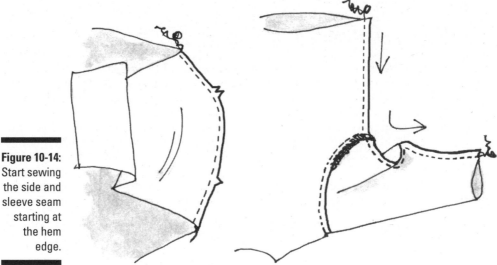

Figure 10-14:
Start sewing the side and sleeve seam starting at the hem edge.

Setting sleeves in the round

Setting sleeves in the round means that you sew together the side seams of the shirt or bodice, stitch the sleeves into tubes at the underarm seam, and then attach the sleeves to the garment.

The information in this section may look more involved than what you see in the pattern guide sheet instructions, but by providing you with these easy steps, I assure you success:

1. **Cut, mark, and easestitch-plus your sleeves as described in the earlier section "Using easestitch-plus to prepare traditional set-in sleeves."**

2. **Place, pin, and sew the garment, right sides together, at the side seams.**

3. **Place, pin, and sew the sleeve, right sides together, following your pattern guide sheet instructions.**

4. **Press the side seams and sleeve seams open or to one side (see Chapter 5 for more on pressing seams).**

5. **Pin the sleeve into the armhole, right sides together, pinning at the notches, dots, and underarm seams as shown in Figure 10-15.**

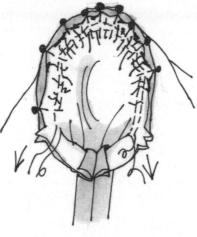

Figure 10-15:
Pin the sleeve into the armhole, matching dots and front and back notches.

Make sure you match notches on the correct side of the garment: double notches at the back of the armhole and sleeve; single notches at the front of the armhole and sleeve. The garment won't look or feel right if you sew in the sleeves backwards.

6. **Stitch the sleeve to the armhole at the ⅝-inch seamline, all the way around.**

   If your sewing machine has a free-arm, slip the sleeve over it, garment side up, and sew. Be sure that the stitches at the beginning and end of the seam cross one another to prevent the underarm seam from coming unstitched.

7. **Starting at the notches, clip into the seam allowance, clipping to within ⅛ inch of the seamline at the inside curves under the arm.**

8. **Trim the seam allowance to ⅜ inch from notch to notch, cutting away the excess seam allowance from both the garment and the sleeve at the underarm seam *only*.**

This way, the sleeve fits comfortably and you don't cut off the circulation under your arms.

9. **Overcast the trimmed underarm seams together from notch to notch. Tie off threads at either end of the overcast edges.**

Overcast the raw edges together by using a three-step zigzag stitch with your sewing machine or three-thread overlock with your serger (see Chapter 6 for more on overcasting).

10. **Press the sleeve seam flat and together all the way around, pressing from the seamline out to the raw edge, and then press the seam open. Gently press the seam back together.**

This pressing process gives the sleeve the proper shape.

If you have a pressing ham, press the armhole seam over the curves of the ham. This handy tool helps to comfortably shape the sleeve into the armhole.

Protective Laptop Sleeve

Our son has a new laptop and wanted to keep it looking new, so I made him a computer sleeve that slips inside his backpack. While I realize this project doesn't have a lot to do with the sleeves used on clothing, I include it in this chapter because it's still a sleeve of sorts. If you start with the right fabric, this little sleeve project can be made in under an hour. Here's what you need:

- Your sewing survival kit (see Chapter 2)
- Thread to coordinate with the fabric
- ½ yard fleece-backed suede

Follow these steps to whip up a stylish computer sleeve in practically no time:

1. **Measure the width, length, and thickness of the laptop and fill in the measurements below:**

   - Width: _____
   - Length: _____
   - Thickness: _____

2. **Calculate the finished measurements.**

   - **Finished width measurement:** Divide the thickness in half and add it to the width measurement, and then add 1 inch to allow for two ½-inch seam allowances.

For example, if the laptop is 11 inches wide and 1½ inches thick, add ¾ inch to 11 inches to get 11¾ inches. Add 1 inch to get a finished width of 12¾.

- **Finished length measurement:** Add 1½ inches to the length.

  If the laptop is 15 inches long, the finished length measurement is 16½ inches.

3. **Using the finished measurements, cut out two sleeve pieces, placing the finished selvage at the top of the sleeve where there will be an opening to slide in the laptop.**

4. **With the *wrong sides* (fleece sides) together, pin the computer sleeve together on three sides, leaving the selvage edges open.**

   Place the pins along the ½-inch seam allowance, parallel with the cut edge. This way, you can slip in the laptop to see if you need to adjust the fit *before* sewing.

   The opening may have more fabric than you think necessary. That's okay, because by boxing the bottom of the sleeve in Step 10, the laptop will fit perfectly into the sleeve without excess fabric at the top.

5. **Set your machine like this:**

   - Stitch: Straight

   - Length: 3 to 3.5 mm/8 to 10 spi

   - Width: 0 mm

   - Foot: All-purpose or Teflon-coated

   - Pressure: Lighten up the foot pressure slightly to make it easier to sew this heavier double thickness fabric

   If your machine has a Teflon-coated presser foot (one of my favorites!), use it to make this project — the suede moves under it like butter. Check your operating manual to see if you have this presser foot.

6. **Place the top end of the sleeve under the presser foot so you guide the edge of the fabric even with the right edge of the presser foot.**

7. **Sew around the three sides of the computer sleeve (see Figure 10-16), pulling out the pins as you go and securely backstitching at the beginning and end of the opening.**

8. **Trim the seam allowance to ¼ inch around the three sides (see Figure 10-16).**

9. **Turn the sleeve inside out.**

10. **At the bottom, fold the two corners as shown in Figure 10-17 and sew across the corner, creating the boxed corners.**

11. **Turn the sleeve right-side out and slip in the laptop.**

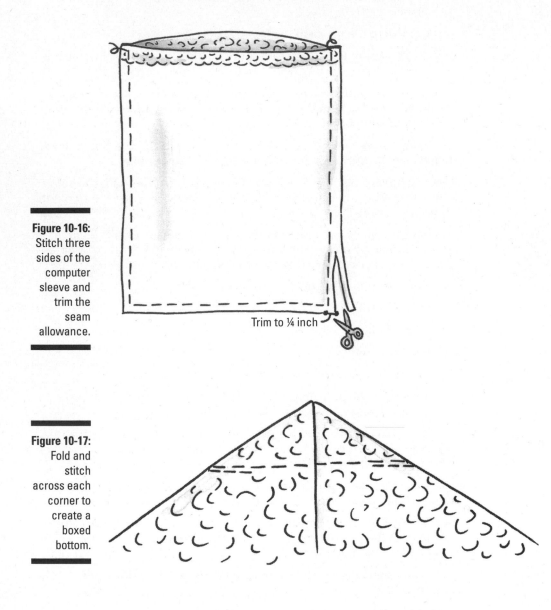

Figure 10-16:
Stitch three
sides of the
computer
sleeve and
trim the
seam
allowance.

Trim to ¼ inch

Figure 10-17:
Fold and
stitch
across each
corner to
create a
boxed
bottom.

Chapter 11

Pockets Full of Ideas

In This Chapter

▶ Making patch pockets for every size and shape

▶ Finding a pocket pattern for everybody

▶ Sprucing up a shirt with a pocket collage

*P*ockets are little pouches sewn into and onto pants, shirts, and other garments, all for the express purpose of holding portable paraphernalia. Although myriad pocket types exist, I focus in this chapter on patch pockets, called such because they're attached to the surface of a project like a knee patch, but with one side left open for the careful toting of your precious possessions.

In this chapter I tell you how to sew patch pockets of all shapes and sizes using the shortcuts that professionals use. I also include a really easy project that lets you use the power of pockets to conceal even the worst of shirt disasters and rescue a stained shirt from the rag pile — with a pocket collage!

Putting Together Patch Pockets

In this section you cut, shape, and stitch unlined patch pockets, one with square corners and another with curved corners. Then you discover the most professional pocket-application technique ever.

But how do you know what pocket style is best to make? Here's my formula: If you want to de-emphasize a round body type, select a pocket and garment style that has square and rectangular lines. To fill out a thin and angular figure, choose pocket and garment styles that are curved and rounded.

Pocket placement is also an important consideration. If you're very busty, placing a curved pocket over the bust is a bad choice. You may want to omit the pocket altogether. For those of us with generous backsides, don't even think about sewing curved patch pockets in that area of the physique . . . they just emphasize the obvious.

Making unlined patch pockets with square corners

I like sewing this pocket on shirts, even when the pattern doesn't call for one. This corner mitering technique works really well, so you can have the squarest corners going. Just follow these steps:

1. **Cut out the square-corner pocket by following the pattern guide sheet instructions or by using one of the pocket patterns found in this chapter (see the section "Using Your Own Pocket Patterns" later in this chapter).**

2. **Using your sewing machine, overcast the top edge of the pocket facing (see Chapter 6 for more information on finishing raw edges).**

3. **Press the pocket side seams toward the wrong side of the pocket.**

4. **Begin to *miter* each corner by folding up and pressing a triangle the width of the seam allowance at both pocket corners, as shown in Figure 11-1.**

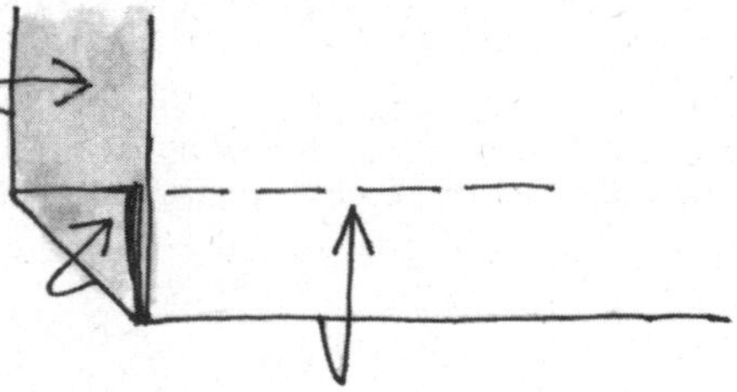

Figure 11-1: Fold up and press a triangle at both pocket corners.

5. **Fold up and press the bottom of the pocket on the seamline, enclosing the triangle in the seam allowance, as shown in Figure 11-2.**

   This is *mitering* a corner. You can use this technique in many different ways when sewing.

6. **Mark the angle of the miter marking both the edge of the fold and the angle (refer to Figure 11-2).**

   The best marker for this is a fabric marker with a felt-tipped point because the ink rubs off all around the felt tip. Draw a line following the angle of the miter so that the ink of the marker touches both fabric edges on the angle.

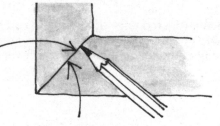

Figure 11-2:
Fold to
enclose the
triangle in
the seam
allowance.

7. **Unfold one pocket corner as shown in Figure 11-3, and darken the marks made in Step 6; this line marks the stitching line.**

   When connected, the marked lines make a large triangle in the corner, which becomes the *stitching line* of the miter.

8. **Trim the seam allowance to ¼ inch as shown in Figure 11-3.**

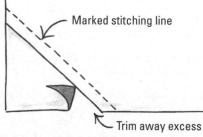

Marked stitching line

Trim away excess

Figure 11-3:
Trim the
seam allow-
ance to ¼
inch at the
pocket
corners.

9. **Set your machine like this:**
   - Stitch: Straight
   - Length: Appropriate for the fabric (see Chapter 5)
   - Width: 0 mm
   - Foot: All-purpose

10. **Fold the triangle in half so that the side and bottom pocket seams are right sides together; stitch the miter on the marked line.**

    Turn the corner right-side out and check that the miter is at a right angle. If not, rip out the seam, adjust, and resew.

11. **Repeat for the other corner of the pocket. Press the corner seams open.**

12. **Fold the pocket facing (the top edge of the pocket) on the foldline toward the right side of the pocket. Sew the seams at both sides of the pocket, backstitching at the top and bottom, as shown in Figure 11-4.**

    The "facing" for this pocket, which gives it a clean, finished look, is simply the hem at the top of the pocket.

Figure 11-4:
Fold the pocket facing toward the right side before sewing the seams.

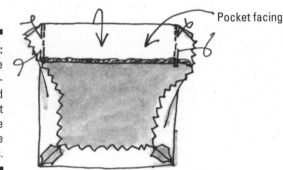

Pocket facing

13. **Trim away the excess seam allowance at the facing corners.**

    This removes the extra bulk so you don't have an unsightly lump in the corners when you turn the pocket right-side out.

14. **Turn the pocket right-side out and press before attaching it to your project.**

Making unlined patch pockets with curved corners

The biggest challenge with a curved corner pocket is making both curves the same shape. Follow these steps and see how easy the job becomes when you use the right tools:

1. **Cut out the curved-corner pocket by following the pattern guide sheet instructions or by using one of the pocket patterns found in this chapter (see Figure 11-8).**

2. **Using your sewing machine or serger, overcast the top edge of the pocket facing (see Chapter 6 for more information on finishing raw edges).**

3. **Set your machine like this:**

   - Stitch: Straight

   - Length: Appropriate for the fabric (see Chapter 5)

   - Width: 0 mm

   - Foot: All-purpose

4. **Fold the pocket facing (the top edge of the pocket) on the foldline toward the right side of the pocket. Sew the seams at both sides of the pocket, backstitching at the top and bottom, as shown in Figure 11-5.**

   This hem at the top of the pocket serves as a facing, giving your pocket a clean, finished look.

5. **Set your machine like this:**

   - Stitch: Straight

   - Length: 3.5 to 4 mm/6 to 7 spi

   - Width: 0 mm

   - Foot: All-purpose

6. **Easestitch-plus to shape the curved corners, as shown in Figure 11-5. (Check out Chapter 10 for instructions on easestitching-plus.)**

   Sewing with the wrong side of the fabric up, easestitch-plus from about 1½ inches above the curve to 1½ inches to the other side of the curve, sewing ¼ inch from the raw edge; then repeat for the other pocket corner.

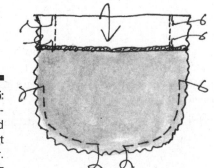

Figure 11-5: Easestitch-plus around each pocket corner.

7. **Press and shape the corners of the pocket around a pocket former (see Figure 11-6).**

Making sure that both pocket corners come out in exactly the same shape is a challenge — to say the least. My favorite tool for this task is a *pocket former,* a flat 4-inch aluminum square that has different curves on each corner. (Check it out in Figure 11-6.) You can find pocket formers at your local fabric store or sewing supply mail-order company.

If you can't locate a pocket former, make one out of a piece of cardboard. Cut a 4-x-4-inch square of cardboard. (Cardboard found on the back of pads of paper or a piece of a manila folder work well.) Set a small round saltshaker or other round container in the corner and then trace around the bottom curve of the container with a pencil, creating a smooth curve at the corner. Trim the corner by following your pencil line, and the resulting pattern is your pocket former. The cardboard deteriorates after a few uses, so if you find yourself making a lot of pockets, buy a pocket former tool.

With the wrong side of the pocket up, snug the gentlest curve of the pocket former into one of the corners and gently steam-press the seam allowance up to the seamline, shaping the curve of the pocket corner around the curve of the pocket former.

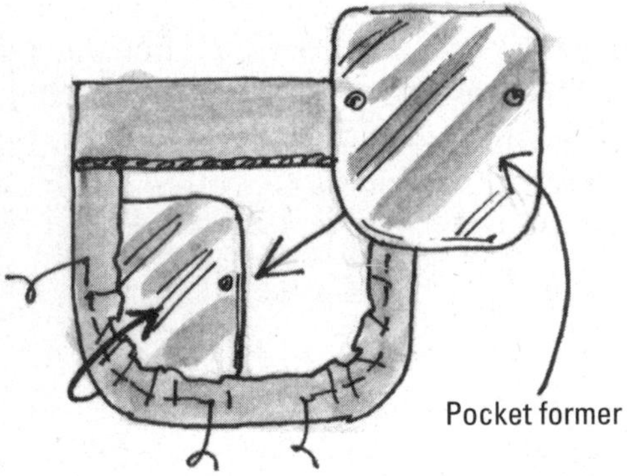

Figure 11-6: Use a pocket former to shape your corners.

Pocket former

8. **Trim away the excess seam allowance at the corners (you can read more about trimming corners in Chapter 6).**

9. **Turn the pocket right-side out and press before sewing it to your project.**

© KREBER

Make over your bedroom with pillows, a duvet cover, and a bed skirt using coordinating prints and matching solid fabrics. Chapter 14 covers everything you need to know to make the pillow covers on the bed, and you can find instructions for the custom duvet cover and bed skirt in Chapter 16.

Starting with fleece-backed faux suede or colorful place mats, make the fold-over clutch in Chapter 9 for any season or any occasion.

Sew a square tablecloth that fits most tables and a set of lapkins to hold your favorite flatware. Chapter 13 has step-by-step instructions.

Dress up your windows by making your own draperies and let them "puddle" to the floor. Turn to Chapter 15 for instructions.

© Kreber

If you're looking to refresh a room in a flash, try sewing flanged pillow covers using a couple of cloth napkins. See how easy this project is in Chapter 14.

© Kreber

With a simple pattern and a little sewing, you can recycle a felted wool sweater into this fashionable winter hat found in Chapter 19.

Plain or enhanced with appliqués, this fleece throw (in Chapter 6) and matching shirt pillow (in Chapter 5) are perfect companions for the family room or school dorm.

Turn a perfectly good shirt into a decorative pillow cover. The sleeves tucked into the back are great for hiding toys or the remote control. You can find step-by-step instructions in Chapter 5.

Have a good shirt with a stain or hole in it? Give it new life by arranging and stitching several pockets over the damage. It's easy to do using the pocket pattern in Chapter 11.

To make this fun, fast, and fashionable apron, you start with a denim skirt and then cut it in half and add some ruffles and a matching tie. You can find the instructions in Chapter 8.

Fashion a reversible table runner and coordinating napkins to add some punch to your next gathering. Find the how-tos for each project in Chapters 12 and 13.

Coordinating prints take these pretty pajama pants out of the bedroom and into the rest of the house. Make them for yourself or someone else — or both! For easy-to-follow instructions, turn to Chapter 8.

© Matt Bowen

Party, shop, or just hang out in this light and airy dress. See how easy and quick this dress is to make in Chapter 19.

© DIYStyle

Keep your laptop in tiptop shape by protecting it with this easy-to-stitch sleeve. Check out Chapter 10 for the how-to.

Fido needs a bed, too, and who says it can't match your décor? Pick out some fun fabric and sew this colorful (and fully washable) pet bed in Chapter 14.

Attaching patch pockets

Attach your pocket the easy way by edgestitching it in place by following these steps:

1. **Pin your finished patch pocket to the project by following your pattern guide instructions.**

   Patch pockets are usually intended to hold something, so instead of placing them so that you have to stitch them flat as a pancake to the project, position them so that they have a little slack at the top, as shown in Figure 11-7.

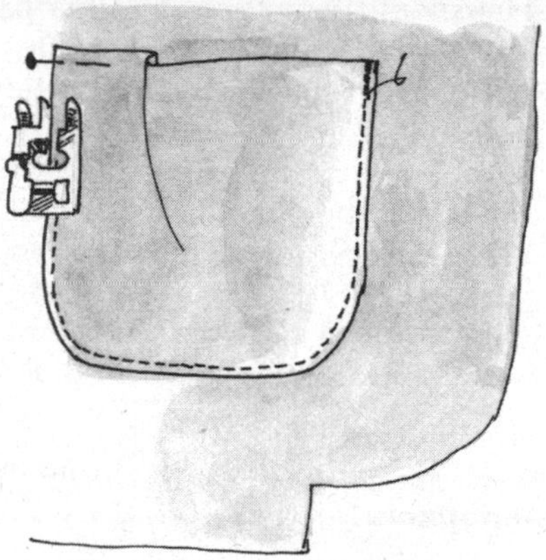

Figure 11-7: Leave a little slack at the top of the pocket to make sure it's functional.

2. **Set your machine like this:**
   - Stitch: Straight
   - Length: Appropriate for the fabric (see Chapter 5)
   - Width: 0 mm
   - Foot: Edgestitch or blind hem
   - Needle position (Optional): Adjust the needle position so that you sew ⅛ inch from the edge of the pocket

3. **Edgestitch around the pocket (read more about edgestitching in Chapter 6).**

   Guide the edge of the pocket along the blade in the foot, backstitching at the top of the pocket. If you topstitched this pocket and don't see it getting a lot of tough wear and tear, don't backstitch. Instead, pull the threads to the back and tie them off (see Chapter 6 for more information on backstitching and tying off threads).

Using Your Own Pocket Patterns

Sometimes I just want to put a pocket on a project, even though the pocket's not part of the original pattern. Instead of rifling through other patterns or buying another pattern to find just the right pocket, I dig into my reserve of pocket patterns when the inspiration strikes. In this section I show you how to make three different pocket patterns.

For instance, you can make three different pocket patterns from the shirt pocket pattern in Figure 11-8: rectangular, rounded, and chevron.

1. **Find a piece of pattern tracing material or leftover pattern tissue that's at least the length of the pocket patterns in Figure 11-8. Fold it in half so that the fold is vertical.**

2. **Place the pocket pattern under the pattern paper, lining up the pattern on the fold of the pattern paper.**

3. **Trace off the desired pocket by following the key in Figure 11-8.**

4. **Cut out your pocket pattern on the cutting line and open up the pattern flat as shown in Figure 11-9.**

While you're at it, why not trace off all three styles? You can have a ready pocket pattern resource for any shape when you need it! After you trace off these pocket patterns, safely store them between the pages of this chapter.

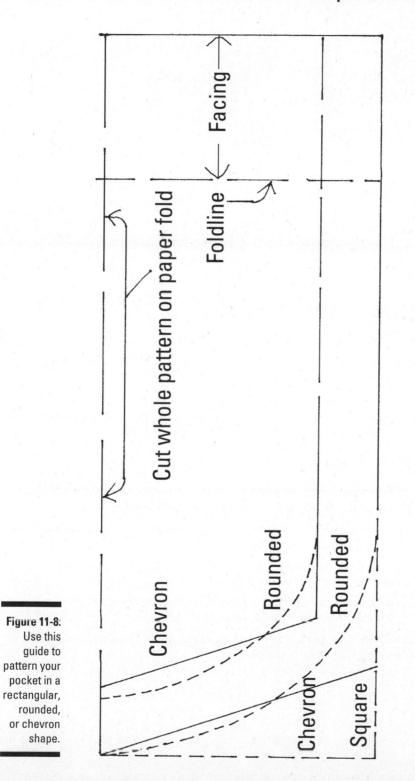

Figure 11-8:
Use this guide to pattern your pocket in a rectangular, rounded, or chevron shape.

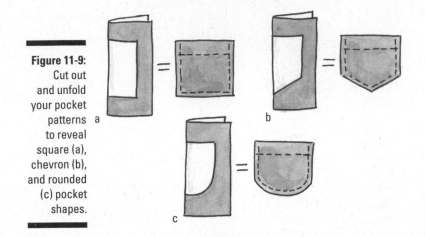

Figure 11-9:
Cut out and unfold your pocket patterns to reveal square (a), chevron (b), and rounded (c) pocket shapes.

Coordinating Pocket-Collage Shirt

My husband ruined three shirts in one week with the same leaky pen. Go figure. So instead of throwing them away (the shirts, not my husband and his leaky pen), I artfully stitched on pocket collages, covering the ink stains on the front of his (now *my*) favorite shirts. Check out the color pages to see an example, and remember that you certainly aren't limited to using damaged shirts for this project. If you're looking to jazz up a new or slightly worn shirt, the pocket collage is a simple change with serious impact.

This is how you stitch on pocket collages:

1. **Dig through your fabric stash for fabric that matches or coordinates with the color or design of your injured garment.**

2. **Trace off the pocket patterns in Figure 11-8 and cut out three different pocket styles from three coordinating fabrics.**

3. **Make the unlined pockets by following the steps in the section "Putting Together Patch Pockets" earlier in this chapter.**

4. **Pin each pocket to the front of the shirt, creatively arranging and overlapping three pockets to cover the stains.**

5. **Edgestitch each pocket to the front of the shirt. (You can read more about edgestitching in Chapter 6.)**

Part IV
Sewing for Your Home

The 5th Wave   By Rich Tennant

"Okay, Ms. Dolan, look closely, take your time, and tell us when you think you can identify a way we can improve this window treatment."

In this part . . .

I know that playing favorites is wrong, but I just can't help it — this part of the book holds probably the coolest chapters you'll ever read! In this part I show you how you can create new looks for just about any room in your house. After you read these chapters, you no longer have to settle for store-bought napkins, tablecloths, table runners, duvet covers, pillows, or window treatments. You can even make over your own bed set — in a weekend! — with the exact colors and fabrics that best fit your décor.

Chapter 12

Do-It-Yourself Decorating: Home Décor Sewing

In This Chapter

▶ Coordinating colors to overcome your fear of decorating

▶ Using home décor braids, cords, trims, and fringes

▶ Making and sewing on piping and cording like a pro

▶ Sprucing up your dining room with a reversible table runner

*W*ouldn't you love your home to look like those you see on TV or a model home? Never fear; your decorating coach is here! In this chapter I cover the important home-decorating basics. And the good news is that sewing for your home is the easiest way to save money when decorating.

First, I give you some strategies for conquering décoraphobia — the fear of decorating. You figure out how to uncover your home's complexion, choose a color scheme that works, use color to create flow from one room into the next, and discover the how-tos of safely putting stripes, plaids, and prints all in the same room — maybe even on the same project. Really!

Overcoming Décoraphobia

Ever bought a piece of clothing and gotten it home only to find out you picked the wrong color or size? You can return that little mistake to the store, no harm done. But a decorating mistake in your home haunts your days and nights until you can afford to change it. Décoraphobia sets in and some folks never, *ever* get over their fear of decorating.

Avoiding costly mistakes (and acute décoraphobia) requires simple planning strategies. You need to

- ✔ Understand how color works
- ✔ Figure out your home's complexion
- ✔ Decorate with the correct color ratios

In this section I walk you through these three color concepts so you can overcome your fear of decorating.

Understanding color

There's more to color than meets the eye. For example, every color has either a blue base or a yellow base. Picture a Red Delicious apple. Compare it to a Beefsteak tomato. Both are red, but when you put them side-by-side, your eyes tell you that they clash. The apple has a blue color base, making it a *cool* red. The tomato has a yellow color base and is considered a *warm* red.

Every color — even blue or yellow — has a warm and a cool version. In stores, home décor fabrics are usually grouped according to their color bases.

How do you identify the warm and cool bases? Start noticing the background colors on a piece of fabric. The color cues are found by finding and identifying the warm and cool neutral colors in the background.

- ✔ Warm neutrals (yellow base) have off-white backgrounds that look like they have been aged and are slightly "yellowed" by being in your grandmother's trunk.
- ✔ Cool neutrals (blue bases) have crisp white backgrounds that look like they have been bleached and whitened by the sun.

When you put both blue-based colors and yellow-based colors in the same room, they clash — just like the apple and the tomato. Your yellow-based sofa looks dirty against the blue-based pillows thrown on top of it. So before hiking off to the paint or fabric store, determine the color base of your home — what I call your home's *complexion* — and then work with the right blue-base or yellow-base colors throughout your home.

Unmasking your home's complexion

Unless you have the budget to decorate from scratch, work with what you have. Look at the largest surfaces — the ones that are more difficult and expensive to change — such as the flooring, countertops, sinks, kitchen appliances, and kitchen and bathroom cabinets. The color of these surfaces determines the complexion of your home.

In general, your home complexion is cool if your

- ✔ Carpet and tile colors are blue, gray, white, or black
- ✔ Cabinets are cool-toned such as those that are painted white, white-washed, pickled (a finish that bleaches the wood to a light gray), maple, or is very dark, such as aged cherry and cabinets that have been painted black
- ✔ Countertops are blue, black, gray, or white
- ✔ Sinks and kitchen appliances are blue, white, black, or stainless steel

Imagine a crisp white sail against the big, blue sea. When selecting print, striped, or plaid fabrics for a cool-complexioned room, choose those with a white background (like the sail).

Your room probably has a yellow-based, or warm, complexion if your

- ✔ Carpet and tile colors are coffee, mustard, off-white, beige, or terra cotta
- ✔ Cabinets are warm-toned woods such as natural oak, pine, or birch
- ✔ Countertops are brown or tan
- ✔ Sinks and kitchen appliances are almond, tan, or off-white

When selecting print, striped, or plaid fabrics for a warm-complexioned room, choose those with an off-white or cream-colored background.

When you use one color base throughout your entire home, your colors work together from room to room, and the wrong color bases that you need to live with for a while aren't as noticeable.

Determining your color odds

When selecting the color scheme for your home, think odd — odd numbers, that is. Start your color scheme using three colors: Use two dominant colors in equal amounts and one accent color. As you gain experience, you can add more colors, but remember that an odd number looks best.

Suppose you want to redo your bedroom and master bath using the color scheme in the fabric on your bedspread — blue and white with lemon-yellow accents. Choosing paint to match a piece of fabric is a whole lot easier than the other way around, so use your bedspread as your inspiration piece and choose your wall paint, pillows, and accessories by following the color cues in the bedspread. This way your color bases won't clash and you get a custom-decorated look to the room.

Your carpet and ceiling are white (the first dominant color), so paint the walls blue (the second dominant color). Find blue and white throw pillows for the bed. Add one yellow pillow as the accent. The lamps on the night tables are blue and white, so you can add yellow tassels as the accent. The draperies match the bedspread, so you can add yellow tiebacks. Place a yellow tulip arrangement in a blue vase on the dresser.

Reverse the colors to keep the scheme flowing through the whole house. Make the accent color in your bedroom the dominant color in your bathroom, for example.

Stumped because you don't have a color scheme? Find something with three colors that you love — a dish, a piece of clothing, a throw pillow, maybe even a picture in a magazine. If it has nothing to do with home décor, that's okay — you're looking for the colors you like and nothing else. Go to the paint store with your treasure and find paint chips that match these same three colors. Now you have your color scheme!

Homing In on Home Décor Fabric

All fabrics are not created equal. The best fabrics for home décor projects are home décor fabrics, for a number of reasons:

- Many home décor fabrics are heavier and more durable than apparel fabrics.

- They run 54 to 60 inches wide, which is 9 to 15 inches wider than apparel fabrics. The additional width is a real advantage for your home décor projects because you get better coverage with a yard of wider home décor fabric than with narrower dressmaking fabric.

- Many home décor fabrics are chemically treated to resist stains and sun damage. Due to the extra width and chemical treatment, décor fabrics are generally more expensive than apparel fabrics. Expect to pay from $15 to $60 per yard.

- Most home décor fabrics have a color strip that may have a circle with a plus sign through it printed on the *selvages* (the finished edges on the long sides of the fabric), so you simply match the color bars and/or symbol when seaming one panel to the next and the design matches perfectly at the seamline.

Always check the bolt end or hang tag of your home décor fabrics for proper cleaning and care instructions, which differ widely from fabric to fabric. See Chapter 3 for more info on specific fabrics used in home décor.

Tackling Trim

Decorator trim is the icing on your home decorating cake and comes in three basic styles — braid, cord, and fringe. In this section I show you some cool ways to use each one.

Braving braid basics

Braid is a flat home décor trim with two finished edges. The two most common types of braid are

- **Gimp:** This flat braid is usually glued to furniture to conceal upholstery tacks (see Figure 12-1). You can also stitch gimp to the edge of decorator cord-edge trim (see the following section for the details on cord).
- **Mandarin:** A dressier, ½-inch dimensional gimp (meaning that it has a texture), this braid is great for outlining pillows, place mats, and other home décor projects. You can also use mandarin braid in crafting by gluing it to handmade boxes and lampshades.

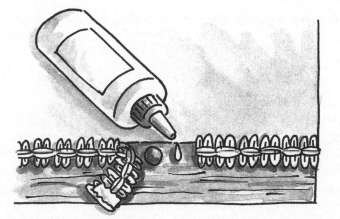

Figure 12-1: Use gimp to cover a join where the upholstery attaches to the furniture frame.

Conquering cord

Cord is a round, twisted strand of fibers that looks like rope. Cord can be anywhere from ⅛ inch to 1¾ inch in diameter and is made out of cotton, shiny rayon, spun satiny rayon, or a combination of fibers, each with a unique texture. See what the different cords look like in Figure 12-2.

The most common kinds of cord include the following:

- ✔ **Cable cord:** A twisted cotton or cotton/polyester cord used as a filling for fabric-covered piping (see the following section for more information on piping). Preshrink the cable cord before you use it in a project. Cable cord is also a key ingredient of *piping* (or *welting*). You make piping by covering the cable cord with a strip of fabric called a *casing*. The casing has a ¼-inch to ½-inch seam allowance so that you can sew it into the seam at the edge of a pillow, slipcover, or sofa cushion cover. Piping gives a crisp, tailored finish to the edge.

  To preshrink cable cord, wrap it around your hand to create a wrapped wad called a hank. Pull the hank off your hand, put a rubber band around the center of it, and throw it in the wash with other fabrics of similar fiber content.

- ✔ **Filler cord:** You use this web-covered, cotton-filled cord inside piping. Filler is softer and fatter than cable cord because of the loose cotton filling. You can find filler cord in diameters up to 1¾ inches thick.

  Because of loose construction, you can't wash filler cord or it turns into a lumpy mess. That means you don't preshrink filler cord before covering it, and you should dry-clean projects made with this cord instead of washing them.

- ✔ **Cord-edge trim:** A twisted cord with a lip edge of flat gimp sewn to it, cord-edge trim is pretty by itself. You don't have to cover it with a casing like cable or filler cord. The lip edge makes it easy to insert the trim at a seam in a pillow or at the edge of a window cornice, swag, or jabot (see Chapter 15 for more information on window treatments).

  Cord-edge trim is dry-clean-only. So even though you may use it with a washable fabric, dry-clean your project to properly care for it.

- ✔ **Chair tie:** A twisted decorator cord 27 to 30 inches long with tassels on both ends, chair ties are traditionally used to attach cushions to chairs. Chair ties also make nice drapery tiebacks.

- ✔ **Tassel tieback:** This twisted decorator cord is shaped into a three-sectioned loop. A color-coordinating ring cinches the loop so that the tassel hangs in the center loop. The side loops encircle a drapery and hold it back by looping over the hardware attached to the wall.

Figure 12-2:
Cable cord,
filler cord,
and chair
tie.

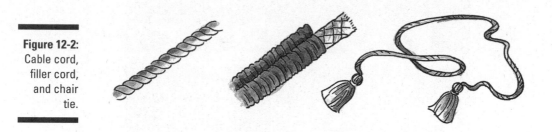

Figuring out fringe

Fringe is a decorative edging made of packed yarns that hang from a band, kind of like a hula skirt. Decorator fringes are a lot of fun to work with and add richness and value to your home décor projects.

Look for these common types of fringe, some of which appear in Figure 12-3, when you want to add a little flair to a project:

- **Ball fringe:** This decorative fringe is constructed with a gimp edge and cotton pompoms. Use it to trim whimsical home décor projects, children's rooms, and costumes.

- **Boucle fringe:** A fringe constructed with permanently kinked, nubby yarns called *boucle yarns*. Boucle fringe can be short, long, looped, or bullion.

- **Bullion fringe:** Sewers use this long fringe with twisted, looped ends on pillows, upholstery, and slipcovers.

- **Butterfly fringe:** This fringe has cut edges on two sides connected by an open threaded area. When you fold butterfly fringe in half the long way and stitch it to a project, you create a double-thick row of fringe.

- **Chainette fringe:** Constructed of many short or long chainette ends, this fringe is great for the edge of pillows, window treatments, and table toppers (see Chapter 13 for instructions for making a table topper).

- **Moss fringe:** This short, cut fringe looks like a brush after you sew it into a pillow or slipcover and remove the chainstitch from the edges.

- **Tassel fringe:** This fringe has many tiny tassels attached to a length of gimp.

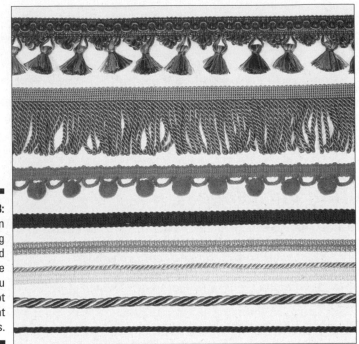

Figure 12-3:
When
selecting
fringe and
decorative
trims, you
have a lot
of great
choices.

A clear chainstitch is found on the edge of several types of trims to keep the fringe flat for easy sewing. As tempted as you may be to remove the chainstitch from the fringe before sewing it into your project, don't do it. If you do, this trim is almost impossible to work with because the little fringe fibers are tough to keep out of the seam.

Dealing with decorator trims

Here are some sewing guidelines to keep in mind as you sew home décor trims onto your projects:

✔ Use a size 14/90 to 16/100 Universal point or sharp needle in your sewing machine. Home décor fabrics can get very thick under the presser foot and need a sharp, heavy needle.

✔ Use a little longer stitch length (3 to 3.5 mm or 6 to 8 spi) than for garment sewing. The longer stitch length makes sewing the extra thicknesses created by the fabric and trim a lot easier.

✔ In certain cases when the fabric moves sluggishly under the presser foot, lighten up the foot pressure (see your operating manual for instructions).

✔ When sewing uneven thicknesses (such as when hemming jeans or attaching decorator trim by sewing up and over the thickness and then back down to the level hem or seam allowance), use a wedge under the presser foot to level it when approaching *and* coming off the heavy seams. You can find wedges like the one shown in Figure 12-4 through your local sewing machine dealer, fabric store, or sewing mail-order source. Look for them by the brand names of Jean-A-Ma-Jig or Hump-Jumper.

If you don't want to buy a wedge, make one by cutting out a 6-inch square of denim. Fold it in half and then in half again until the wedge is thick enough to keep the foot level when it rests on the wedge and the thick seam.

✔ Prevent unnecessary needle breakage by sewing slowly over thick areas.

✔ Start sewing trim at the center of any side of a pillow or cushion unless the project instructions say explicitly to do otherwise.

✔ Fabric and trim must be equal lengths. If you pull or stretch the trim to fit an edge, the edge puckers, and no amount of pressing can straighten it out.

✔ When making pillows and slipcovers or covering cushions, sew the trim to the top pillow piece first. Sew the back pillow piece to the trimmed front fabric piece afterward. This way if you get any stitch distortion, it shows on the back, rather than the front, of the project.

Figure 12-4:
Use a wedge under the presser foot when sewing uneven thicknesses.

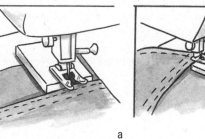
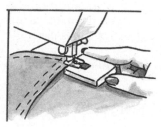

a   b

Attaching Piping, Cording, and Fringe

Call me crazy, but I love sewing piping and cording in a seam. I like the way these trims set off style lines in a garment, and I love seeing trim or fringe at the edge of a pillow or cushion because it says *quality* (see Figure 12-5).

Piping

Figure 12-5:
Piping gives
this pillow
a finished
look.

Making your own piping

If you're lucky enough to find piping to match your project, buy it. If not, this section tells you how to make your own piping to match your project.

You make piping by covering a cable or filler cord with a strip of fabric called a *casing*. (Refer to "Conquering cord," earlier in this chapter, for more about cable and filler cord.) The casing has a ¼-inch to ½-inch seam allowance so that you can sew the casing into the seam at the edge of a pillow, slipcover, or sofa cushion cover. If you make bias trim from a coordinating stripe or plaid fabric, the design looks like a barber pole.

To make your own piping, just follow these steps:

1. **Measure the perimeter of the area you want to pipe and add 2 inches or so for overlap and seaming for each length of piping you want to insert.**

   For example, if you want to pipe the edge of a pillow that has a perimeter of 30 inches, you need 32 inches of piping.

2. **Preshrink your cable cord (refer to "Conquering cord," earlier, for instructions) and cut it to the measurement you determined in Step 1.**

   You can also use filler cord, but remember *not* to preshrink it. (I explain the difference between cable cord and filler cord in the earlier section "Conquering cord.")

   Prevent the cable or filler cord from uncontrolled fraying by taping around the end of the cord with masking tape before cutting through it. As long as you use masking tape, the tape can stay on the project, but other types of tape get gummy, deteriorate, and melt with cleaning.

3. **To determine how wide to cut the fabric casing that covers the cording, find the circumference of the cord and add 1 inch for seam allowances.**

   Wrap your tape measure snugly around the cording. This length is the circumference of the cord.

4. **Cut a fabric strip long enough to cover the length of the cable or filler cord.**

   If you can't cut one strip of fabric long enough to cover the entire length of the cord, cut as many small strips as you need and sew them together with a ½-inch seam allowance.

   You cover cable or filler cord with either a straight- or bias-cut fabric casing, depending on the shape of the seam you put it in.

   • If you want to sew the piping to straight seams (such as the edges of a rectangular slipcover or square pillow), cut the fabric into strips either across the grain or on the lengthwise grain (see Chapter 4 for more information on grainlines).

   • If you want to sew the piping to a curved edge, like a round pillow, cut the fabric strips on the bias (the next section tells you exactly how to do this).

Cutting bias strips for covering cable cord

Cut bias fabric strips the easy way following these steps:

1. **Fold down a corner of the fabric so that the cut edge is parallel to and even with the selvage and then press a crease in the fold, as shown in Figure 12-6.**

Figure 12-6:
Find the bias.

2. **Open up the fold; the foldline marks the cutting line.**

3. **Using the foldline as a starting point, measure the width of the strip desired and mark off more strips, using a straight edge and pencil or dressmakers chalk.**

4. **Cut the fabric strips along the marks you made in Step 3 and as shown in Figure 12-7.**

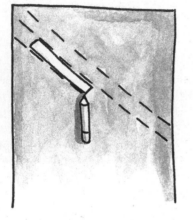

Figure 12-7:
Use a straight edge when you mark cutting lines.

5. **Set your machine like this:**

   • Stitch: Straight

   • Length: 3 mm/9 spi

   • Width: 0 mm

   • Foot: All-purpose

6. **Place the short ends of the two fabric strips right sides together and seam them using a ½-inch seam allowance (see Figure 12-8).**

   Repeat this step with each strip, creating a long chain, until you have a fabric strip of the proper length.

7. **Press open the seams.**

8. **Set your machine like this:**

   • Stitch: Straight

   • Length: 3 mm/9 spi

   • Width: 0 mm

   • Foot: Zipper or piping

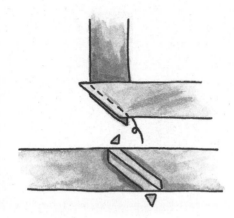

Figure 12-8:
Seam bias-cut fabric strips to create a casing for piping.

If you sew on a lot of piping, buy a piping foot. The underside of the foot has a deep groove that automatically guides over the cording for straight sewing and even piping application. I like and use the Pearls 'N Piping Foot manufactured by Creative Feet. It's designed to fit any brand or sewing machine model. Visit www.creativefeet.com for more information.

9. **Starting at one end, sandwich the cord in the casing — like you would put a hot dog in a bun.**

   The cord nestles into the wrong side of the fabric; the right side faces out.

10. **Working at a slow and steady pace, sew the casing closed along the length of the cord by snugging the zipper foot against the cord (as shown in Figure 12-9).**

   Use your hands to guide the fabric and cording together as you sew.

   Don't pin the casing around the length of the cable cord before sewing. Pinning takes forever, and you'll never want to look at another piece of piping as long as you live.

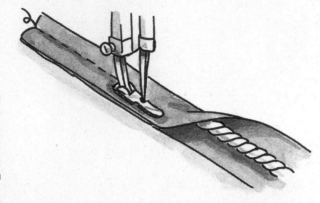

Figure 12-9:
Sew the cording into the fabric.

Sewing on piping and fringe

Piping and fringe add pizzazz to your home décor projects. Both trims have a lip edge that is sandwiched between two seams to hold them in place, but because fringe has a braid as its lip edge, you can also sew it to the surface of a project as a decorative treatment where the braid shows.

Getting started and turning corners

When attaching piping, fringe, or other decorator trim to a pillow or cushion, attach the trim to the front piece first and then sew the pillow back to the front.

1. **Starting anywhere but at a corner, pin the piping or fringe to the right side of the fabric so that the lip edges of the piping or fringe and the fabric are almost even.**

   Keep the trim in one long length until you're absolutely sure that you have enough to go around the project.

   Don't stretch the trim to fit the edge, or the seamline ends up puckered.

2. **Set your sewing machine like this:**
   - Stitch: Straight
   - Length: 3 mm/9 spi
   - Width: 0 mm
   - Foot: Zipper or piping

3. **Sew on the trim at the ½-inch seamline, as shown in Figure 12-10, pulling out the pins as you get to them. Stop sewing about 2 inches before the end of the trim.**

   If you're sewing trim to a straight edge, skip to Step 6 under "Joining piping ends in a casing."

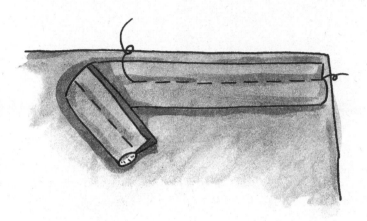

Figure 12-10:
Sew the
trim onto
the fabric.

4. **When you reach a corner, clip the seam allowance of the lip edge up to, but not through, the stitching line as shown in Figure 12-11 (see more about clipping into seam allowances in Chapter 6).**

   This allows the lip edge of the trim to easily bend around the corner without buckling.

5. **Sew around the corner.**

   • **If you're using piping:** Stop sewing with the needle in the fabric, raise the foot and pivot slightly, nudging your index finger into the corner of the piping so that it bends around your finger and away from the needle.

   • **If you're using fringe:** Stop sewing with the needle in the fabric, raise the foot and pivot the fabric, pulling the fringe around the corner so the lip edge is even with the raw fabric edge.

   Lower the presser foot and continue stitching. You may have to stitch a gentle curve rather than a sharp corner to accommodate the bulk of the piping or fringe.

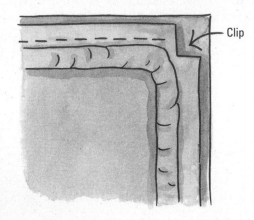

Clip

Figure 12-11:
Using your scissor tips, clip through the piping or fringe seam allowance to turn the trim around the corners.

When you reach the starting point of the fringe, overlap the two ends of the fringe. If you're using moss or brush fringe, just butt the fringe ends together at the join so that you don't make it so thick.

Joining fringe ends

Fringe is the easiest trim to join. When you reach the starting point around a pillow, tablecloth, or cushion, butt the fringe ends together at the join and simply pin and sew the fringe in place, sewing ½-inch from the raw edge and backstitching.

Remember to start sewing the fringe and bring the ends together on a straight edge as shown in Figure 12-12. If you start in a corner, there is too much bulk created by the trim when turning the project right side out and you'll end up with an unsightly bulge in the corner.

Joining piping ends in a casing

This join is a little trickier than the one you use for fringe, and I've tried a lot of different techniques. The following process works and looks best, time after time:

1. **Follow Steps 1 to 3 from the earlier section "Getting started and turning corners."**

2. **Open the casing about 1 inch on both ends by ripping out the stitching that holds the fabric casing around the cable or filler cord as shown in Figure 12-13a and b.**

3. **Cut one end of the cable cord so that it butts the other end, and then tape the ends of the cable cord together.**

4. **Turn under one short end of the casing, overlapping the folded end over the flat end (shown in Figure 12-13c and d). Pin the casing at the overlap.**

5. **Finish stitching on the rest of the piping so that you secure it around the perimeter of the project.**

Figure 12-12:
Sew fringe to the outside edge of a project, beginning and ending on a straight side.

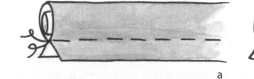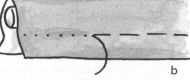

a

b

Figure 12-13:
Join fabric-covered piping at the ends.

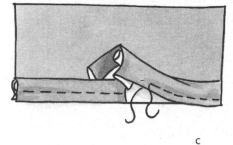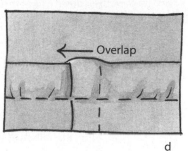

Overlap

c

d

6. **Pin the piped seam allowance to the non-piped seam allowance of the back piece of the project, with the right sides together and at the ½-inch seamline.**

7. **Place the project under the presser foot so that the stitching from Step 5 is where you can see it, and start sewing.**

   The needle should fall just to the left of the stitching line. You want to sew close enough to the piping or fringe that the previous row of stitching doesn't show when you turn the project right side out.

Attaching and joining cord-edge trim

You attach cord-edge trim the same way you attach piping and fringe (see the preceding section). The difference is that when you reach the starting point to join the trim, you need to overlap the two ends of the cord rather than butting them together so they don't fray.

Follow these steps to make a clean join with your cord-edge trim:

1. **Using a tape measure and your scissors, cut the cord-edge trim 6 inches longer than the finished area it must go into.**

   The trim has a 3-inch tail on each end that can be overlapped and beautifully finished.

2. **On the 3-inch tail pieces, separate the lip edge from the cord with a seam ripper.**

3. **After the cord is cut, the plies of the cord want to unwind from each other and unravel, so gently separate and wrap masking tape around the end of each ply to prevent raveling.**

4. **Trim each lip to 1 inch, leaving enough to overlap on each end; tape each lip end with masking tape.**

5. **Arrange the plies of the decorative cord so they look like twisted plies of one continuous decorative cord, as shown in Figure 12-14.**

   Pull the right-side plies under the lips, twisting and arranging the cord until it returns to the original shape. Secure with tape.

6. **Set your sewing machine like this:**
   - Stitch: Straight
   - Length: 3 to 4 mm/6 to 9 spi
   - Width: 0 mm
   - Foot: Zipper or piping

7. **Stitch through all the layers to secure the cord edge trim and loose plies to the fabric at the ½-inch seam allowance.**

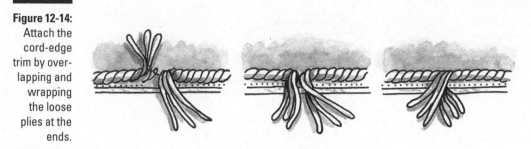

Figure 12-14:
Attach the
cord-edge
trim by over-
lapping and
wrapping
the loose
plies at the
ends.

Reversible Table Runner

Try your hand at by making this easy table runner. You can create this pretty runner to *run* either the width or the length of a table — use it instead of place mats or a tablecloth.

To make the runner, you need the following supplies (in addition to the tools in the sewing survival kit that I tell you about in Chapter 2):

- ½ yard of 60-inch-wide, solid-colored home décor fabric
- ⅔ yard of 60-inch-wide print home décor fabric
- Thread that matches the fabric
- One yardstick

Follow these steps to make your runner:

1. **Cut a piece of the solid-colored side fabric 16 inches by 60 inches.**

2. **Cut a piece of the print fabric 24 inches by 60 inches.**

3. **Set your machine like this:**
   - Stitch: Straight
   - Length: 3 mm/8 to 9 spi
   - Width: 0 mm
   - Foot: All-purpose

4. **With the right sides together, pin and sew together the two long sides of the runner, leaving an 8-inch opening on one long side as shown in Figure 12-15.**

   Because the two pieces of fabric are different widths, the wider piece has extra slack.

Figure 12-15:
Pin and sew the long sides of the table runner, leaving an opening to turn the runner though.

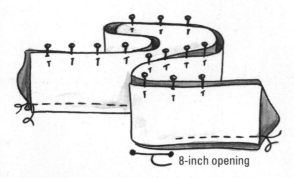

8-inch opening

5. **Lay the runner wrong-side out so the print side is down against the table and the solid side is on top facing you, and fold the seams in toward the center so that the runner lays flat and the solid-color fabric has an even border of print fabric down each length.**

   Because the print fabric is cut wider than the solid, the extra print fabric creates extra slack that pulls to the front creating a contrasting band on both long sides of the runner. (Check out the color pages for a closer look.)

6. **Press the long seams to one side toward the outside edges of the runner.**

7. **Pin and sew the short ends as shown in Figure 12-16a.**

8. **Clip each corner as shown in Figure 12-16a.**

9. **Turn the runner right-side out though the 8-inch opening, as shown in Figure 12-16b, and press.**

10. **To close the opening and to give the runner more structure, topstitch the length of the runner along the long sides, guiding the presser foot ⅜ inch from the print as shown in Figure 12-16b.**

Figure 12-16:
Sew the short ends and clip each corner (a), then topstitch down each print side to close the opening (b).

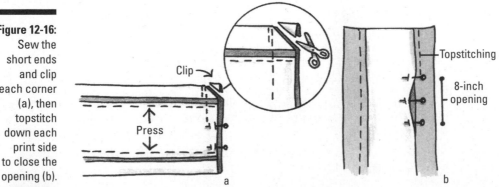

Clip

Press

Topstitching

8-inch opening

a

b

Chapter 13

Quick-Change Table Toppers

. . . .

In This Chapter

▶ Picking the best fabrics for your table toppers

▶ Creating all sorts of napkins

▶ Cranking out a decorative tablecloth

. . . .

*O*ne of the fastest, easiest, and most colorful ways to cozy up a room is by making table toppers. What are table toppers? They're napkins and tablecloths that liven up any mealtime or add a little punch of color to that boring end table in the corner of the family room or den. And with more folks eating at home, these projects are guaranteed to keep dinner interesting.

I know what you're thinking: "Cloth napkins are only for special occasions." But I say every day the family eats together *is* a special occasion and should be celebrated, and — who knows — in a nice setting, table manners may even improve. So if you want to beautify any tabletop in your home, start by making the napkins and tablecloths in this chapter. I cover the fastest and easiest edge-finishing techniques so you can make your toppers and set your table with them, all in one afternoon.

Selecting Fabric for Table Toppers

Whether you want to make napkins, table runners, or a tablecloth, you should keep these things in mind when selecting fabric:

> ✔ Before buying a fabric simply because you like the color or design, consider the fiber content, the fabric finish, and what you want to make. Fabrics such as all-cotton or all-linen are absorbent but very wrinkle-prone, so you may want to choose fabrics blended with a little polyester. A fabric finish such as Scotchgard repels stains and spills, so a fabric that has been Scotchgarded may not have the absorbency needed for napkins but works great as a tablecloth.

- ✔ Don't use fabrics that consist of more than 50 percent synthetic or man-made fiber. These fabrics aren't absorbent, and stains and odors remain in the fabric even after repeated washings.

- ✔ Providing that the fabric is printed on-grain, using fabrics with pre-printed stripes, plaids, or checks helps you cut straight, and hemming is as easy as following the lines in the fabric.

- ✔ Don't use knits. Tightly woven fabrics work better and last longer as napkins and tablecloths.

- ✔ Look at the wrong side of the print. Does it limit your napkin-folding possibilities because of bad looks? If so, choose another fabric or use it for something other than a napkin, where the wrong side doesn't matter.

- ✔ For napkins, stick with small prints or textures so you don't have to worry about matching a design from one napkin to another.

- ✔ If you want a light- to medium-weight fabric that works well for napkin-making, look for bandannas, broadcloth, calico prints, chambray, chintz, duck, gingham, kettle or weaver's cloth, light- to mid-weight linen, and denim, muslin, percale, poplin, and seersucker.

- ✔ For heavier-weight fabrics better suited for tablecloths, look for damask, double-sided fabrics, linen, sailcloth, and terry cloth.

Making Easy Napkins

Friends and family members usually expect handmade gifts from me, and I've made some really gorgeous things through the years. But the most appreciated gifts were also the simplest — cloth napkins that I made several years ago. I sewed 160 napkins (20 sets of eight) one holiday season. I used fabric that coordinated with my friends' color schemes and lifestyles. Sally works with chimpanzees, so she got a jungle print. My classically tailored pal Carol got the black and white stripes. I used a cheerful juvenile print for our son's day-care provider.

Cloth napkins are fast and easy to make, and good for the environment to boot. The following sections talk you through how much fabric you need to purchase and how to create napkins in a few different ways.

Figuring out fabric yardage

If you're just making fabric napkins for your own use, you may take advantage of an opportunity to use up some decent-size scraps of fabric you already have. But if your goal is to make a matching set or give the napkins as gifts, you probably want to shop for new fabric.

Tables 13-1 and 13-2 tell you how much fabric you need to make napkins of various sizes, including a little extra for shrinkage and evening up the squares. The size of each unfinished napkin is listed in inches; the amount of fabric for each set of napkins is listed in yards.

Table 13-1		Yardage for 45-Inch Fabric		
Unfinished Napkin Size	Six Napkins	Eight Napkins	Ten Napkins	Twelve Napkins
15 inches	⅞	1⅜	1¾	1¾
18 inches	1⅝	2⅛	2⅝	3⅛
20 inches	1¾	2¼	2⅞	3½
22½ inches	2	2⅝	3¼	3⅞

Table 13-2		Yardage for 54- to 55-Inch Fabric		
Unfinished Napkin Size	Six Napkins	Eight Napkins	Ten Napkins	Twelve Napkins
15 inches	⅞	1⅜	1¾	1¾
18 inches	1⅛	1⅝	2⅛	2⅛
20 inches	1¾	2¼	2⅞	3⅜
24 inches	2⅛	2¾	3⅜	4⅛

Sewing basic table napkins

I discovered a fast, efficient way to make napkins while I was cranking out 160 of them for the holidays. These little beauties come together so quickly that you may be tempted to create sets for special dinner parties, family celebrations, and holidays. To make these napkins, you need the following materials in addition to your sewing survival kit (see Chapter 2):

- ✔ Napkin fabric (refer to Tables 13-1 and 13-2 for yardage)
- ✔ Thread that matches the napkin fabric

Just follow these steps to have napkins in no time:

1. **Cut the napkin squares according to the unfinished napkin sizes listed in Tables 13-1 and 13-2.**

2. **Set your sewing machine like this:**
   - Stitch: Three-step zigzag
   - Length: 1 to 1.5 mm/24 to 30 spi
   - Width: 5 mm
   - Foot: All-purpose

   If you're using a serger, set your serger like this:
   - Stitch: Balanced three-thread overlock
   - Length: 2 mm
   - Width: 3 to 5mm
   - Foot: Standard

3. **Overcast the opposite edges of the fabric squares by placing the raw edge under the foot so that the needle catches the fabric on the left and swings off the raw edge at the right.**

   See Chapter 6 for more information on overcasting raw fabric edges.

4. **Repeat Step 3 on the other two opposite edges of each napkin.**

5. **Pin and press a ¼-inch hem on two opposite edges of the fabric square.**

   When you pin the hems on opposite edges, the corners turn out sharp and square.

6. **Set your machine like this:**
   - Stitch: Straight
   - Length: 3.5 mm/9 spi
   - Width: 0 mm
   - Foot: All-purpose

7. **With the wrong side of the fabric up, topstitch a ¼-inch hem on the opposite edges, as shown in Figure 13-1a.**

8. **Continue sewing from one napkin to the next without cutting the threads in between, as shown in Figure 13-1b.**

   Stringing the napkins together this way saves time and lets you hem a lot of them at once.

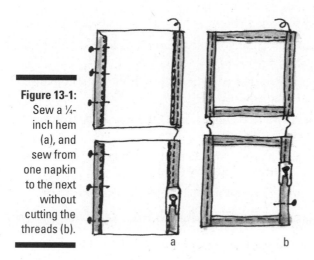

Figure 13-1:
Sew a ¼-
inch hem
(a), and
sew from
one napkin
to the next
without
cutting the
threads (b).

a   b

9. **Cut the connecting threads between each napkin at the fabric.**

10. **Repeat Steps 7 and 8 for the opposite hem edges, backstitching at the end of each corner.**

11. **Cut the connecting threads between each napkin at the corners.**

Serging napkins with narrow rolled edges

Have you ever noticed the neatly finished edges on restaurant napkins? If you have a serger, you can duplicate this finish and have a basket full of napkins done in no time.

To make these napkins, you need the following materials in addition to your sewing survival kit (see Chapter 2):

✔ Napkin fabric (refer to Tables 13-1 and 13-2 for yardage)

✔ Serger thread that matches the napkin fabric

✔ Seam sealant (such as Fray Check)

Read your operating manual to set your serger for a narrow rolled edge and then follow these steps:

1. **Set your serger like this:**
   - Stitch: Three-thread
   - Length: 1.0 to 1.5 mm
   - Foot: Narrow rolled edge

- Needle plate: Narrow rolled edge
- Upper looper: Loosen so that you see the stitches form a smooth row of satin stitches
- Lower looper: Tighten so that you see a straight line of stitching forming on the underside of the stitch

2. **Before starting your narrow rolled edges, test the edge finish on a scrap first to get the perfect stitch.**

3. **Cut out your napkin squares using your favorite cutting tools (refer to Tables 13-1 and 13-2 for yardage requirements).**

   The narrow rolled edge takes up about a ¼-inch hem allowance all the way around, so remember to cut your napkins large enough so that they end up the desired finished size.

4. **Place all the napkin squares in your lap so that the right side of the fabric faces up.**

5. **Place the first napkin edge under the foot so that when you serge, you trim away about ⅛ inch.**

   This fabric placement ensures proper stitch formation and prevents the stitches from pulling off the edge of the fabric with repeated washings.

6. **Serge the first edge of the napkin and then, in a continuous step, butt the next napkin up to the first and finish one edge of the second napkin.**

   Continue in this way, butting one napkin up to the next, until you finish off one side of all the napkin squares in your lap. Your napkins resemble a kite tail connected with serged thread chains.

7. **Repeat Steps 4 through 6 for the opposite (parallel) side of the napkin squares.**

8. **Apply a drop of seam sealant (like Fray Check) at the base of the chain at each corner of the napkin squares.**

9. **After the seam sealant dries, cut apart the napkins, cutting the chains at the base of each corner as shown in Figure 13-2.**

10. **Rotate all the napkins 90 degrees, and serge the narrow rolled edges of the remaining opposite sides of each napkin, following Steps 5 through 9.**

Napkins as no-sew pillow covers

Make a quick-change pillow cover by covering a throw pillow with two napkins. Simply rubber-band the napkins together at the corners and pop in the pillow. Prevent the rubber bands from showing by covering them with ribbon or cord. Now you have a great way to change the look of a room and then change it back in an instant.

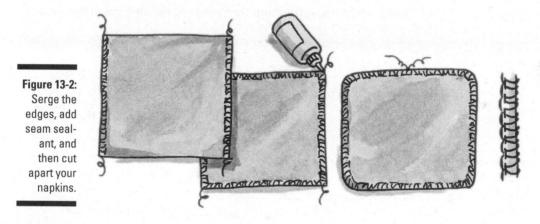

Figure 13-2:
Serge the edges, add seam sealant, and then cut apart your napkins.

TIP

Serging opposite edges makes the corners turn out square. To serge each napkin individually and create round corners, start by tracing around a dime at each corner. Trim off the excess fabric in the corners, cutting on the traced line. Starting in the center of one napkin edge, serge carefully, guiding the rolled edge toward and then around each corner.

Party-Ready Lapkins

Lapkins are cool double-duty napkins that have stitch channels sewn to hold silverware in place, perfect for portable picnics, barbecues, and buffets. You can create lapkins from napkins that you make or buy. You can see some in the color section that I made from linen napkins my mom wasn't using anymore.

To make these utensil-holding napkins you need the following materials in addition to your sewing survival kit (see Chapter 2):

- ✔ Set of finished napkins
- ✔ Thread that matches the fabric
- ✔ Flatware to fit each lapkin

Just follow these steps to create lapkins from napkins:

1. **Fold a napkin in half, creating a triangle, and press.**

2. **Turn back one corner, pressing the crease at the bottom of the smaller triangle shown on the left in Figure 13-3.**

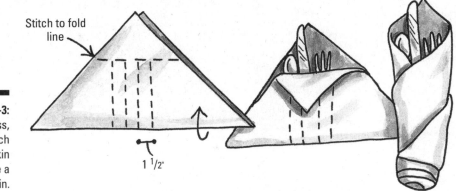

Stitch to fold line

1 1/2"

Figure 13-3: Fold, press, and stitch a napkin to create a lapkin.

3. **Using your fabric marker, draw four lines perpendicular to the long fold, about 1½ inches apart (see Figure 13-3).**

   Center the four marked lines so that the slots are centered in the napkin triangle.

4. **Set your machine like this:**
   - Stitch: Straight
   - Length: 3 to 3.5 mm/7 to 9 spi
   - Width: 0 mm
   - Foot: All-purpose

5. **Straight stitch over the marked lines, sewing from the bottom fold up to the crease and backstitching at the top and bottom of each row.**

6. **Slip in the flatware, roll up the lapkin, and you're ready for a feast.**

Hip to Be Square Tablecloth

After you sew this square tablecloth, simply place it on your table so that the points are centered on the sides and ends of the table — a process called *setting the square on point*. You can also use this tablecloth over another tablecloth to add color accents and dimension to your eating space.

To make the tablecloth, you need the following materials in addition to your sewing survival kit (see Chapter 2):

✔ Tablecloth fabric (see "Selecting Fabric for Table Toppers" earlier in this chapter for some suggestions). You need 1¼ yards of 45-inch-wide fabric for a 43-inch table square or 1½ yards of 54- to 55-inch-wide fabric for a 52-inch table square.

✔ Thread that matches the fabric.

✔ Four tassels (optional).

These few simple steps create a tablecloth you're proud to eat on:

1. **Cut the tablecloth fabric square.**

   For example, if you're working with 45-inch-wide fabric, cut a square 45 by 45 inches; if you're working with 54-inch fabric, cut a 54-inch square.

2. **Set your sewing machine like this:**

   - Stitch: Three-step zigzag
   - Length: 1.5 to 2 mm/13 to 15 spi
   - Width: 5 mm
   - Foot: All-purpose

   If you're using a serger, set your serger like this:

   - Stitch: Balanced three-thread overlock
   - Length: 2 mm
   - Width: 3 to 5 mm
   - Foot: Standard

3. **Finish the edges of the square.**

   Place the raw edge under the foot so that the needle catches the fabric on the left and swings off the raw edge at the right. After you finish the first edge, finish the edge on the opposite side. Do the same thing with the two remaining opposite edges.

4. **Pin and press a ½-inch hem on two opposite edges of the fabric square, as shown in Figure 13-4. Repeat for the other two sides.**

   This step ensures that the corners fold in correctly for secure hemming.

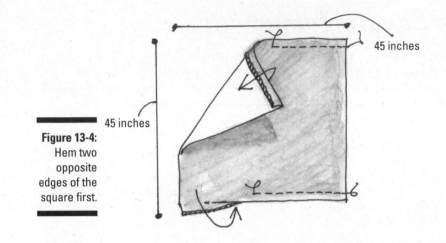

45 inches

45 inches

Figure 13-4:
Hem two
opposite
edges of the
square first.

5. **If you want to add a little razzle-dazzle to your tablecloth with tassels, slip in and pin one tassel at each corner, as shown in Figure 13-5.**

   For more on attaching long and short-looped tassels, see Chapter 12.

6. **Set your machine like this:**

   - Stitch: Straight
   - Length: 3.5 mm/7 spi
   - Width: 0 mm
   - Foot: All-purpose

7. **With the right side of the fabric up, topstitch around the hem edge, guiding the foot an even distance from the edge. Backstitch at the end of the topstitching.**

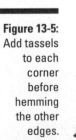

Figure 13-5:
Add tassels
to each
corner
before
hemming
the other
edges.

Chapter 14

Praiseworthy Pillows

. . . .

In This Chapter

▶ Starting with the right materials

▶ Covering a pillow form

▶ Creating an easy reversible pillow cover

▶ Making a flanged pillow cover from napkins

▶ Crafting a pillow-style pet bed

▶ Producing a modern box-edged pillow cover

. . . .

*P*illows prop us up, cushion our falls, and comfort weary heads. Pillows are also perfect palettes for playing with shape, color, texture, and design, and you can easily put together a pillow project in one stress-free sitting. In this chapter you discover the secrets of making praiseworthy pillows perfect for both people and their privileged pets.

Selecting Materials for Pillows

Achieving pillow perfection starts with using the right materials. Keep these tips in mind as you shop for materials for your pillows:

✔ **Fabrics:** For easy-care pillows, buy home décor fabrics that have a cotton fiber content of 50 percent or more. Also look for washable cotton/polyester blends and Polarfleece. Fabric napkins are another fabric option (and a great shortcut).

If you use a cotton novelty print, corduroy, denim, duck, chintz, twill, or poplin to make your pillow, preshrink the fabric before making the pillow cover.

The amount of fabric you need depends on the size of the pillow you want to cover and the kind of pillow cover you want to make. Because pillow forms are soft and pliable, the pillow cover pieces you cut are cut the same size as the pillow form without seam allowances (so a cover made to fit a 16-inch pillow form is 16 inches square). Adding seam allowances to your pillow covers makes them too big.

✔ **Thread:** You need all-purpose thread to match your pillow fabric.

✔ **Trims:** You have to use trims that are compatible with your fabric from a fiber and washability standpoint. When in doubt, have a sales associate at your local fabric store take a look at your trim and fabric choices to confirm their compatibility.

Many home décor fabrics recommend dry-clean-only care. If you choose such a fabric, make the pillow covers removable by adding a zipper or buttons and buttonholes (see Chapter 9 for specifics on several types of closures) and have them dry-cleaned to preserve their appearance. If you don't, fabrics may shrink, trims may disintegrate, and you may find that you spent all your time and creative energy for nothing.

✔ **Pillow forms:** The easiest stuffing to work with is a premade pillow form. This timesaving fabric-covered pillow is a given size, shape, density, and stuffing type (polyester or goose down) and pops into a decorative pillow cover. You can find pillow forms in many sizes and a variety of price ranges.

✔ **Stuffing:** For creating more free-formed pillow shapes like the bolster you make for the pet bed later on in this chapter, you need loose stuffing for filling and shaping. It comes in bags, and I refer to it as Polyfill because the loose fibers are made of polyester.

A Basic Cover Fit for a Pillow Form

In this section you see how easy making a pillow cover from start to finish can be. This pillow cover is the easiest way most pillow covers are made. It uses front and back pillow pieces that are stitched together. An opening is left large enough for the pillow form to slip through, and then the cover is slipstitched closed by hand (see Chapter 5 for more on slipstitching). When you want to wash or clean the pillow cover, you just loosen the hand stitching and remove the pillow.

The amount of fabric you need for this project depends on the size of the pillow you want to cover. Measure your pillow form (see the next section), or take it with you to the fabric store and ask the sales associate to cut enough yardage so you can cut two fabric squares exactly the size of your pillow form.

Measuring your pillow form and cutting the pillow front and back

Measure your premade pillow form from seam to seam across the middle before cutting the fabric for the pillow cover. Even though the package may say the pillow form is a 16-inch square, for example, dimensions do vary.

After you measure your pillow form, cut two squares the same size as the pillow form. For example, if you have a 16-inch pillow form, you cut two squares of fabric 16 x 16 inches — one for the front and one for the back.

Sewing the seams

Follow these steps to put the pillow cover together:

1. **If you want cord-edge trim, fringe, a ruffle, or piping sewn on the edge of the pillow, sew it onto the front pillow piece.**

   Read more about cutting, sewing, and joining these trims in Chapter 12.

2. **Place and pin the pillow front and back right sides together, leaving an opening half the width of the pillow form on one side of the cover.**

   If you're making a 16-inch pillow cover, leave an 8-inch opening.

   If the fabric has a directional design, leave the opening at the bottom edge so it doesn't show as much.

3. **Set your sewing machine like this:**
   - Stitch: Straight
   - Length: 3 to 3.5 mm/8 to 10 spi
   - Width: 0 mm
   - Foot: All-purpose

4. **Using a ½-inch seam allowance, sew the seam opposite the opening; then sew the side with the opening, backstitching on either side of the opening as shown in Figure 14-1a.**

   To make sure you can easily push the pillow form through, the opening should be half the width of the form. So if the form is 16 inches square, the opening should be at least 8 inches.

5. **Press the seams flat and together. Using your scissor tips, clip through one seam allowance to within ¼ inch of the backstitching on both sides of the opening (see Figure 14-1b).**

   This clipping trick makes it easier to slipstitch the opening closed, as you see later on in the project (see Chapter 6 for more on clipping using your scissor tips).

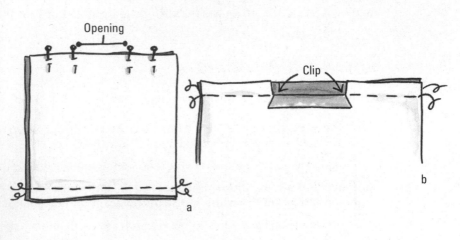

Wrapping the corners

You want nice-looking corners on your pillow covers, and this wrapped corner technique is one of my personal favorites. I love it because it's fast and easy and you're guaranteed to get square corners every time.

1. **Fold over and pin each corner at the stitching line (see Figure 14-2).**

2. **With a ½-inch seam allowance and same machine settings as before, sew the two remaining seams as shown in Figure 14-2, backstitching at the beginning and end of each seam.**

   Press the seams flat and together.

3. **Put your hand through the opening and turn the pillow cover right-side out, smoothing and squaring up the seams in each corner with your thumb and index finger.**

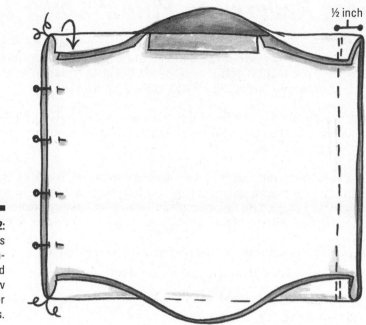

Figure 14-2:
Fold corners
at the stitch-
ing line, and
then sew
the other
two seams.

½ inch

Stitching the closure

Because you clipped through one layer of the opening seam allowance in "Sewing the seams" above, stitching the closure is a snap.

1. **Put the pillow form into the pillow cover through the opening on one side of the pillow cover.**

2. **Pin and hand sew an even slipstitch to close the opening:**

   1. Thread a hand needle and fasten the thread, bringing the needle out at the edge of the fold. (See Chapter 5 to find out about fastening the thread.)

   2. Taking fine stitches, slip the needle through the fold on one edge and draw the thread taut.

   3. Take another stitch, slipping the needle through the opposite folded edge. (See Chapter 5 for an illustration.)

   4. Continue to the end of the opening; then fasten the thread and trim the excess.

The Easiest Reversible Pillow Cover Ever

This pillow cover really is what the name says. I used some extra fabric left over from other projects to make the example in the bedding ensemble pictured in the color section of this book — it's the little rectangular pillow positioned in the place of honor smack dab in the center of the bed.

To get the right amount of fabric for this project, measure your pillow form or take it with you to the store and ask the sales associate to cut enough yardage so that you can cover it.

To make this clever pillow cover, you need the following supplies (in addition to the tools in the sewing survival kit that I tell you about in Chapter 2). The fabric yardage is based on my example, a 12-x-20-inch pillow form. To use a form of a different size or shape, adjust the amount of fabric as needed.

- ⅓ yard of 60-inch-wide, solid-colored home décor fabric
- ⅓ yard of coordinating 60-inch-wide print home décor fabric
- One 12-x-20-inch rectangular pillow form
- Thread that matches the fabric

Follow these steps:

1. **Cut each of your pillow-cover fabrics the size of your pillow form.**

2. **Your sewing machine settings depend on the type of fabric you're using, so start with a 2.5 mm/10 to 12 spi stitch length. Sew a test strip and then adjust your stitch length if you need to.**

3. **Placing the right sides together, pin and stitch the two short sides of the pillow cover with a ½-inch seam allowance as shown in Figure 14-3.**

   Press the seams flat and together; then press them open.

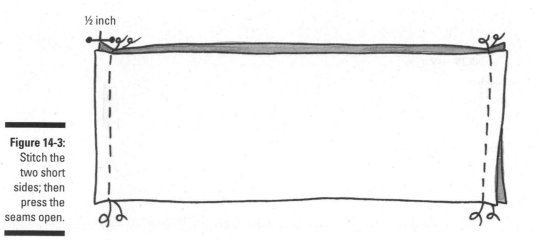

½ inch

Figure 14-3:
Stitch the two short sides; then press the seams open.

4. **Fold the pillow cover in half so the side seams are positioned as shown in Figure 14-4.**

5. **Pin and stitch the two long sides of the pillow cover, leaving an opening as shown in Figure 14-5.**

   Press the seams flat and together.

6. **On either side of the opening, clip through one of the seam allowances up to within ¼ inch of the stitching line (see Figure 14-5).**

7. **Trim away the excess fabric in each corner as shown in Figure 14-5.**

   This makes turning the pillow cover easier and the corners sharp and crisp.

8. **Turn the pillow cover through the opening, pushing out the corners smoothly with your index finger.**

   If you turn into a pillow-making whiz and want an easier way to make your corners square, buy a point turner. Several models are on the market, but they work essentially the same. Simply snug and gently push the triangular-shaped point of the tool into the corner. You get great-looking corners every time.

9. **Insert the pillow form into the cover, and evenly slipstitch the opening closed (see "Stitching the closure" above).**

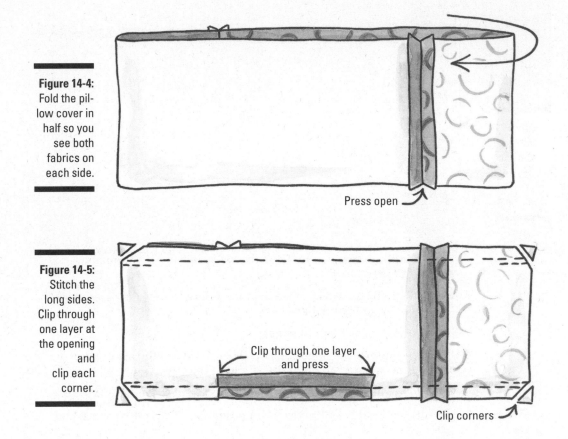

Figure 14-4:
Fold the pillow cover in half so you see both fabrics on each side.

Press open

Figure 14-5:
Stitch the long sides. Clip through one layer at the opening and clip each corner.

Clip through one layer and press

Clip corners

Put the pillow on the bed or sofa one way and most of one fabric shows; turn it over and the other fabric is the star. One pillow, two great looks.

15-Minute Flanged Pillow Cover

I made the bright orange and yellow pillows shown in the color section in 30 minutes by covering two pillow forms with napkins. When the covers are dirty, simply loosen a few stitches, remove the pillow forms, wash the covers (you can wash napkins, after all), press the wrinkles out, pop in the forms, and then restitch. Easy, easy, easy.

Follow these simple steps to become a pillow-cover pro:

1. **Buy two 20-inch napkins to cover one 16-inch pillow form.**

   With these measurements, the flange measures 2 inches all the way around the pillow cover.

2. **Preshrink the napkins and press them.**

3. **Place and pin the napkins wrong sides together.**

4. **Set your sewing machine like this:**

   • Stitch: Straight

   • Length: 2.5 to 3 mm/10 to 12 spi

   • Width: 0 mm

   • Foot: All-purpose

5. **Stitch a 2-inch seam around the napkins, leaving an 8-inch opening in one side.**

6. **Pop the pillow form through the opening in the stitched napkin cover.**

7. **Machine stitch the opening closed, backstitching at the ends.**

Plush Pet Bed

Make this really easy pet bed, shown in the color section of the book, using Polarfleece and a washable fabric that complement your décor. After making this project designed by my friends at DIYStyle (www.diystyle.net), you may amaze even yourself with your newfound creativity and sewing skills, and your favorite four-legged friend will be so happy.

You need the following materials in addition to your sewing survival kit (See Chapter 2 for a kit rundown):

✔ One 18-inch pillow form

✔ 1 yard of 45-inch washable cotton/polyester print fabric for the bolster

✔ ⅝ yard Polarfleece for the pillow

✔ 1 bag of Polyfill stuffing

✔ ¼ yard (9 inches) of hook-and-loop fastener

✔ Thread that matches the fabric

Making the bolster

Follow these steps to create the pillow. Be sure to preshrink the print fabric first so if Fido has an accident on his bed, it won't shrink in the wash. Note that Polarfleece doesn't need to be preshrunk because it doesn't shrink.

1. **Cut the print fabric into two 18-x-45-inch pieces.**

2. **Cut the fleece fabric so it measures 18 x 50 inches.**

3. **Set your machine like this:**

   - Stitch: Straight

   - Length: Appropriate for the fabric (see Chapter 5)

   - Width: 0 mm

   - Foot: All-purpose

4. **Place the two pieces of print fabric right sides together. Pin and sew them together on one of the short ends (see Figure 14-6).**

Figure 14-6: Place, pin, and sew two short ends of print together. Press 1-inch hems on the remaining two short ends.

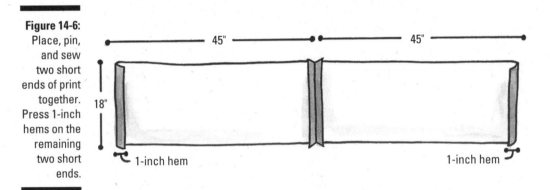

5. **Press, pin, and stitch 1-inch hems on the remaining short ends, as shown in Figure 14-6.**

6. **Fold the strip made in Step 5 in half lengthwise and with right sides together.**

7. **Place, pin, and stitch the long seam, right sides together, leaving an 8-inch opening as shown in Figure 14-7. Press the long seam open and so it is centered in the strip as shown (see Figure 14-7).**

   This piece (used to make the bolster of the bed) should look like a long skinny tube, inside out.

Figure 14-7:
Sew the
print fabric
into a long
skinny tube,
leaving an
opening
to put the
Polyfill stuff-
ing through.

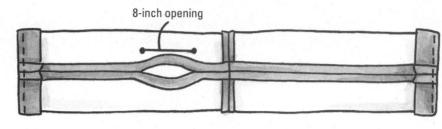

Figure 14-7:
Sew the
print fabric
into a long
skinny tube,
leaving an
opening
to put the
Polyfill stuff-
ing through.

8-inch opening

8. **Turn the tube right-side out through one of the openings at either end.**

9. **Stitch each end closed, and then sew the hook-and-loop strips to both ends of the tube as shown in Figure 14-8.**

10. **Stuff the bolster with Polyfill and set it aside until you've completed the fleece pillow cover that it fits around (see the next section).**

Figure 14-8:
Turn the
tube right-
side out
and sew
the hook-
and-loop
fastener on
both ends.

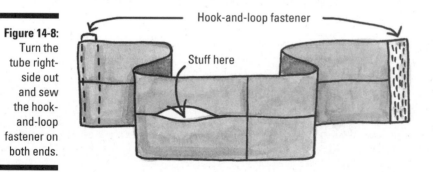

Hook-and-loop fastener

Stuff here

Creating the fleece pillow cover

The bolster from the previous section fits around the cozy fleece pillow that you create by following these steps. Note that instead of stitching two pieces together to make the cover, this pillow cover wraps around the pillow form.

1. **Set your machine like this:**

   • Stitch: Zigzag

   • Length: 2.5 to 3 mm/9 to 11 spi

- Width: 4 to 5 mm

- Foot: Embroidery

2. **Turn under one short end of the fleece yardage to create a 4-inch hem. Pin and stitch using a zigzag stitch, as shown in Figure 14-9.**

Figure 14-9:
Fold and zigzag stitch 4-inch hems on both short ends of the fleece yardage.

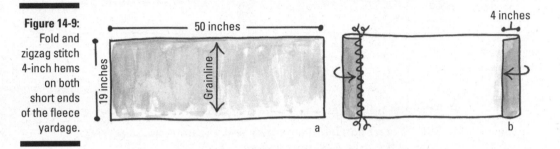

3. **Repeat Step 2 on the other short end of the fleece.**

4. **With right sides together, lap the fleece over the pillow form as shown in Figure 14-10; pin the cover in place, then slip out the pillow form.**

Figure 14-10:
From the wrong side, fold and overlap the short ends, pin together, and remove the pillow form.

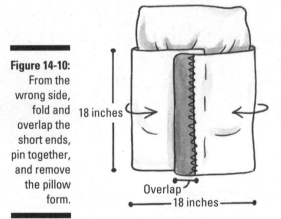

5. **Set your machine like this:**

- Stitch: Straight

- Length: 3 to 4 mm/6 to 9 spi

- Width: 0 mm

- Foot: All-purpose

6. **Sew a ½-inch seam along the top and bottom openings of the pillow cover, backstitching at both ends of each seam. Take out the pins holding the overlapped flaps together.**

   The stitching at the top and bottom holds the pillow cover in shape, and the overlapping fabric flaps form an "envelope" that the pillow form can be inserted through.

7. **Turn the pillow cover right-side out and pop the pillow form into the cover through the overlapping opening in the back.**

Putting the bed together

Here comes the fun part: putting everything together. Your little prince or princess will be napping in a new bed in no time.

1. **Connect the hook-and-loop fastener on the two short ends of the bolster, creating a skinny fabric inner tube.**

2. **Firmly push the bolster over the fleece-covered pillow; you may need to squish the pillow form in and pull it up into the bolster a little bit to get the bed to look like Figure 14-11.**

3. **Remove the bolster from around the pillow and add or remove some fiber fill so the bolster fits; then adjust the hook-and-loop fastener if it's too snug or too loose around the center pillow.**

4. **Slipstitch the opening of the bolster closed (see "Stitching the closure" above for instructions), and then reposition it around the center pillow.**

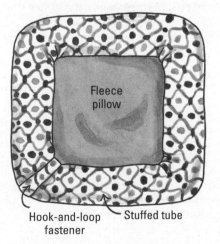

Figure 14-11:
Push the bolster over the pillow, and voilà — a very cool and stylish pet bed.

Fleece pillow

Hook-and-loop fastener — Stuffed tube

Box-Edged Pillow

Box-edged pillows, popular in the 1950s, have popped back onto the decorating scene. They look like small sofa cushions — two rows of piping with a strip of fabric in between called a *boxing strip* that runs around the outside edge. (Check out the cream-colored pillows on the bed in the color section.) For a tufted look, they often have fabric-covered buttons stitched in the center.

To make a box-edged pillow, you need the following supplies in addition to the sewing survival kit (see Chapter 2 for details):

- One 14-inch pillow form (If you can find a box-edged pillow form the size that you need, buy it; otherwise, use a regular pillow form.)
- ½ yard of 48- to 54-inch-wide home décor fabric
- One 60-x-2-inch contrasting home décor fabric for the boxing strip
- Thread that matches the fabric
- Four yards of piping that coordinates with the pillow and boxing strip fabric. (See Chapter 12 for piping instructions.)
- Two ½- to 2-inch covered button sets; one button goes on each side of the pillow (optional)
- Long hand-sewing needle used in doll making (optional)

Follow these steps to create the pillow:

1. **Cut two 14-inch squares of home décor fabric; set one aside.**

   You don't need to allow extra fabric for seam allowances because the boxing strip adds the room you need for creating the flat sides. Because of the softness of the pillow forms, if you add seam allowances, the pillow cover comes out too big.

2. **Set your sewing machine like this:**
   - Stitch: Straight
   - Length: 3 mm/9 spi
   - Width: 0 mm
   - Foot: Zipper or piping

3. **Using a ½-inch seam allowance, pin and stitch the piping to the right side and all the way around the first pillow square (see Chapter 12 for a more detailed explanation of attaching piping).**

4. **Repeat Step 3 for the other pillow square.**

5. **Pin the boxing strip to the first pillow square as shown in Figure 14-12a.**

   Starting anywhere but at a corner, pin the boxing strip to the right side of the pillow square so that the raw edges of the piping and the fabric are even.

   The boxing strip is intentionally cut longer than needed to go around the pillow square. This way, you don't run short of boxing strip fabric, and you can cut it to fit.

6. **Sew on the boxing strip at the ½-inch seamline. Stop sewing about 2 inches before the end of the boxing strip.**

   When pinning and sewing around a corner, clip the seam allowance of the boxing strip up to, but not through, the seamline. With the needle down in the fabric, raise the foot and pivot slightly. Lower the presser foot and continue sewing a gentle curve rather than a sharp corner to accommodate the bulk of the piping and boxing strip fabrics.

Figure 14-12: Starting anywhere but a corner, pin on the boxing strip (a). For additional detail, add piping on the edges and buttons to the center of the pillow (b).

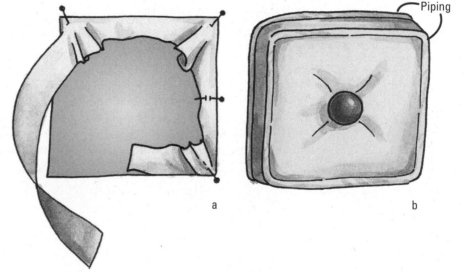

Piping

a   b

7. **Pin and seam the short ends of the boxing strip together and then press the seam open.**

8. **Stitch the rest of the boxing strip to the edge of the first pillow square.**

9. **Repeat Steps 5 and 6, attaching the second piped pillow square to the other side of the boxing strip but this time leaving a 5- to 6-inch opening for the pillow form to fit through.**

   If the fabric has a directional design, leave the opening at the bottom edge so it doesn't show as much.

10. **Turn the pillow right-side out and push the pillow form through the opening of the pillow cover and slipstitch it closed.**

    See "Stitching the closure" above and Chapter 5 for more on slipstitching.

11. **If you want to add buttons to the center of the pillow, sew them on by following these steps:**

    1. Cover the buttons with matching or contrasting fabric as directed in the button-covering kit.

    2. Poke the end of a long thread through the eye of a long needle, pulling it so both thread ends are even. Treating them as one, tie a knot (see Chapter 5 for knot-tying instructions).

    3. Push the needle through the center of one side of the pillow and bring it through to the other side.

    4. Thread one button onto the needle, snugging the button down to the surface of the pillow.

    5. Push the needle back through to the other side of the pillow, and repeat Step 4 with the second button. Now both buttons are secured to the pillow and each other.

    6. Repeat Steps 3 through 5 several times so that you secure both buttons together through the pillow, as shown in Figure 14-12b. Then secure the stitch by sewing a knot (see Chapter 5 for instructions).

Chapter 15

Adding Wow to Your Windows

In This Chapter

▶ Working with windows and window treatments

▶ Finding out how much fabric you need

▶ Creating wonderful window panels

*I*f you're transitioning to a new apartment or home or updating your current abode, making your own window treatments is a great way to save money and get the look you want. This chapter tells you how to work with all kinds of window treatments, and you find out how to create a drape that fits almost any window that's easy on the eyes — and the pocketbook!

The Wide World of Window Treatments

When starting your journey through the vast world of window treatments, you first need to consider some basic design elements. No matter what room you work in, remember that every room has three common elements: *eye-level* décor, *mid-level* décor, and *floor-level* décor.

Most people do a great job on the floor-level décor, which includes flooring, carpet, area rugs, and floor pillows. Just about everyone does a good job with the mid-level décor, which includes sofas, chairs, tables, and lamps. The most neglected design element in a room (and the one that makes the most impact) is the eye-level decor — or the window treatments.

If you've checked out custom window treatments and their prices, you're probably not surprised at the number of naked windows in so many homes and apartments. But before you take out a second mortgage for your window treatments, I want you to know that affordable alternatives are available. In fact, sewing your own window treatments can save you up to 75 percent of custom treatments. So no more excuses — now's the time to dress those naked windows.

Dealing with draperies and curtains

Use *curtains,* or short treatments that stop at or just below the windowsill, for shorter, narrower windows (see Figure 15-1). Use *draperies,* long treatments that stop at the floor or *puddle* onto the floor, for longer, wider windows.

Figure 15-1: Double cafe curtains (a) and sheers (b) look great on short windows.

Window treatments can attach to the rod in a variety of ways. The pinch pleat (Figure 15-2a) is a more formal treatment great for formal living rooms, formal dining rooms, and master bedrooms. Grommetted treatments (Figure 15-2b) are modern and informal, great for family rooms and kid's rooms. Both shirred and tab-top treatments (Figure 15-2c and d) are informal and have more of a country or lodge feeling, great for family rooms and kitchens.

Use the following ideas alone or together with curtains or draperies for just about any window:

✔ **Puddles:** A puddle uses drapery fabric that measures 12 to 20 inches longer than a standard drapery from the top of the rod to the floor. The hem edge is shirred in with a rubber band or cord and then spreads out or "puddles" onto the floor (see Figure 15-3a).

✔ **Cornice:** A rigid box covered with fabric and padded with a soft batting or contoured foam (see Figure 15-3b). Use a cornice alone over the top of a window, over draperies, or over vertical blinds mounted on a traverse rod (see the next section for information on the different rod types).

✔ **Scarf or swag:** A soft, usually sheer fabric that drapes over the top of swag holders at each corner of the window (see Figure 15-3c). (You can find several types of swag holders where drapery hardware is sold.)

✔ **Bishop sleeves:** You create these sleeves by tying back drapes and then pulling up slack so that the drapery blouses over the tieback and looks like a puffed sleeve when gathered in at the cuff (see Figure 15-3d).

✔ **Poufs and rosettes:** Short lengths of fabric pulled into a loop along the length of a drapery scarf that fan out, creating soft, roselike poufs that look sort of like puffed sleeves at the corners of the window.

✔ **Tiebacks:** Made of fabric or drapery cord and tassels, tiebacks hold a drapery open at the side of a window.

✔ **Window topper:** Any treatment mounted at the top of the window — from a cornice to a short skirt shirred onto a rod.

If you're itching to know more about other aspects of design, check out *Home Decorating For Dummies,* 2nd Edition, by Katharine Kaye McMillan and Patricia Hart McMillan (Wiley).

Figure 15-2:
Draperies can feature pinch pleats (a) or grommets (b); they may be shirred (c) or have tab tops (d).

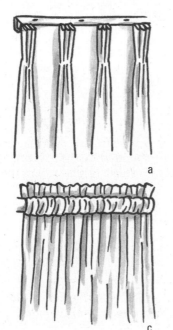

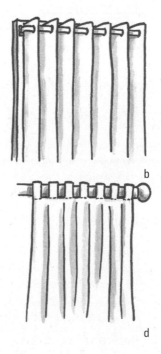

a

b

c

d

Figure 15-3:
Puddled
draperies
(a), cor-
nices (b),
swags (c),
and bishop
sleeves (d)
add drama
to your
windows.

Exploring the anatomy of windows and rods

The mullion's connected to the . . . window sash; the sash slides into the . . . window frame; the window frame is surrounded by the . . . trim mold. If you know the tune but these words makes no sense to you, now's the time to dis-cover the language of windows (as shown in Figure 15-4).

Check out these standard window parts:

- ✔ **Apron:** A piece of wood that attaches under the windowsill. On windows that don't have sills, the apron looks like a continuation of the trim mold.

- ✔ **Overlap:** The piece of hardware attached in the center where one drap-ery crosses over the other on a two-way draw traverse rod.

- ✔ **Return:** Where the rod or cornice turns the corner and returns to the wall. Depending on the depth of the return, you may have enough room for another rod to fit behind it, allowing you to layer your draperies.

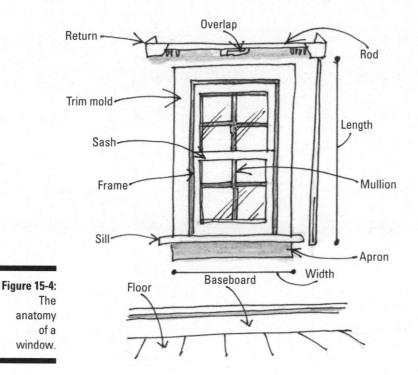

Figure 15-4:
The anatomy of a window.

- ✔ **Rod:** Holds the drapery or curtain in place over the window.

- ✔ **Trim mold:** The wood that has been nailed around the window to trim or finish the opening.

- ✔ **Window length:** The distance measured from the top to the bottom of the window. Outside window length is measured from the outside edge of the trim mold to the bottom of the apron. If the window doesn't have an apron, the outside window length is from the outside edge of the trim mold to the bottom of the sill. Inside length is the distance from the top of the window frame to the top of the sill.

- ✔ **Windowsill:** A piece of trim extending from the window and running parallel to the floor, usually at the bottom of the window. This is the part you set your coffee cup on.

- ✔ **Window width:** The distance measured across the window. Outside window width measures from one outside edge of the trim mold to the other outside edge of the trim mold. Inside window width measures from one side of the window to the other, inside the window frame.

Rods come in a variety of shapes and sizes (see Figure 15-5). The type of rod you use depends on what sort of window treatment you want to make:

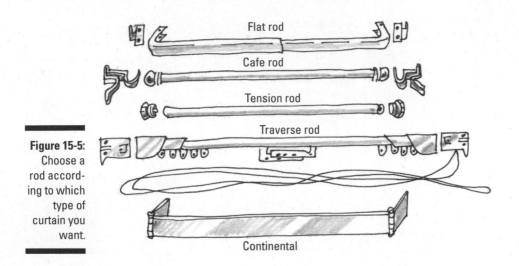

Flat rod

Cafe rod

Tension rod

Traverse rod

Continental

- ✔ **Cafe rods:** Mounted either inside or outside the window frame. Cafe rods work well for straight, shirred, or pleated curtains.

- ✔ **Flat rods:** Hold shirred drapery panels by threading the rod through the casing at the top of the panels. This very basic window treatment needs a cornice, valance, or other window topper to go over the curtain at the top of the window frame.

- ✔ **Tension rods:** Best for lightweight curtains. Tension rods are held between walls or inside a window frame by a spring-type mechanism inside the rod rather than by a bracket that you screw into the wall.

- ✔ **Traverse rods:** Include a drapery cord that you pull to open or close the draperies. Some traverse rods let you pull the draperies across to one side, and others move the drapery panels from the center so that one ends up on each side.

Determining Window Treatment Dimensions

After you select the curtain or drapery style you want to use for your window and determine the sort of rod you need, you need to determine what size your window treatments need to be and how much fabric is required for the finished look.

Measuring the finished width and length

The first step is measuring your windows to determine the *finished* width and length of the treatment — the width and length of the curtain or drapery when you finish it and hang it over the window.

Keep these guidelines in mind for accurate measurements:

- **Install the curtain rod first.** If you have the rod installed when you take your measurements, you're able to accurately measure the needed width and length. Rods can attach to the window frame inside the window frame (called an *inside mount*), outside the window frame or trim mold (called an *outside mount*), or on the ceiling (called a *ceiling mount*). As of publication, today's interior fashion trend is for rods to hang well above the top of the window trim. This helps to make ceilings look higher and let more light into the room.

- **Use a substantial metal measuring tape.** Cloth measuring tapes, which may stretch or sag, and flimsy metal tapes, which are difficult to use, can both cause inaccurate measurements.

- **If you're making window treatments for several windows, take measurements for each window.** Even when the windows look the same size, their measurements may vary. You want to make sure each treatment fits the window it's intended for.

To determine the finished length to make your curtains and draperies, measure from the top of the rod to the desired length. To determine the finished width, measure the rod from end to end plus returns (the part of the rod that "returns" to the wall).

Curtains for a window without an apron should have a finished length that's at least 4 inches below the windowsill or below the bottom of the frame. This way, your curtain is in proportion to the window. (See "Exploring the anatomy of windows and rods" earlier in this chapter.) If the window does have an apron, the finished length of the drape should be 1 inch below the bottom of the apron.

Calculating cut fabric length and width

After you know the finished measurements for your window treatment (see the previous section), you need to calculate the cut length of the fabric.

Pattern instructions for curtains and draperies tell you to cut so many *panels* for a particular project. Panels are simply a certain length of fabric used at the widest width of the fabric.

Looking for length

You determine the cut length of the curtain or drapery by taking the finished length (the length of the curtain or drapery when you finish it and hang it over the window) and adding additional fabric to allow for the following parts (some of which are shown in Figure 15-6):

- **Casing:** A fabric tunnel at the top of a curtain or drapery panel that you thread onto a rod

- **Heading:** Decorative extra fabric above the casing that looks like a little ruffle after you thread the casing onto the rod

- **Doubled lower hem:** Twice-folded hems to give the curtain weight

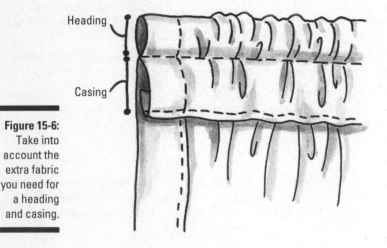

Heading

Casing

Figure 15-6:
Take into account the extra fabric you need for a heading and casing.

When you begin making window treatments, choose fabric that is a solid color or has a very small design. Treatments become much more difficult to work with when you have to try to match a large-pattern design.

Follow these easy steps to determine how much extra fabric to add to the finished length of your curtain or drapery:

1. **Using your tape measure, measure the curtain rod's diameter.**

2. **Add an inch to the measurement you determined in Step 1.**

   This extra inch accounts for a ½-inch seam allowance, and you also have plenty of extra room for the rod to slide smoothly through the casing.

3. **Decide how high (if at all) you want the heading to extend above the rod, and double that length.**

   For example, if you want a 2-inch heading, add another 4 inches to the length of the fabric you need to cut.

   If you don't want a heading, go on to Step 4.

4. **Determine how much extra length to add for the doubled hem, according to the following guidelines:**

   - **Sheer and lightweight fabrics:** Use a 6-inch double-fold hem by adding 12 inches to the cut length.

   - **Mid-weight fabric:** Use a 4-inch double-fold hem by adding 8 inches to the cut length.

   - **Heavyweight fabric:** Use a 3-inch double-fold hem by adding 6 inches to the cut length.

5. **If you're making a drapery and you want it to puddle on the floor, add 18 to 20 extra inches.**

   Skip this step if you don't want the drapery to puddle or if you're making a curtain.

6. **Add the measurements from Steps 2 through 5 to the finished length of your curtain and you have the cut length needed for one drapery panel.**

Determining width

To determine the cut curtain or drapery width, you need to take the following into account:

- **Fabric weight:** The lighter the fabric weight, the more fullness you want in the treatment. Lightweight fabric is more likely to look skimpy. Follow these general guidelines to figure out the ideal drapery width for your situation:

  - **Sheer and lightweight fabric:** Use 2½ to 3 times the rod width (including the returns).

  - **Mid-weight fabric:** Use 2 to 2½ times the rod width (including the returns).

  - **Heavyweight fabric:** Use 1½ to 2 times the rod width (including the returns).

- **Fabric width:** Most treatments use more than one fabric width, or panel, so that you have enough fabric spanning across the window for pulling up the gathers, pleats, and shirring. For example, in a set of sheer panel draperies, you may see three separate panels shirred onto a rod and each finished panel may be made from two cut panels.

If a fabric is 54-inches wide and you need two and a half widths to make a drapery, that means you need two 54-inch panels and one 27-inch panel.

✔ **Seam allowances:** Seam allowances for home décor projects are usually ½ inch. For easy pattern matching, home décor fabrics have match points and/or color bars printed in the selvages (the finished edges that run the length of the fabric), and if the fabric is printed, the print usually starts ½ inch in from the selvage (see Figure 15-7 to see the selvage match points).

✔ **Side hems:** The right and left edges of the drapery are called side hems. Side hems are created using narrower drapery lining (as in the following drapery project). This helps the fabric hang straight and even on the edges.

Custom Draperies

This project, shown in the color section of the book, uses one home décor fabric and drapery lining. Lining your draperies makes them hang better and wear longer. The lining also acts as another barrier between the window glass and the rest of the room to prevent drafts. Who knew such a decorative accent could be good for your heating bill?

To make this drapery, you need your sewing survival kit (which I tell you about in Chapter 2), plus the following items:

✔ One solid-colored mid-weight drapery fabric and one drapery lining up to 60 inches wide. (See "Determining how much fabric you need" in the next section to calculate the specific yardage.)

✔ A drapery rod and hardware. (See the section earlier in this chapter called "Exploring the anatomy of windows and rods" that describes the different types of rods.)

✔ Enough drapery rings with *mitten clips* (which pinch together to attach the rings to the top of the drapery panel, similar to those your mom used to attach your mittens to your winter jacket) to fit across the panels(s).

✔ Enough drapery header tape (a special interfacing that's sewn into the top of the drapery for stability) to span across the top of each drapery. (See more on drapery headers in the later section "Heading off rips with the drapery header.")

✔ Thread that matches the fabric.

Determining how much fabric you need

Follow these steps to determine how much mid-weight fabric you need to buy for your curtain or drapery.

For your first drapery project, remember to choose a fabric that is either a solid color or a texture. If you don't, you won't have enough fabric to match the design.

1. **Install your drapery rod following the manufacturer's instructions.**

2. **Measure the width of your drapery rod in inches.**

3. **Multiply the width of your drapery rod by 2.**

   For example, if your rod is 58 inches wide, 58 inches × 2 = 116 inches.

4. **Determine how many panels of fabric you need by dividing the number you get in Step 3 by the width of your fabric.**

   Using the same example, 116 inches divided by 60-inch width fabric = 1.93, which you round up to 2 panels. So one panel goes on the left side of the window and the second panel goes on the right side of the window.

   If you get an uneven number of panels, you'll cut one in half and sew the remaining panels together evenly into two larger panels.

5. **Measure from the top of the rod to the place you want your curtains or drapery to end.**

   If your rod is a foot below the 8-foot-high ceiling and you want the drapes to skim the floor, you measure 84 inches.

6. **Add 6 inches to the measurement in Step 5 for the double hems.**

   For example, 84 inches in length + 6 inches for hems = 90 inches in total length.

7. **Multiply the number you get in Step 6 by the number of panels you need (see Step 4). This is the length of fabric you need in inches.**

   Using the same example, you need 90 inches × 2 panels = 180 inches of fabric.

8. **Divide the number you get in Step 7 by 36. This is the length of fabric you need in yards.**

   You would need to buy 5 yards of 60-inch fabric. You need the same amount for the lining.

Putting the drapery together

Follow these steps to create a great-looking drapery:

1. **If you're using more than one panel per side of the window, seam the fabric panels together at the selvages and match points as shown in Figure 15-7, using a ½-inch seam allowance. (See Chapter 6 for more information on seaming.)**

2. **Double hem the lining by turning up and pressing a 2-inch hem, then turning it up again and topstitching it in place (see more on topstitching in Chapter 5).**

3. **Double hem the drapery fabric by turning up and pressing a 3-inch hem, then turning it up again and blind hemming it in place (see more on machine blind hemming in Chapter 7).**

4. **Press both hems smooth.**

5. **Place the lining and drapery fabric right sides together so the hemmed lining is 2 inches shorter than the hemmed drapery.**

6. **Cut the lining fabric 4 inches narrower and even with the top edge of the drapery fabric as shown in Figure 15-8.**

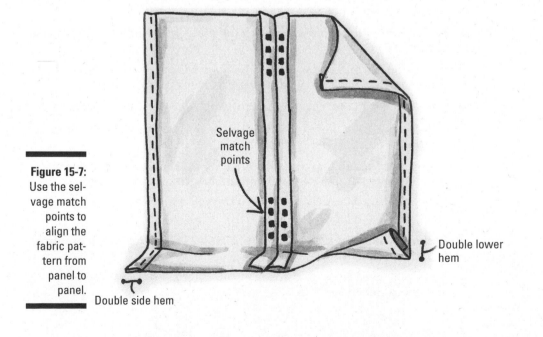

Figure 15-7: Use the selvage match points to align the fabric pattern from panel to panel.

Selvage match points

Double lower hem

Double side hem

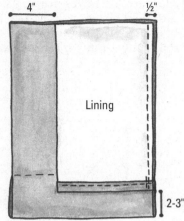

Figure 15-8:
Place the lining and drapery fabrics right sides together and sew a ½-inch seam along one side.

7. **Sew a ½-inch seam attaching the lining to the side of the drapery fabric as shown in Figure 15-8, stopping the seam 1 inch above the top of the lining hem.**

8. **Shift the fabrics so that the free edge of the lining aligns with the free edge of drapery fabric. Repeat Step 7 along this edge, as shown in Figure 15-9a.**

   When you shift the lining and the drapery fabric in order to sew the second lengthwise seam, you create the foldover hem that you see along the right side of Figure 15-9a.

9. **Press the seams flat and together and toward the lining.**

10. **Center the lining on the drapery fabric and baste across the top of the drapery (see Figure 15-9b).**

Figure 15-9:
Sew the other side of the lining to the face fabric (a); baste across the top of the drapery, centering the lining on the panel (b).

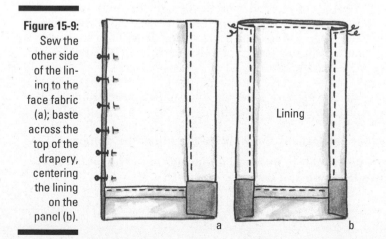

11. **For sharp-looking corners, turn under the lower drapery hem so it makes a miter at one corner and hand slipstitch as shown in Figure 15-10 (see more about mitering corners in Chapter 11 and slipstitching in Chapter 5). Repeat for the other side of the drapery hem.**

Figure 15-10:
Sew the drapery and lining together, stopping 1 inch above the lining hem (a); then miter each corner and slip-stitch (b).

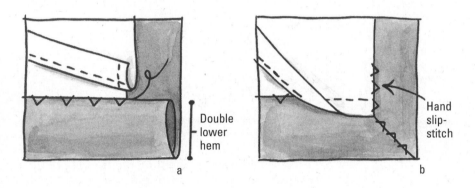

Double lower hem

Hand slip-stitch

a

b

12. **Repeat Steps 1 through 11 for the drapery on the other side of the window.**

Heading off rips with the drapery header

Not to confuse things — or anything — but a drapery *heading* is at the top of a shirred drape that is gathered onto a drapery rod or pole (refer to Figure 15-6). A drapery *header* is a stiff strip of interfacing-like tape that's 4 to 5 inches wide and is used at the top of the drapery panel to reinforce the top so the drapery hardware (hooks, rings, mitten clips, or whatever you use to attach the drapery panels to the rod) won't rip through the fabric when they're attached to the drapery. For this project the header is sewn inside the drape and the mitten clip–type rings attach over the top of the header before the panel goes onto the rod.

Follow these steps on one drapery panel at a time to finish the drapes and transform your room from boring to beautiful:

1. **Cut the header tape exactly the width of the top of the drapery.**

2. **Pin and sew the header to the seam allowance at the top of the drapery as shown in Figure 15-11a.**

3. **Turn the drapery right-side out and press.**

4. **Topstitch around all four sides of the drapery header as shown in Figure 15-11b (read more about topstitching in Chapter 7).**

Figure 15-11:
Pin and stitch the header to the top of the drapery (a); then turn it right-side out and finish by topstitching around all four sides of the header.

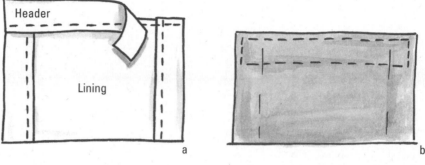

5. **Clip the mitten clips that are attached to the drapery rings over the top of the curtain, spacing them equidistantly across the width of the drape.**

6. **Thread the rod through the rings and hang up your creation.**

If your rod has a knob or *finial* (a decorative doodad) on the end, remove it by gently pulling it off or unscrewing it. Thread your drapery rings onto the rod, and then put the knob or finial back onto the rod and hang up your treatment. Follow these same simple steps to remove your drapery for cleaning.

Chapter 16

Giving Your Bed a Makeover

In This Chapter
▶ Giving your bedroom a makeover the easy way
▶ Making the easiest tailored bed skirt ever
▶ Creating a duvet cover

The bed is the focal point of most bedrooms, so the easiest way to give your bedroom a fresh new look is to transform the bedding. From the bed skirt and the duvet cover to the shams and throw pillows, changing one or all these elements is guaranteed to make a huge difference in your room. And even though they may seem like daunting projects, bedroom sewing projects can actually be very simple, and the satisfaction and pride you'll get from making over your bedroom will make you want to show it off to all who enter your home.

In this chapter I show you how to make a crisp pleated bed skirt and a simple duvet cover from flat sheets. To complete your bedroom makeover, turn to Chapter 14 to create matching pillow shams and a clever reversible accent pillow using your leftover bedding fabric. Finally, dress your naked windows with one of the terrific window treatments from Chapter 15. Putting your sewing skills to work to give your bedroom a new look is easier than you think, and you'll get exactly what you want.

Saving Money by Crafting a Bedding Set

Sure, you can by one of those "bed-in-a-bag" bedding sets from big-box stores or online — and they can be quite reasonably priced — but you can't count on finding one you're really wild about. Either the fabric is poor quality, the color is wrong, or the bed skirt is too short and flimsy. You can get exactly the look you want by creating your own bedding set, using flat sheets to make the duvet cover. Sheets are large, so you don't need to do a lot of matching or seaming, and they're available in many colors and designs. And because a duvet cover is easy to launder and change, if you keep the bed skirt and drapes a neutral color, you can have a wardrobe of duvet covers that can be changed for the season or on a wild decorating whim.

The biggest challenge with most home décor projects is handling the length, bulk, and weight of the larger pieces of fabric. Clear away some space on the floor, move everything off the dining room table, and gather up an extra folding table and ironing board before you get to sewing! If you don't, you'll be scrambling at the last minute trying to find this extra space, so plan on it now to save some frustration later.

Pleated Bed Skirt

A bed skirt, sometimes called a dust ruffle, fits between the mattress and box spring and drops to the floor, covering up the unsightly box spring, bed frame, and side rails. I like making my own bed skirts because I use better fabric for a really rich look to the bedroom. (If you're in quandary about how to coordinate your bed skirt fabric with the other fabric in your room, see Chapters 12 and 20 for advice.)

When working with extra-long seams like those in both of this chapter's projects, hold the fabric taut in front of and behind the presser foot as you sew. Sew a few inches and then reposition your hands, keeping even tautness in front of and behind the presser foot as you proceed along the length of the seam. Doing so keeps the seams flat and easier to press and helps you keep the excess fabric out of your way.

Thanks to my friend Devin Knuu, owner of dk design studio in Toronto, Canada (and designer par excellence), the clever bed skirt that you create in this project is not only easy to make, it's easy to press. Most bed skirts have a large, flat piece of fabric positioned between the mattress and box spring with a skirt around three sides. When storing or moving this type of bed skirt, you can't fold everything flat or hang it on a hanger, so it gets full of wrinkles. Then when you try pressing it, the bulky flat piece of fabric weighs everything down and the skirt slides off the ironing board, so pressing out all the wrinkles is tough. The following bed skirt does away with the large, flat middle section, making it easier to store and press with minimal wrinkling, and also easy to put on the bed.

This bed skirt is three-sided (the headboard side doesn't have a skirt on it) and is designed for a bed without posts or a footboard. If your bed has either a footboard or posts, you can buy a bed skirt pattern specifically suited to fit around those pieces.

To make the bed skirt you need the following materials in addition to your sewing survival kit (see Chapter 2):

- Solid-colored woven fabric (see Table 16-1 below to find out the right amount of fabric for your bed size).
- Thread that matches the fabric.

✔ A heavy, ultrafirm, nonwoven stabilizer (a stiff, almost cardboard-like fabric available in the interfacing section of your local fabric store) like Pellon's Peltex70 (see "Buying your fabric" later in this chapter to find out how much you need).

Some nonwoven stabilizers have a fusible (iron-on) coating on one or both sides. Be sure to use nonfusible stabilizer so you don't gunk up your iron.

✔ Twist pins (they look like a pin with a little pig tail).

✔ Masking tape.

Measuring the box spring

To make sure the skirt entirely covers the box spring and the space beneath the bed, you need to take the measurements shown in Figure 16-1. Take the mattress off your bed and measure and write down the measurements of the box spring on the bed. You're looking for the width, the length, and the *drop,* which is the measurement from the top of your box spring to the floor.

✔ Width: _____

✔ Length: _____

✔ Drop: _____

You need these measurements to help determine how much fabric to buy and cut out for the base and the skirt.

Figure 16-1:
For a perfect fit, measure your box spring after taking off the mattress.

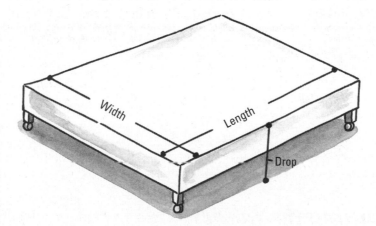

Don't think you can shortcut this measuring step by leaving the mattress on the box spring, or you'll end up scrapping the first bed skirt and starting over (ask me how I know)!

Buying your fabric

To provide structure to this bed skirt you need a stiff nonwoven base fabric (buy 2 yards for twin- and full-sized mattresses; buy 2¼ yards for queen- and king-sized mattresses). I used a product called Peltex70 by Pellon. This stiff fabric is cut into 6½-inch strips, stitched to the edge of the skirt, and then attached to the box spring, so you need something firm and stable.

You make the skirt itself by sewing strips of fabric together. The amount of fabric needed depends on the size of your bed and the width of your fabric. For this project, use a quality home décor fabric at least 54-inches wide. Narrower fabrics don't work unless you want to waste a lot of fabric. A normal drop (the distance the bed skirt measures from the top of the box spring to the floor) is 14 inches, and 54-inch fabric allows you to cut strips that are at least 18-inches long to allow for nice 2-inch double hems.

I recommend that you stick to polyester-cotton blends (for easy care) in solid colors or textures (tasks get more complicated when you have to match patterns). Using the guidelines in Table 16-1, buy enough fabric to fit your bed. Note that I err on the side of too much, so you have a little leftover just in case you make a mistake.

Note: The approximate size of each mattress is listed below. Compare these measurements to the box spring measurements you took to make sure they're the same. If your measurements are larger, go for the higher amount of fabric in the range. If yours are smaller, stick to the smaller end of the range.

Table 16-1	Yardage Chart for Pleated Bed Skirt
Bed Size	*Length of 54- to 60-Inch-Wide Home Décor Fabric Needed*
Twin (39 x 75 inches)	2½ yards
Full (54 x 75 inches)	2½ to 2¾ yards
Queen (60 x 80 inches)	2¾ to 3 yards
King (76 x 80 inches)	3 to 3¼ yards
California king (72 x 84 inches)	3 to 3¼ yards

Cutting the fabric

This skirt part of the bed skirt is constructed using five separate fabric strips — three straight sides with a pleat positioned at each corner at the foot of the bed. Because you want each side of the bed skirt to be made of a long continuous piece of fabric, you lay out and cut the fabric the long way — parallel with the selvages. In the biz we call this *railroading* the fabric because you cut long continuous pieces of fabric, like a railroad track.

Cutting the width of the skirt and pleat pieces

Use these guidelines to cut the fabric strips:

1. **Cut three 6½-inch wide strips of fabric stabilizer.**

   Peltex is 20-inches wide, so cut three strips by folding the Peltex in half (as shown in Figure 16-2) and cutting three equally wide strips the length of the fabric.

2. **Cut three 18- to 20-inch-wide home décor fabric strips.**

   Home décor fabric is 54 to 60 inches wide, so cut three 18- to 20-inch-wide strips by folding it in half (as shown in Figure 16-2) and cutting three equally wide strips the length of the fabric. You will have a little fabric left over from the part of the skirt that is at the foot of the bed to make the two pleat pieces that go in the corners.

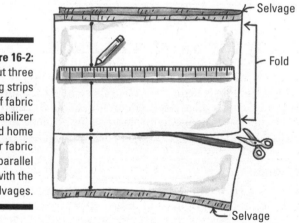

Figure 16-2:
Cut three long strips of fabric stabilizer and home décor fabric parallel with the selvages.

Selvage

Fold

Selvage

Cutting the length of the skirt and pleat pieces

Table 16-2 indicates how to finish cutting the home décor fabric strips you cut in the preceding section. You may think the measurements are too large, but these dimensions ensure you have enough fabric to turn double side and lower hems. Rather than creating traditional pleats at the feet of the bed (way too much trouble and very bulky), you cut, hem, and attach separate pleat pieces to give the illusion of a pleat with much less work. Because of this, you will be making separate double hems on all five of the skirt pieces.

Note: To get the measurements in Table 16-2, I added 4 inches to the width and the length of the box spring to allow for the seam and side hems. This gives you enough fabric to turn generous 1-inch double side hems and a 2-inch double lower hem.

Before cutting the home décor fabric strips to length, remember to double-check that the box spring mattress dimensions in Table 16-1 are the same as yours.

Table 16-2	Cutting Lengths for Bed Skirt and Pleats		
Bed Size	*Cut 1 Strip (For the foot of the bed skirt)*	*Cut 2 Strips (For the sides of the bed skirt)*	*Cut 2 Strips (For the pleats)*
Twin	43 inches	79 inches	12 inches
Full	58 inches	79 inches	12 inches
Queen	64 inches	84 inches	12 inches
King	80 inches	84 inches	12 inches
California king	76 inches	88 inches	12 inches

Double hemming the skirt and pleats

Home-decorating projects are made with double side and lower hems (see Chapter 15 for more on side and lower hems). Because these hems are turned up twice, you don't need to finish the edge before hemming. All of the home décor fabric strips that you cut get two side hems and one lower hem. This gives the fabric extra weight at the hem edges and a professional, finished look.

Double hem the short sides

Double hem both sides of each strip. The goal is for the foot and side strips to match the box spring size you recorded earlier in the chapter (see "Measuring the box spring"). For example, if your cut side strip for a twin bed is 43 inches, by double hemming each short end 1 inch, the finished strip measures the desired 39 inches. Follow these steps for both sides of all five fabric strips:

1. **Place the fabric on the ironing board wrong-side up so that the side hem edge is on the board the short way.**

2. **Press up the width of the finished side hem (approximately 1 inch).**

3. **Turn up and press the side hem again so that it's doubled. Pin in place.**

   Your finished side hem width should be approximately 1 inch (for more on double hemming, see Chapter 15).

4. **Set your machine like this:**

  - Stitch: Straight
  - Length: 3 mm/9 spi
  - Width: 0 mm
  - Foot: All-purpose

5. **Sewing with the wrong side of the fabric strip up, topstitch your double hem, guiding an even distance from the hem edge.**

   For a 1-inch hem, guide approximately ¾-inch from the folded hem edge. For more on hemming, see Chapter 7.

   To help guide you, stick a strip of masking tape across the bed of the machine so that the left edge of the tape is the finished hem width to the right of the needle and parallel to the lines marked in the needle plate. Use the edge of the tape as your stitching guide.

6. **Iron over the hem to smooth out the stitching.**

Double hem the long edges

Before double hemming the long edges of your bed skirt, try it on the bed for size. Pin up the lower edge 4 inches of a strip to simulate a 2-inch double lower hem. Starting at the raw top edge, measure down ½-inch and mark. Hold the strip so the mark is even with the top edge of the box spring and let it hang down to the floor. If the length isn't right, lengthen or shorten your hem allowance as needed so that the hem edge touches the floor. Then hem the skirt and pleat pieces according to the following steps:

1. **Place the fabric on the ironing board wrong side up so that the hem edge is on the board the long way.**

2. **Press up the width of the finished hem width (approximately 2 inches) along the length of the strip.**

3. **Turn up and press the hem again so that it's doubled, and pin in place as shown in Figure 16-3a.**

   Your finished hem width should be approximately 2 inches (for more on double hemming, see Chapter 15).

4. **Set your machine like this:**
   - Stitch: Blind hem
   - Length: 3 mm/9 spi
   - Width: 2 mm to 2.5 mm
   - Foot: Blind hem

5. **Sewing with the wrong side of the skirt strip up, blind hem the lower hem as shown (see Figure 16-3b).**

6. **Iron over the hem to smooth out the stitching.**

The completed hems on a pleat piece are shown in Figure 16-4.

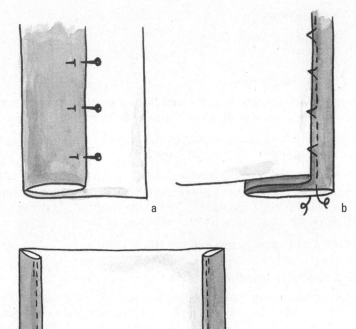

Figure 16-3:
Double the lower hem by pressing, pinning (a), and blind hemming (b).

a

b

Figure 16-4:
The completed hems, as shown on a pleat piece.

Attaching the skirt and pleats to the base fabric

As you follow these steps, you join the five fabric pieces to form a very long strip. As the skirt takes shape, fold it up and let it rest in your lap to keep it out of the way.

1. Set your machine like this:

- Stitch: Straight
- Length: 3.5 to 4 mm/6 to 8 spi
- Width: 0 mm
- Foot: All-purpose

2. **Sew all the Peltex strips together end to end so you have a long, skinny strip.**

   This creates the facing strip that the skirt is attached to. Since this strip can end up over 250 inches long, you need to trim it to length after sewing on the skirt pieces.

3. **Pin the facing strip to the three hemmed skirt strips, right sides together, as shown in Figure 16-5a.**

4. **Place and pin the pleat pieces right-side down on the wrong sides of the skirt strips, centering them where the short and long strips adjoin, as shown in Figure 16-5b.**

5. **Sew the skirt and pleat pieces to the facing strip using a ½-inch seam allowance.**

   Hold the fabric taut in front of and behind the presser foot as you sew. Sew a few inches, removing pins before sewing over them. Then reposition your hands, keeping even tautness in front of and behind the foot and along the length of the seam to keep the seam smooth and pucker-free.

6. **Press the long seam to one side so it's smooth and straight.**

Figure 16-5:
Pin (a) and stitch (b) the skirt strip and pleat pieces to the wide facing strip.

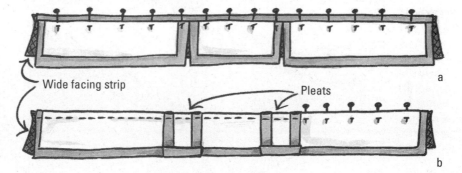

Wide facing strip

Pleats

a

b

Positioning the bed skirt on the box spring

This is the exciting part: attaching the finished project to the box spring. It's as easy as 1, 2, 3:

1. **Place the foot of the bed skirt on the box spring. Using a twist pin, pin the skirt to the box spring at the foot of the bed and at each pleat as shown in Figure 16-6.**

   Turn the twist pins clockwise into the fabric just like you turn a small screw.

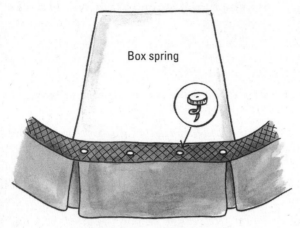

Figure 16-6:
Place the wide facing piece on the box spring so the skirt drops to the floor; then put twist pins at the foot and at each pleat.

2. **To turn the corners, pinch up the excess facing strip at each corner and fold it down as shown in Figure 16-7.**

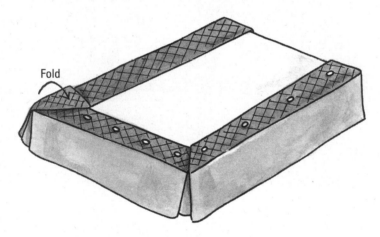

Figure 16-7:
Pinch and pin the facing strip at each corner and at the sides to attach the bed skirt to the box spring.

3. **Secure the remaining sides of the skirt with twist pins.**

Custom Duvet Cover

A *duvet* is a fluffy cotton-covered comforter filled with natural or synthetic down that you slip into a separate, decorative duvet cover. The cover made in this section starts with flat bedsheets and has a buttoned envelope closure. The finished sheets save work by eliminating seaming and hemming steps and are as easy to care for as the sheets on your bed. You utilize the finished hems on both ends of the sheet as firm and stable places to sew on buttons and make buttonholes.

Handcrafted duvet covers are much cheaper than a duvet itself, so you can afford to have several color-coordinated covers — a wardrobe of room accessories to match your moods or the changing seasons.

Before you start, measure the length and width of the duvet you intend to cover (there's no industry standard, so duvets vary in size from brand to brand). You need this measurement to buy sheets in the right size.

To make a duvet cover, you need the following materials in addition to your sewing survival kit (see Chapter 2):

- ✔ Two flat sheets larger than the length and width of your duvet
- ✔ Thread that matches the sheets
- ✔ Six to eight ¾-inch buttons that coordinate with the fabric

Cutting out the front of the duvet cover

The front of the duvet cover is a solid piece of sheet, with most of the work happening on the back of the duvet (described in the following section). Follow these simple steps to make the front piece:

1. **Lay one sheet on the table or floor, wrong side up. Center your duvet on the sheet so that the edges of the duvet are inside the hemmed edges of the sheet.**

   If you need a little more length, rip out the hems at the top and bottom of each sheet and then press the hems flat.

2. **Cut the sheet so that it's ½-inch bigger than the duvet on all four sides.**

   Cut off the excess fabric from the bottom, sides, and top. This piece is the duvet front.

Constructing the back of the duvet cover

Follow these steps to make the back of your duvet cover:

1. **Lay the second sheet flat and on top of the front cover piece. Using the cut piece as a pattern, trim the long sides of the second sheet as needed to match. Do *not* cut the top or bottom.**

2. **Cut off the top 12 inches of the second sheet, using the edge with the widest hem. This 12-inch piece becomes the buttonhole strip.**

   The extra fabric in this hem is a nice sturdy place to sew the buttonholes.

3. **Lay the front of the duvet cover flat and right-side up. Place the buttonhole strip on it, right-side down, with the raw edge aligned with the top edge of the front piece. Pin together as shown in Figure 16-8a.**

4. **Lay the large remainder of the second sheet right-side down on top, overlapping the remaining narrow hem with the wide hem of the buttonhole strip. Cut the bottom of the sheet so that it's even with the raw edge of the first sheet.**

   Overlap the hems enough to allow room for buttons. The buttons are sewn to the narrow hem of the second sheet so they won't pull off with the wear and tear of sleeping and bed-making.

5. **Using the buttonhole strip with the wide hem, mark and make six to eight buttonholes spaced evenly across the hem and parallel to the hem edge (see Figure 16-8 to see the buttonhole position and Chapter 9 for more on marking and making buttonholes).**

6. **Using the buttonholes made in the previous step as a guide, mark and sew the buttons on the right side of the narrow hem of the back duvet piece.**

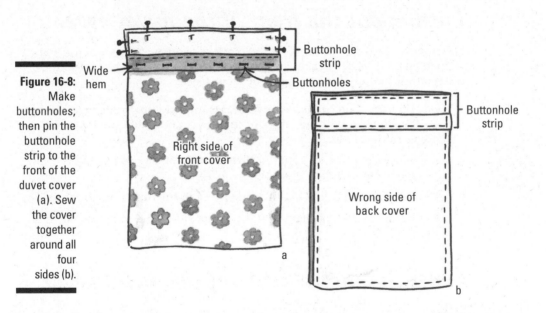

Figure 16-8: Make buttonholes; then pin the buttonhole strip to the front of the duvet cover (a). Sew the cover together around all four sides (b).

Position the buttons so they are centered rather than at either end of the buttonholes for less stress on the button thread. (See Chapter 9 for more on marking and sewing on buttons.)

Putting everything together

Follow these steps to put your duvet cover together. Remember, the side with the buttons is the back of the duvet, and the one-piece sheet is the front.

1. **Button the larger back duvet piece to the buttonhole strip.**

2. **With the right sides of the fabric together, pin the sides and bottom of the front and back pieces together.**

3. **Set your machine like this:**

   • Stitch: Straight

   • Length: 3 to 3.5 mm/8 to 9 spi

   • Width: 0 mm

   • Foot: All-purpose

4. **Sew the duvet cover together on all four sides, using a ½-inch seam allowance as shown in Figure 16-8b.**

   Iron all the seams smooth and flat.

5. **Unbutton the buttons and put your duvet into its very cool cover.**

If you struggle to get the duvet into the cover, try this: Place the duvet cover wrong-side out on the floor, and then place the duvet on top. Wrap rubber bands around the cover and the comforter at each corner (like you would wrap a ponytail — see Figure 16-9). Wrap the corners very tightly. Then turn the duvet cover right-side out through the opening. The rubber bands keep the corners of the comforter and the corners of the cover together and prevent the duvet from moving around and bunching up inside the cover.

Put your new duvet cover on your bed, stand back and admire your work for a moment, and then hop in for a nap.

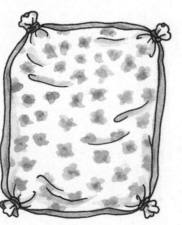

Figure 16-9: Rubber-band the corners of your duvet to the cover before turning the cover right-side out.

Part V
Making Alterations and Quick Fixes for a Sustainable Wardrobe

The 5th Wave   By Rich Tennant

"I see that you're still collecting scraps for your reconstructing projects."

In this part . . .

Y ou know the old expression: Stuff happens. Well, it happens to your clothes, too. Holes show up in your favorite shirt, and one day you may try on your lucky pair of pants and discover that the fit just isn't the same.

When bad stuff happens to your favorite garments, don't throw them away. Read the chapters in this part and give them a second lease on life. Some of the projects I show you in this part may actually make your garments look better than they did before the bad stuff happened!

Chapter 17

When Clothes Are Too Short, Too Long, Too Tight, or Too Loose

. . . .

In This Chapter

▶ Lengthening and shortening pants, skirts, and sleeves

▶ Adding some breathing room in jackets and pants

▶ Snugging up too-loose pants

▶ Helping pants fit the easy way with an adjustable belt

. . . .

Are you suffering from the *terrible toos?* You know, clothes that are too long, too short, too tight, or too loose? I have the toughest time getting rid of clothes that are still wearable, especially when I know if I just lose five pounds, they'll fit. So if you're like me and don't want to throw away perfectly good clothes despite their imperfect fit, you can use the creative shortcuts in this chapter to whip them back into shape — into your shape, that is.

When It's Too Short

You can reduce shrinkage of most fabrics by not cooking washable fabrics in the dryer on the hottest, cotton setting. Fabrics last longer and don't shrink as much when you dry them on your dryer's permanent-press setting.

But what if that information is water under the bridge and your garment is too short to be respectable? Read on to find out what to do.

Cutting off pant legs and re-hemming them

You can turn some short pants into capri-length pants or shorts by simply cutting off the legs and re-hemming them (see Chapter 7 for more information on hemming). Look at the width of the pant legs and imagine them cut off at the length where you normally wear your cropped pants or shorts. Are the pant legs in question full enough for you to cut off? Or, are they narrow like you like them? The answer lies in your personal preference. As for the fabrics, stick with woven fabrics, such as denim, corduroy, gabardine, or poplin. Chapter 7 contains full instructions for hemming.

Letting down and facing the hem

If your pants or skirt are too short, the hem allowance may be generous enough that you can let it down and increase the length. Look at the hem allowance on the garment:

- ✔ Is the hem double turned and then stitched?
- ✔ Is the hem allowance a generous 2 inches or more?

If so, you may be able to let down the hem, giving you the extra hem depth (minus a ¼-inch seam allowance needed to attach the bias hem facing).

For this project, you need bias *hem facing tape,* which you can find at your local fabric store. The tape is made of a light weight cotton/polyester blend woven fabric, has pre-pressed ¼-inch hems on both long edges, and is almost 2-inches wide. It's cut on the bias so it can be sewn on and pressed to conform to almost any hem edge. The color choice is limited, but you should be able to find one that's close to the color of your project.

Follow these steps to lengthen your hem by facing it:

1. **Using your seam ripper, rip out your existing hem (see more about ripping in Chapter 6).**

2. **Using a steam iron, press over the hem to press out the old hem crease.**

Sometimes the hem crease doesn't disappear entirely. You can usually press out a tough crease by sprinkling a mixture of equal parts white vinegar and water on a press cloth (see Chapter 2), laying the dampened press cloth over the hem crease, and then pressing until the press cloth is dry.

3. **Unfold one edge of the pre-folded hem facing tape and pin the tape edge even with the hem edge, placing the right sides together as shown in Figure 17-1.**

Figure 17-1:
Unfold the hem facing tape, sew it to the hem edge, and then sew the ends of the hem facing tape together.

Leave the hem tape in one long piece. You cut it off after you seam the ends.

4. **Set your machine like this:**

   - Stitch: Straight
   - Length: Appropriate for the fabric (try some test stitches to find the one that most closely matches the stitch length used in the other seamlines)
   - Width: 0 mm
   - Foot: All-purpose

5. **Starting an inch from the end of the tape, stitch around the hem on the fold of the hem tape, with the tape side up (refer to Figure 17-1).**

6. **Stop sewing on the tape about 1 inch from where you started.**

   Don't cut the tape yet. Remove your work and head to the ironing board.

7. **Fold up the faced hem the width of the tape and, using a steam iron, gently press over the hem facing.**

   Press from the wrong side of the garment, using a little steam and a press cloth, to help shape the hem facing so it becomes part of the garment.

8. **Cut off the extra length of hem facing tape, leaving enough length on each end for a seam allowance.**

9. **Sew together the ends of the hem facing tape, press the seam open, and then finish stitching the hem facing to the hem edge (refer to Figure 17-1).**

10. **Re-hem the garment using one of the hemming methods I describe in Chapter 7.**

Adding ribbing into an opening

The knitted bands found on the necklines and cuffs of T-shirts and sweatshirts are called *ribbing*. My favorite type of ribbing has spandex blended with cotton or nylon (see more about fibers and fabrics in Chapter 3) and doesn't bag out of shape with a lot of washing and rough wear.

When my son was little and had frequent growth spurts, my favorite way to add length to a pair of pants or a shirt sleeve was to let down the hems and add ribbing. After doing this a couple of times for him, I ended up using the same technique for myself with great results.

Seaming knit ribbing

Before you can use ribbing to fix the problem of a garment being too short, you have to prepare the ribbing for the opening by seaming it. The following steps show you how to create the flattest and most invisible seam for ribbing:

1. **Cut the ribbing the proper width and length:**

   - **Ribbing length:** For necklines, cut the ribbing three-fourths the length of the opening's circumference (if the opening is 20 inches around, cut the ribbing 15 inches long). For sleeves, ankles, and waistlines, cut the ribbing two-thirds the length of the opening's circumference (if the opening is 12 inches around, cut the ribbing 8 inches long).

   - **Ribbing width:** Double the desired finished width and add ½ inch (if you want a 2-inch finished width, cut the ribbing 4½ inches wide).

2. **Set your machine like this:**
   - Stitch: Overlock
   - Length: Longest
   - Width: 5 to 6 mm
   - Foot: Embroidery

3. **Fold the ribbing as shown in Figure 17-2 and, using a ¼-inch seam allowance, sew the short ends together.**

Figure 17-2:
Seaming
knit ribbing.

4. **Finger press the seam to one side, and then turn the ribbing so when turned right-side out it makes a circle with the seam on the inside of the band.**

Sewing or serging ribbing into place

When you see how fast and easy applying ribbing into an opening is, you'll want to put ribbing on everything in sight.

Follow these steps to attach your ribbing like a pro:

1. **Use pins to mark off the opening into quarters.**

   This process is called *quarter marking*.

   Until you get more practice, you may find that marking the opening and ribbing into eight equal parts, rather than four, is easier.

2. **Quarter mark the ribbing.**

3. **With the garment inside out and the ribbing tucked inside the opening so the two pieces are right sides together, line up and pin together the ribbing and the opening so seams and the pin marks match up.**

4. **Set your sewing machine like this:**

   - Stitch: Overlock

   - Length: Longest

   - Width: 5 to 6 mm

   - Foot: Embroidery

   Or, set your serger like this:

   - Stitch: Four-thread overlock

   - Length: 2.5 to 3 mm

   - Width: 4 mm

   - Foot: Standard

5. **Sew a ¼-inch seam with your sewing machine or serger, following the steps outlined in Chapter 6.**

When It's Too Long

Of course, you can simply re-hem pants and skirts that you find too long to the right length (see Chapter 9). But when it comes to sleeves and thicker fabrics like denim, the following solutions are my favorite ways of solving the too-long problem.

Moving the button on a sleeve cuff

A fast way to take care of a slightly too-long sleeve on a dress shirt is to move the button over so that the cuff fits snugly around the wrist. This adjustment keeps the cuff from sliding down over your hand as shown in Figure 17-3.

Review the information in Chapter 9 on the ways to sew on a button.

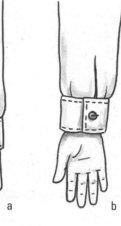

Figure 17-3:
Move the
button over
to shorten
a too-long
sleeve:
before (a)
and
after (b).

Removing the cuff to shorten the sleeve

My husband's arms are shorter than manufacturers think they should be, apparently, so I constantly shorten shirtsleeves for him by moving the cuff higher up the sleeve. (I offered to take up some tucks in his sleeves, but he just wasn't interested — a little too puffy and pirate-y.)

You can easily shorten sleeves at the cuff when you follow these steps:

1. **Using a seam ripper, rip off the cuff, carefully cutting the stitches that hold it onto the sleeve.**

   Leave the cuff with the seam allowance pressed toward the inside.

   As a frame of reference, remove one cuff at a time. This way, if you need to check how the shirt manufacturer stitched the cuff on in the first place, you can check the one that you haven't removed.

2. **Pin the cuff back onto the sleeve so that the finished edge of the cuff is in the desired position.**

   Try on the shirt and bend your arm to be sure that the cuff is positioned in exactly the right spot.

3. **Using a fabric marker, mark along the top of the cuff, establishing the new cuff position.**

4. **Unpin the cuff and cut away the excess sleeve fabric, leaving a ½-inch seam allowance at the bottom of the sleeve, below the cuff placement marks that you made in Step 3 (see Figure 17-4).**

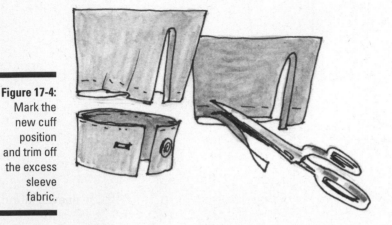

Figure 17-4:
Mark the
new cuff
position
and trim off
the excess
sleeve
fabric.

5. **Re-pleat and pin the bottom of the sleeve, using the original pleats as a guide and deepening the pleats as needed to fit the fullness of the sleeve to the cuff.**

6. **After shortening one cuff, repeat Steps 1 through 5 for the other cuff.**

   Double-check that you pleated the other sleeve like the first. (Read more about pleats in Chapter 8.)

7. **Pin on each cuff (see Figure 17-5) so the seamline is even with the marks you made in Step 3.**

Figure 17-5:
Pin on
the cuff.

8. **Set your machine like this:**

   - Stitch: Straight
   - Length: 2.5 to 3 mm/10 to 12 spi
   - Width: 0 mm
   - Foot: All-purpose

9. **Edgestitch the cuff to the sleeve, guiding the stitches so that they sew over the original stitching line (see Chapter 6 for more on edgestitching). Repeat for the other sleeve.**

Shortening jeans

Shortening and re-hemming jeans presents some real challenges unless you have the right tools and technique. Some doubled jean seams cannot fit under the presser foot of home-use sewing machines. And if the presser foot coasts down off the thicknesses, you have a big mess on your hands — unless you use a wedge.

You put a wedge under the presser foot to help you sew over an uneven fabric thickness. Sewing wedges, which come in several varieties, work like a shim under a dresser leg by stabilizing the presser foot as it travels over troublesome seams.

Follow these steps to shorten too-long jeans:

1. **Before taking up the hem on your jeans, wash and dry them on the high or regular cotton setting.**

   After re-hemming, wash and dry your jeans on the permanent-press setting to ensure that they don't shrink any further.

2. **Measure and mark the desired hemline with your dressmaker's chalk.**

3. **Cut off the excess fabric, leaving at least ½- to ⅝-inch for the hem allowance.**

4. **Finish the raw edge, using one of the overcasting stitches on your sewing machine or a three-thread overlock on your serger (see Chapter 7 for the best way to finish raw edges).**

5. **Fold up and press the hem allowance on the mark you made in Step 2.**

   Even though your jeans may have been double-hemmed, this excess thickness is often too much for many sewing machines. You can sew your hem more easily and it looks better if you turn it up only once.

6. **Set your machine like this:**

   - Stitch: Straight
   - Length: 3 to 4 mm/6 to 9 spi
   - Width: 0 mm
   - Foot: All-purpose, Teflon, or roller

- • Needle: Size #90/14 Jeans
- • Accessories: Wedge (sometimes called a button reed) or a Jean-a-ma-Jig (brand name)

7. **Sew the hem, starting in either the front of back of the leg (not at an inseam or outseam).**

8. **When you get to an inseam or outseam, sew until the presser foot toe tips up on the fabric thicknesses created by the seam allowances. Stop with the needle in the fabric and lift the foot.**

9. **Place the wedge under the heel and lower the foot.**

   The wedge lifts up the back of the foot so that the foot is elevated to the thickness of the fabric.

10. **Stitch across the thickness until the toes start tipping down. Stop with the needle in the fabric and lift the foot again.**

11. **Remove the wedge from under the heel, place it under the toe of the foot, and lower the presser foot, as shown in Figure 17-6.**

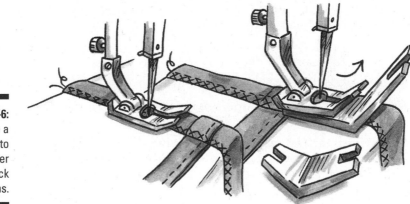

Figure 17-6:
Use a wedge to maneuver over thick seams.

12. **Sew until the needle and the back of the foot are off the thickness.**

    As you come off the thickness, the wedge levels the foot for even feeding and even better stitching.

13. **Lift the foot and remove the wedge, and then lower the foot and sew until you get to the next thick seam.**

    Repeat Steps 8 through 12 until you finish hemming.

When It's Too Tight

The tidbits in this section can help you get just a little bit more wear out of your clothes without forcing you to lose weight or start that exercise program.

Moving the buttons over on a jacket

An easy way to get more room in a jacket is to simply move the buttons over. Moving a button over even ½ inch makes a big difference in the way a garment looks and feels.

Turn a double-breasted jacket into a single-breasted jacket by eliminating one row of buttons and moving the other row so that the buttons and buttonholes are centered (see Figure 17-7). You get more room, and the single-breasted styling is usually more slimming. (See Chapter 9 to find out about sewing buttons by hand and machine.)

Figure 17-7:
Add room to a double-breasted jacket by moving over the buttons.

a   b

Adding room to the waistband

You typically cut waistbands on the lengthwise grain (see Chapter 4 for more information on grainlines). When washed and dried on the high cotton setting, fabric often shrinks on the lengthwise grain, and it keeps shrinking even after you've washed the garment several times. No wonder those waistbands feel a little tight lately! Here's how to give yourself up to ¾-inch of extra room:

1. **Find a place in the garment where you can steal a little bit of fabric to make an extension.**

   Extra hem allowance, an extra belt loop, or the lower edge of an inseam pocket (if it matches the garment fabric) all work well.

2. **Cut the extension as long as possible and the same width as the waistband, and interface it with fusible interfacing (see Chapter 3).**

3. **At the back of the pants, carefully rip out any belt loops that might be in the way (see Chapter 6 for more on safely ripping out stitches).**

4. **Rip out the stitching that holds the waistband to the waistline, removing the stitching 3 to 4 inches on either side of the center back. Cut through the waistband the short way, as shown in Figure 17-8.**

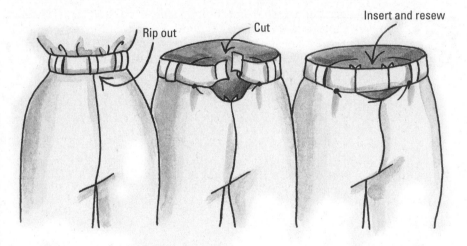

Rip out   Cut   Insert and resew

Figure 17-8:
Waistband
too tight?
Add a fabric
extension to
the center
back.

5. **Cut your fabric extension.**

   Try on the garment and figure out how much of an extension you need. Cut the extension long enough to fit the waistband *plus* the seam allowances.

   Add generous seam allowances so that you can press open the seams on both ends of the extension, making the extended waistband smooth and comfortable.

6. **Set your machine like this:**

   - Stitch: Straight

   - Length: Appropriate for the fabric (try some test stitches to find the one that most closely matches the stitch length used in the other seamlines)

- Width: 0 mm

- Foot: All-purpose

7. **Sew the extension to the center back of the waistband (refer to Figure 17-8).**

   Place the right side of the short, open end of the waistband to the right side of the interfaced extension and sew a seam. Repeat for the other end of the extension.

8. **Sew the waistband back on and attach any belt loops as they were before.**

   Because the original waistband shrinks and the waistline of the garment doesn't, adding this little bit of length to the waistband "relaxes" the fit so you have extra room and comfort.

When It's Too Loose

Here are a couple of tricks that I use when things are too loose. When hips are proportionally bigger than the waistline, this quick fix takes in the waistline. If your waistline yo-yos from season to season, using an adjustable belt over a too-big waistline just may be the ticket.

Taking in the waistline works well when taking in casual men's or ladies' slacks that have a front zipper and that don't have the traditional center back seam in the waistband. Just follow these steps:

1. **With the pants inside out, pinch in and pin-baste the necessary amount out of the center back, from the waistband down as far as needed.**

   To pin-baste, place the pins close together and along the new seamline. You may also want to mark the new seamline with dressmaker's chalk.

2. **Sew along your pin line, taking in as much fabric as needed for the fit determined in Step 1.**

3. **Starting at the crotch and sewing up through the waistband, edge-stitch (see Chapter 6 for more about edgestitching) next to the seamline, which causes the seam allowance to lay down smoothly and to one side (see Figure 17-9).**

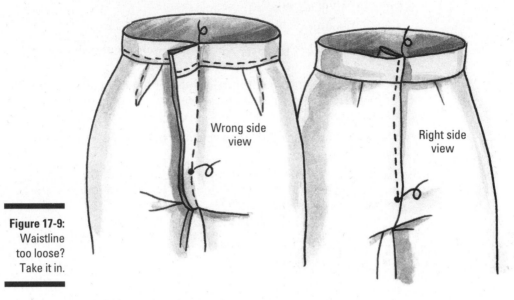

Figure 17-9:
Waistline
too loose?
Take it in.

Crossover Belt

Adding a belt to your outfit can help take up extra room in a shirt, blouse, or dress, creating a truly quick and easy fix to a fitting issue! Want a belt that shrinks or grows with you? Quickly craft this very comfortable belt of woven cotton belting.

In addition to your sewing survival kit (which you can read about in Chapter 2), you need the following materials:

- 41 inches of 2-inch Guatemalan belting (see the appendix for sources)
- Two 2-inch hook-side Velcro strips
- Two 8-inch loop-side Velcro strips
- Thread to match the belting
- Fabric glue, such as Fabri-Tac
- Seam sealant, such as FrayCheck

To create the belt, follow these steps:

1. **Dribble a line of seam sealant on each end of the belting to prevent the ends from fraying, and let it dry for about 5 minutes.**

2. **Set your machine like this:**
   - Stitch: Straight
   - Length: 3.5 mm/7 spi
   - Width: 0 mm
   - Foot: All-purpose

3. **Fold, press, pin, and sew small pleats at each end of the outside of the belting, as shown in Figure 17-10.**

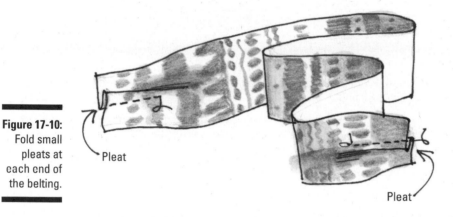

Figure 17-10: Fold small pleats at each end of the belting.

Pleat

Pleat

4. **Pin the two short strips of hook-side Velcro over the pleats on the outside of the belting and sew the Velcro in place around all four sides (see Figure 17-11).**

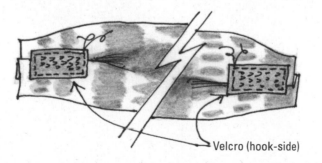

Figure 17-11: Sew Velcro over the pleats on each end.

Velcro (hook-side)

5. **Place and glue the two long, loop side strips of Velcro 4 inches in from each end and on the inside (or the other side) of the belting strip, as shown in Figure 17-12.**

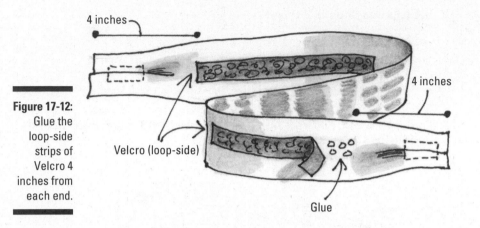

Figure 17-12:
Glue the loop-side strips of Velcro 4 inches from each end.

You glue the long strips so that stitches don't show through to the outside of the belt.

6. **Let the glue dry as directed by the manufacturer (usually at least 24 hours for a permanent bond) before using the belt.**

7. **Place the belt around your waist, tucking the loose end under and attaching it to the Velcro, as shown in Figure 17-13.**

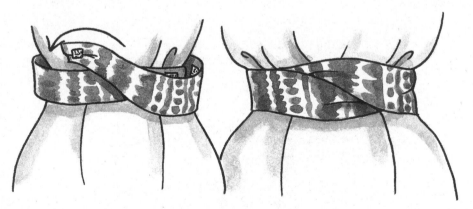

Figure 17-13:
This belt adjusts with you, even when you eat too much.

Chapter 18

Making Repairs on the Run

In This Chapter

▶ Fixing split seams

▶ Covering holes the easy way

▶ Closing up tears

▶ Replacing a fly-front zipper

Have you looked in your closet and discovered you have nothing to wear? Maybe you're running short on wearable clothes because your favorite shirt has a split seam or your jeans need a new zipper. In this chapter I share some of my favorite shortcuts for painlessly cutting your repair pile down to size. Find out how to fix a split seam, patch a hole, repair a tear, and replace a zipper. If you're looking for information on the most basic (and common) repair of all — sewing on a new button — turn to Chapter 9.

Repairing a Split Seam

If you have a simple split seam, where the stitches in a seam are ripped or broken, your repair job is an easy one. The type of fabric — woven or knit — determines the stitches you use to repair the seam; I cover the possibilities in the following sections.

If the fabric has deteriorated, pulled away from the stitches, or is totally obliterated at or around the seam allowance, you use a different technique to fix things up. Check out "Patching Holes and Rips" later on in this chapter for more information.

Repairing a seam on woven fabrics

Follow these steps to repair a simple ripped seam in woven fabric, which doesn't have much stretch (if any):

1. **Turn the item inside out so that you can easily access the seam allowances.**

2. **Using your seam ripper and embroidery scissors, remove the broken and ripped stitches (for more on unsewing, see Chapter 6).**

3. **Pin the seam allowances back together in their original position (see Figure 18-1a).**

4. **Set your machine like this:**

   • Stitch: Straight

   • Length: 2.5 to 3 mm/10 to 12 spi

   • Width: 0 mm

   • Foot: All-purpose

5. **Starting ½ inch before the split in the seam, sew over the intact seam, over the split, and ½ inch over the intact seam on the other side of the split, as shown in Figure 18-1b.**

   Backstitch at the beginning and end of the repairing stitches.

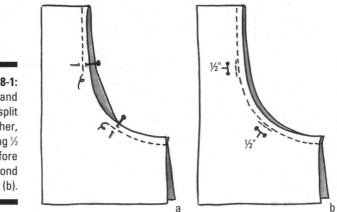

Figure 18-1:
Pin (a) and sew the split together, sewing ½ inch before and beyond the split (b).

Repairing a seam on knit fabrics

Knit fabrics have varying degrees of stretch to them. In order to keep the stretch in a repaired seam, you have to use a zigzag stitch. For a really secure mend, follow these steps:

1. **Turn the item inside out so that you can easily access the seam allowances.**

2. **Using your seam ripper and embroidery scissors, remove the broken and ripped stitches (for more on unsewing, see Chapter 6).**

3. **Pin the seam allowances back together in their original position.**

4. **Set your machine like this:**

   - Stitch: Zigzag

   - Length: 1 to 1.5 mm/20 to 24 spi

   - Width: 1 to 1.5 mm

   - Foot: All-purpose or embroidery

5. **Starting ½ inch before the split in the seam, sew over the intact seam, over the split, and ½ inch over the intact seam on the other side of the split (see Figure 18-1).**

Patching Holes and Rips

My brother is a commercial salmon fisherman in Alaska. Before he was married, he handed me a pile of mending whenever I visited. Talk about holes! He had so many shirts with holes in the elbows that he finally gave up and started cutting the sleeves off his long-sleeved shirts before they could get holey.

Even if you don't give your clothes quite the workout that a fisherman does, you may find holes that need patching in your clothes and other sewing projects from time to time.

Covering holes with patches

I find the following technique to be the very best way to patch holes. You can use this method to patch over holes in elbows, knees, or anywhere that holes find their way into a piece of fabric.

You can make large or small patches and arrange them artfully to cover other messes besides holes. In the color section you can see how I used small pocket patches arranged in a collage to cover an indelible ink stain. (See Chapter 11 for more on sewing pockets.)

Iron-on patches are too good to be true: Experience has taught me that, after a little washing and wearing, the adhesive quits and the patch falls off. If you're using iron-on patches, also stitch them on.

Follow these steps to sew on a patch:

1. **Find a fabric similar to the garment you're patching.**

   If possible, steal some of the original fabric by stitching shut a pocket that doesn't get a lot of use and cutting away the fabric from underneath.

Save worn-out jeans so that you have a plentiful supply of used denim for patching.

2. **Cut out a patch ½ to ¾ inch larger than the hole, all the way around. You can cut the patch to any shape that you like.**

   Before cutting the patch to size, inspect the fabric around the hole. You may decide that you need a bigger patch to cover any frays in the area.

3. **Pin the patch in place, centering it over the hole so that the right side of the patch fabric is up, as shown in Figure 18-2.**

   Pin around the edges of the patch, through the patch and the garment underneath.

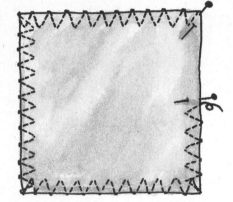

Figure 18-2:
Pin the patch in place and sew it on with a three-step zigzag stitch.

4. **Set your sewing machine like this:**

   • Stitch: Three-step zigzag

   • Length: 0.5 to 0.8 mm/fine setting or 60 spi

   • Width: 5 mm (or the widest width you have)

   • Foot: Embroidery

   • Needle: #90/14 HJ denim or jeans (for heavy fabrics); #80/12H Universal for everything else

5. **Place the garment and patch under the presser foot, right-side up.**

   The patch should be under the foot so that the edge is slightly to the right of the needle.

6. **Start sewing so that when the needle travels across the patch fabric to the right, the last stitch formed is on the outside edge of the patch.**

   Remember to pull out the pins before sewing over them. This stitch is very dense and helps to meld the two pieces of fabric together so the patch is as strong as the fabric it patches.

7. **If the patch is a circle, sew all the way around it. If the patch is a rectangle or square, sew to the corner and pivot by following these steps:**

   1. Sew to the corner, stopping with the needle in the far right side of the stitch. Doing so positions the patch so that you reinforce it in the corner.

   2. Lift the foot, pivot 90 degrees, lower the foot, and sew the second side of the patch, again stopping with the needle in the far right side of the stitch and pivoting.

   3. Continue like this until you've sewn around the patch.

8. **Pull the threads to the back of the fabric and tie them off (see Chapter 6 for more information on tying off threads).**

Patching with appliqués

You can get creative by making or purchasing a ready-made *appliqué* — a shaped piece of fabric that may be partially or completely covered by embroidery stitches and that may have a row of close-together zigzag stitches called *satin stitches* on the edge. Use it as a patch in a low-stress area. Before patching with an appliqué, though, consider where you want to position it on the garment. Appliqués usually aren't large enough for patching knees, elbows, and other high-wear areas, and they can be lumpy and not very comfortable. Your best bet is to use them to disguise smaller holes.

Appliqués make short work of repairing holes. Just follow these steps to patch with an appliqué:

1. **Pin the appliqué over the hole.**

   If the appliqué is too thick to pin through, temporarily glue it into place, using your fabric glue stick.

2. **Set your sewing machine like this:**

   • Stitch: Straight

   • Length: 3 mm/10 spi

   • Width: 0 mm

   • Foot: Embroidery

3. **Using thread that matches the appliqué, straight stitch around it, sewing just inside the satin-stitched edge. (See Chapter 5 for more information on these two stitches.)**

4. **Pull the threads to the wrong side and tie them off.**

Sometimes you can disguise your appliqués and make them look like decorations. For example, I've patched a hole with an appliqué and then placed another appliqué or two on the garment in other places so that the appliqués looked like they were on the garment all along.

Mending Tears in Fabric

The goal in mending a tear is to make the repair as flat and invisible as possible. You accomplish this smooth repair using the three-step zigzag stitch and some lightweight fusible interfacing. (See Chapter 3 for more information on interfacing.)

If you're lucky enough to find a lightweight cotton darning or embroidery thread through your local sewing machine dealer in the color that matches your garment, use that instead of all-purpose sewing thread. This finer weight of thread works beautifully for an almost invisible repair.

To mend tears on woven fabric, just follow these steps:

1. **Cut a ½-inch-wide strip of lightweight fusible interfacing the length of the tear plus 1 inch.**

For a more invisible mend, use a pair of pinking shears and pink the edges of the interfacing. The irregular edge is less noticeable and may not shadow through to the right side of the fabric when pressed.

2. **Trim off the loose threads from the tear.**

3. **Lay the repair wrong-side out on the ironing board.**

4. **Push the raw edges of the tear together; place the interfacing over the tear.**

5. **Using your iron, fuse the interfacing to the back of the tear according to the manufacturer's instructions.**

6. **Set your machine like this:**

   • Stitch: Three-step zigzag

   • Length: 0.5 to 0.8 mm/fine setting or 60 spi

   • Width: 5 to 7 mm

   • Foot: Embroidery

7. **With the fabric right-side up, position your needle ¼ inch before one end of the tear and lower the foot, centering it over the tear.**

8. **Sew so that the stitches go back and forth over and ¼-inch below the tear as shown in Figure 18-3.**

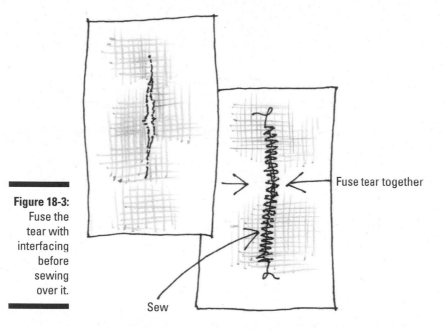

Fuse tear together

Figure 18-3:
Fuse the tear with interfacing before sewing over it.

Sew

If the tear is wider than the width of the mending stitch, sew two rows of stitching next to each other so that the second row meshes into the first.

9. **Pull the threads to the back and tie them off.**

Replacing a Fly-Front Zipper

I bet you have a pair of pants, jeans, shorts, or a skirt in the repair pile badly in need of a zipper replacement. Don't put off this repair another minute! It's actually much easier than you think. The fabric is already shaped, pressed, and stitched with the original zipper, so the work is all figured out for you. You just have to rip out the old zipper and then slip in and stitch the new one.

You don't have to find a zipper that measures exactly the same length as the one you want to replace. Use a zipper that measures longer than the opening. Using a longer zipper allows you to maneuver the presser foot without running into the pull.

Follow these instructions to replace a zipper:

1. **Take notes or a digital picture of how the manufacturer originally installed the zipper.**

   Those notes and photos come in handy when you put everything back together.

2. **Unzip and remove the old zipper by carefully ripping out the stitches that attach it to the garment using a sharp pair of embroidery scissors or a seam ripper (check out Chapter 6 for more on ripping).**

3. **Rip back the waistband just far enough to remove the old zipper.**

4. **Mark the original topstitching line on the garment with transparent tape (see Figure 18-4).**

   Even though you removed the stitches, you can still see where the top-stitching used to be.

5. **Set your machine like this:**

   - Stitch: Straight
   - Length: 2.5 to 3 mm/10 to 12 spi
   - Width: 0 mm
   - Foot: Zipper

6. **Secure the zipper to the fly-front facing extension.**

   Open the fly-front facing extension (the part of the garment used to make the flap that covers up the zipper). With the right side of the zipper to the right side of the extension, pin or hand-baste the zipper so that the left edge of the zipper tape is even with the left edge of the facing extension, as shown in Figure 18-4.

7. **Sewing from the bottom of the zipper tape, stitch all the way along the left edge of the zipper tape, sewing about ⅛ inch from the edge.**

8. **Pin the other side of the zipper.**

   Unzip the zipper. Pin the side that you haven't sewn yet so that the zipper tape is sandwiched between the underlap and the underlap extension (the fabric piece behind the zipper that keeps you from catching your underwear in the zipper) and the fold is next to the zipper teeth, as shown in Figure 18-5.

9. **Zip the zipper and check that the zipper and the fly front are smooth.**

   If they aren't smooth, reposition the pins.

10. **When everything is smooth, unzip the zipper again and stitch the other side of the zipper, sewing close to the teeth.**

11. **Unzip the zipper, cut off the excess zipper tape, tuck the underlap end of the zipper under the waistband, and pin the waistband back to the top of the pants with right sides together.**

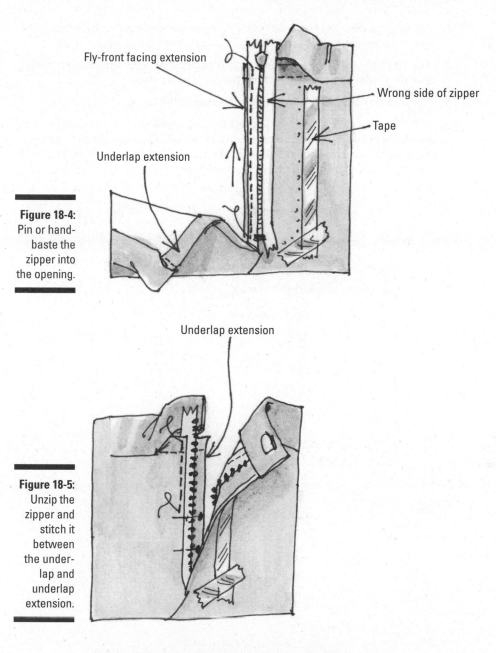

Fly-front facing extension

Wrong side of zipper

Tape

Underlap extension

Figure 18-4:
Pin or hand-
baste the
zipper into
the opening.

Underlap extension

Figure 18-5:
Unzip the
zipper and
stitch it
between
the under-
lap and
underlap
extension.

12. Topstitch the fly front as shown in Figure 18-6.

Slide the toe of the foot to one side so that it avoids the zipper teeth.
Lower the foot, placing it on the fly front and guiding the needle next to
the transparent tape on the inside edge. The tape is a template to keep
you sewing straight.

13. Pin the waistline opening to one side of the waistband so that the right sides are together and enclosing the top of the zipper in the seam.

14. Sew the other side of the zipper, guiding the needle over the stitching line that was there before you replaced the zipper.

15. Put your all-purpose foot back on the machine.

16. Restitch the back of the waistband to the opening on both sides of the zipper opening by either topstitching or stitching in the ditch in the crack of the waistband seamline as shown in Figure 18-6 (see Chapter 5 for the how-tos of stitching in the ditch).

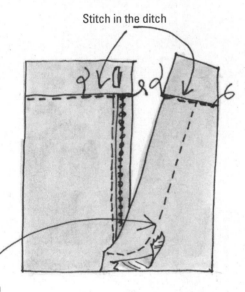

Stitch in the ditch

Figure 18-6:
Topstitch over the zipper and stitch in the ditch to reattach the waistband.

Topstitch

Chapter 19

Eco Fashion: Giving Existing Garments New Life

. . . .

In This Chapter

▶ Making the most of clothing you already have by shopping in your own closet

▶ Finding out how to felt a wool sweater and recycle it into a hat

▶ Turning a bra into an innovative and imaginative party dress

. . . .

"Green is the new black" — but what does that really mean? I believe it means that our culture's newfound awareness of conservation is now appealing and appropriate in just about everything we do. People are planting gardens, shopping at resale and vintage shops as well as Goodwill and Salvation Army stores, and recycling almost everything in sight. The idea of altering or remaking a piece of clothing is something that came naturally to my mom and grandmother — survivors of the Great Depression — and they passed on their knowledge to me.

Why should you care about eco fashion? Several reasons. First of all, when you start with a finished garment, the hard stuff is already done for you; secondly, it saves time; and thirdly, you end up with a stylish, repurposed piece of clothing that will stay out of the landfill a while longer. Take the ruffled apron project in Chapter 9, for example. You can start off (like I did) by spending a mere $3 at Goodwill on a denim skirt, or you may only need to look in your own closet for something similar. An old skirt already has a waistband, pockets, belt loops, and a zipper (time-consuming sewing, wouldn't you agree?). In about three hours you can cut the skirt apart, add ruffles and belting, and end up with two different aprons ready to dazzle any apron fashionista worth her salt.

In this chapter I share two eco-friendly projects with you. The first is a felted wool hat made from one of my wool sweaters that was accidentally machine washed and dried. The second project comes from my friends at DIYStyle (www.diystyle.net) — a bra dress. You read it right — a dress that starts with a bra. Very stylish, cute, and easy to make.

Felted Wool Hat

What do you do with a wool sweater that accidentally made a trip through the wash and dry cycle? Recycle it. Whether intentional or not, washing and drying results in *felted wool,* which is a wonderful material for making everything from tea cozies and oven mitts to this warm, easy-to-make hat, which appears in the color section. Thanks much to Judy Raymond and the Simplicity Pattern Company (www.simplicity.com) for supplying the pattern for this very cool project.

Besides your sewing survival kit (see Chapter 2), you need the following materials for this project:

- ✔ One wool sweater ready to be felted
- ✔ A 2-inch button that coordinates with the sweater
- ✔ ½ yard of yarn or narrow trim that complements the hat
- ✔ All-purpose, cotton/poly thread to match
- ✔ Tracing paper
- ✔ Pencil

Sourcing and preparing the wool

I remember learning in elementary school about how wool is sheared off sheep then carded to clean and straighten out the wool fibers so they can be spun into yarn for sweaters and woven into fabric. Wool shrinks and felts when washed in hot water because it returns to its curly, original shape — like it grows on the sheep. For this project, you use a felted sweater. The looped nature of knitted wool when it's washed and dried creates a smooth, thick, and thus excellent piece of fabric to work with.

If you don't have a felted sweater on hand (or one in your own closet that you're willing to felt for the cause), check out your local thrift stores, yard and tag sales, and the back of your friends' and family's closets. Make sure the sweater you use is wool, because synthetic fibers and cashmere don't felt. Some wool fibers felt better than others, so use these guidelines to achieve the look you're going for:

- ✔ Lambswool and angora/lambswool combos make very fine and soft felted wool.
- ✔ Blends of lambswool, angora, and nylon can be used as long as the nylon fiber content is 20 percent or less.

✔ Merino and alpaca wool are favorites of the felting pros because of the silky felted texture.

✔ Shetland wool creates a rougher, thicker felt.

✔ Icelandic wool — like the naturally-colored fisherman knit sweaters of Iceland — produce very thick felted wool that is tough to get under the foot of the sewing machine, so steer clear for this project.

Felting the wool

Follow these steps to felt one wool sweater:

1. **Slip the sleeves into the body of the sweater, but keep the sweater turned right-side out.**

2. **Set your washer on the hot water setting and run the first wash cycle three to five times until you get the desired felted texture.**

   You don't need detergent when felting a sweater. Unless, of course, the sweater is dirty.

   Stop the washer every few minutes either to clean out the lint from your washer's lint trap or to skim the lint from the surface of the water. If you don't, you may wreck your washer with continued unfiltered feltings.

3. **Machine-dry the sweater in a moderately hot dryer.**

For a supply of felted wool fabric, you can felt multiple sweaters simultaneously. Depending on their size, you can wash six to ten sweaters at a time. Divide them into lights and darks to wash each color group separately (as you would do for regular laundry). Then follow the same steps as for felting one sweater (see the preceding list).

Laying out and cutting the hat pieces

Follow these steps for a very warm felted hat.

1. **Using the tracing paper and a pencil, trace off the hat pattern in Figure 19-1.**

   The pattern is the actual size that you need to make a hat that will fit just about any head size.

   You need to cut six hat pattern pieces, so I recommend that you trace off three pattern pieces. This way you can lay them out on the doubled sweater and cut all six pieces at once (see Figure 19-2).

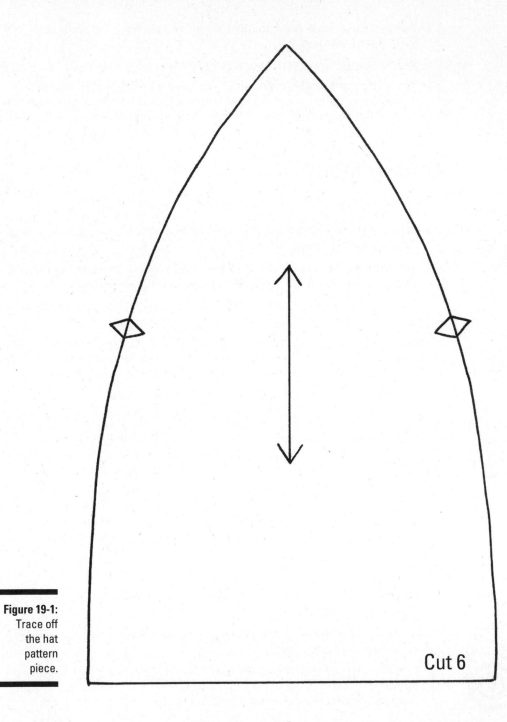

Figure 19-1:
Trace off
the hat
pattern
piece.

Cut 6

2. **Cut off the ribbing from the bottom of the sweater and set it aside for use later in the project.**

3. **Lay the sweater out flat on a table; then place, pin, and cut out the six hat pattern pieces as shown in Figure 19-2.**

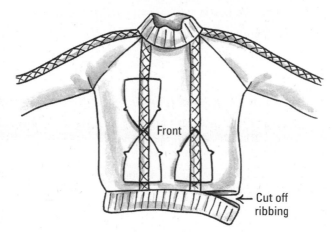

Front

Cut off ribbing

Figure 19-2: Cut six hat pieces from the front and back of the felted sweater.

Assembling the hat

You can assemble this simple yet chic project in one short sitting. First you sew three pattern pieces together to create one side of the crown, and then you repeat to make the other half of the crown. After that, you sew both halves together at the center front and back.

Making the two halves first

Follow these steps for creating two halves of the hat:

1. **Set your machine like this:**

    - Stitch: Slight zigzag

    - Length: 3.5 to 4 mm/4 to 6 spi

    - Width: 1 mm

    - Foot: Embroidery or all-purpose

   Felted sweater thicknesses vary, so test your stitch length on a scrap. If the fabric puckers, lengthen the stitch; if it waves out of shape, shorten the stitch length.

2. **Place the right sides of two of your hat pattern pieces together, matching the notches as shown in Figure 19-3a, and then sew them together using a ⅝-inch seam allowance.**

3. **Press the seam open using steam and a slight up-and-down pressing motion (for more on pressing, see Chapter 5).**

4. **Set your machine like this:**

    • Stitch: Straight

    • Length: 3 to 4 mm/3.5 to 6 spi

    • Width: 0 mm

    • Foot: Embroidery or all-purpose

5. **From the wrong side, topstitch on either side of the seam guiding the raw edge even with the edge of the presser foot (see Chapter 5 for more on topstitching tips and tricks).**

6. **Repeat Steps 1 to 5 to sew the third hat piece to the first two; this creates one side of the hat as shown in Figure 19-3b.**

Figure 19-3:
Make each side of the hat separately, sewing and topstitching three pattern pieces to create each side.

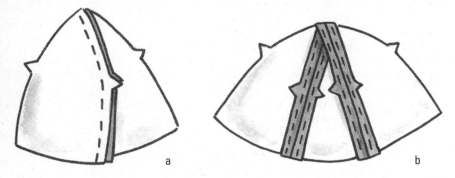

a   b

7. **Repeat Steps 1 to 6 with the remaining three hat pattern pieces to create the other half of the hat.**

Sewing the halves together

The preceding section creates two halves of your felted wool hat. This section puts them all together and creates a smooth crown. Just follow these steps:

1. **Set your machine like this:**
   - Stitch: Slight zigzag
   - Length: 3.5 to 4 mm/4 to 6 spi
   - Width: 1 mm
   - Foot: Embroidery or all-purpose

2. **Place the two pieces of the hat right sides together, matching the notches. Sew the hat together by starting at one edge and sewing a ⅝-inch seam up and over the crown and then down to the opposite edge, as shown in Figure 19-4a.**

3. **Press the seam open.**

4. **Set your machine like this:**
   - Stitch: Straight
   - Length: 3 to 4 mm/3.5 to 6 spi
   - Width: 0 mm
   - Foot: Embroidery or all-purpose

5. **Turn the hat right-side out and topstitch on either side of the seam as shown in Figure 19-4b.**

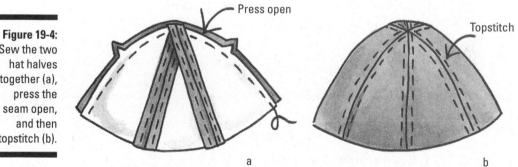

Figure 19-4: Sew the two hat halves together (a), press the seam open, and then topstitch (b).

Press open

Topstitch

a   b

Adding the ribbing

The ribbing you cut off the bottom of the sweater is used to create the hat band, which is sewn to the bottom of the hat. Follow these easy steps:

1. **Stretch the ribbing around your head to determine the length needed for a snug, comfortable fit, and then cut it to length, adding ½ inch to allow for the seam allowance.**

2. Using a ¼-inch seam allowance, seam the two short ends together using the slight zigzag stitch you used to seam the hat pieces together (see Step 1 in "Sewing the halves together"), and then press the seam open.

3. Pin-mark both the hat opening and the ribbing into eighths as shown in Figure 19-5.

4. With the hat right-side out, pin the ribbing to the bottom edge of the hat, matching the pin marks and aligning the ribbing seam at the center back of the hat.

   To find the center back, examine the two seams that join the two hat halves together. Use whichever one looks worst at the center back.

5. Set your machine like this:

   • Stitch: Wide zigzag stitch

   • Length: Longest

   • Width: 5 to 6 mm

   • Foot: Embroidery

   • Upper tension: Loosen

6. Using a ¼-inch seam allowance, machine-baste the ribbing to the body of the hat (see Figure 19-5).

   By basting the ribbing on first, you can check the fit and make the appropriate adjustments before the final stitching.

7. Set your machine like this:

   • Stitch: Overlock

   • Length: Longest

   • Width: 5 to 6 mm

   • Foot: Embroidery

   • Upper tension: Normal

   If you're using a serger, use these settings:

   • Stitch: ¾ thread

   • Length: Appropriate for the fabric

   • Width: 4 mm

   • Foot: Standard

8. Using a ¼-inch seam allowance, sew the ribbing and hat together as shown in Figure 19-5 (for more on sewing ribbing see Chapter 6).

9. Hand sew the button on the crown where all the hat pieces come together using the yarn or decorative trim. Use one of the button-sewing methods shown in Chapter 9.

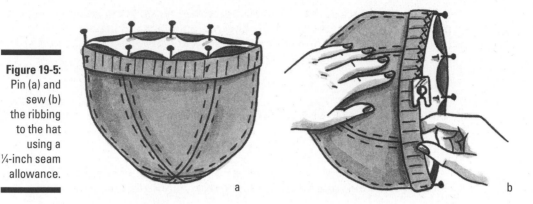

Figure 19-5:
Pin (a) and
sew (b)
the ribbing
to the hat
using a
¼-inch seam
allowance.

a

b

(Almost) Instant Party Dress

One of my favorite sewing Web sites is DIYStyle (www.diystyle.net) because it shows me what's really going on in the world of fashion sewing as seen through the eyes of up-and-coming designers. The inspiration for this project came from DIYStyle staffers who saw ready-to-wear baby-doll dresses with what looked like built-in bras. These innovative designers discovered brightly colored and trimmed bras that could be paired up with coordinate prints, and the (Almost) Instant Party Dress was born. Check it out in the color section.

Besides your sewing survival kit (see Chapter 2), you need:

- ✔ One bra (see the next section for what type works best)
- ✔ 2¼ yards of a coordinate cotton or cotton-polyester print
- ✔ Thread to coordinate with your project

Finding the perfect bra and fabric

You want this dress to look like a party dress, not a piece of underwear you stitched a skirt to. So look for a bra with the same or similar fabric and trim in the back as in the front — not with the elastic that looks like a standard bra. You also want one that closes in the back and has enough coverage (padded or not is fine) that you're comfortable wearing it out in public. Don't choose one with an underwire; the skirt is stitched to the bra and the machine can't sew through it.

For the skirt, choose a woven, cotton/polyester fabric in colors and graphics that coordinate with the bra. Most lingerie requires hand laundering, so preshrink the skirt fabric the way you intend to care for the finished dress (for more on preshrinking your fabric, see Chapter 3).

Cutting out the skirt and straps

Follow these steps to get this party (dress) going:

1. **To determine the width to cut the front and back skirt panels, measure the bra band from end to end, and then double this measurement.**

2. **To determine the length to cut the front and back skirt panels, measure from under the bra line to where you would like the finished dress hem, and then add 1 inch (½ inch for the seam allowance and ½-inch for the hem).**

3. **Cut two skirt panels the width and length determined in Steps 1 and 2, as shown in Figure 19-6.**

4. **Cut two strips 6 inches wide by 36 inches long for the straps (see Figure 19-6).**

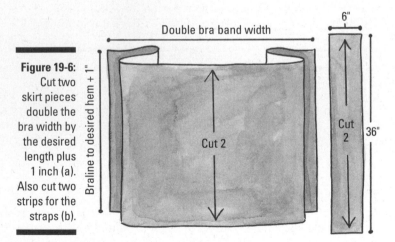

Figure 19-6: Cut two skirt pieces double the bra width by the desired length plus 1 inch (a). Also cut two strips for the straps (b).

Making the skirt

The skirt is gathered and then attached to the bottom of the bra, creating a flirty, flowy look. Here's how:

1. At the top and center back of the back skirt panel, mark a 4- to 5-inch long vertical line (see Figure 19-7).

2. Set your machine like this:

    • Stitch: Straight

    • Length: Appropriate for the fabric (see Chapter 5)

    • Width: 0 mm

    • Foot: All-purpose

3. Starting at the edge of the fabric ½ inch to the left of the line, straight stitch a *V* around the mark, coming to a point below the bottom of the line and finishing back at the top ½ inch to the right of the line. (See Figure 19-7.) Press the stitching line.

4. Using your scissor tips, cut along your marked line at the center of the *V*, being careful not to cut through the stitches at the point.

5. Double fold the fabric on either side of the cut, and sew down one side then up the other side of the "V" in one continuous line of stitching as shown in Figure 19-7 to finish it. Press.

    This creates the center back opening of the skirt.

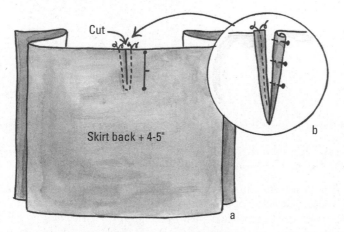

Figure 19-7:
Mark a straight line, stitch a *V*, and cut and narrow hem it to create the center back opening.

6. To prevent the fabric from raveling, finish the raw edges of the side seams on the front and back skirt panels (see Chapter 6 for more on seam finishes).

7. Pin the front and back skirt panels right sides together and sew them at the ⅝-inch seam allowance. (For more on seaming techniques, see Chapter 6.)

    Press the seams open. (For more on pressing seams, see Chapter 5.)

8. **Run gathering stitches ½-inch from the raw edge at the top of the skirt, and then pull up about one fourth of the fullness into even gathers (see Chapter 8 and choose the gathering technique you like best).**

There isn't a lot of stretch under the bra cups, so make the gathers at the center front a little denser than the rest of the skirt.

9. **Pin-mark the bra band and skirt into quarters as shown in Figure 19-8.**

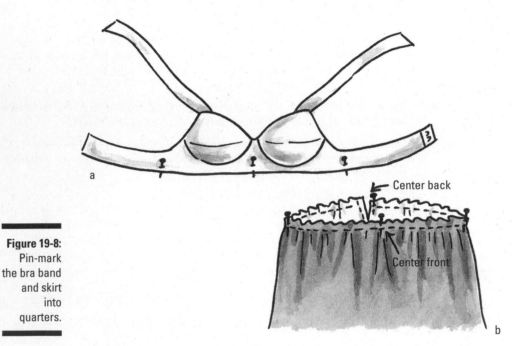

Figure 19-8:
Pin-mark the bra band and skirt into quarters.

10. **Lay the wrong side of the bra on top of the right side of the skirt panel and pin the bra band to the skirt.**

At this point, the skirt is larger than the bra — that's okay for now. Make sure that one edge of the finished "V" is even with the bra hooks on one side and even with the loosest eyelets on the bra back on the other. This way even if the bra is hooked on the loosest setting, the dress covers you in the back.

11. **Set your machine like this:**

- Stitch: Three-step zigzag
- Length: 1.5 to 2 mm or fine setting
- Width: 4 to 5 mm
- Foot: Embroidery

12. With the right side up, place the project so the bottom of the bra is under the presser foot and the skirt is to the left.

13. Starting at one end and sewing from one pin mark to the next, pull the bra band taut in front of and behind the foot as you sew, stretching the bra band to fit the loosely-gathered skirt. Pull the threads to the wrong side and tie them off.

Sewing the straps

The dress is nearly done; just a few finishing touches to go. Here's how to make the straps:

1. Remove the original straps from the bra by snipping the stitches holding them onto the bra. Discard the straps.

2. Using the 6-x-36-inch strips of cut fabric, fold each strip in half lengthwise, right sides together (see Figure 19-9a).

3. Sew a ½-inch seam on each strip as shown in Figure 19-9b, angling the seam down to the fold at one end and leaving the other end open.

Figure 19-9:
Placing right sides together (a), stitch each seam (b) and then turn each strap right side out (c).

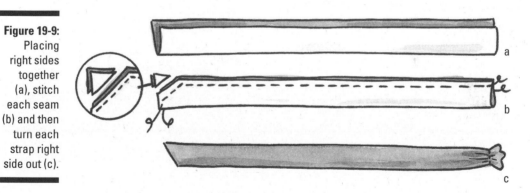

4. Turn each strap right-side out (see Figure 19-9c), press, and finish the raw edge using one of the seam finishes found in Chapter 6.

5. Using a hand needle and thread, gather the finished ends of each strap and pin one to each side of the bra, at the underside of the front where the original straps were sewn.

6. Straight stitch the new straps in place so they can tie comfortably around the neck halter-style. Backstitch at each end of the seam.

Hemming the dress

This little number sports a narrow hem. Follow these steps to put the final touch on the dress (and see Chapter 7 for more on hemming techniques):

1. **While wearing the dress, even up and adjust the length as needed.**

2. **Finish the raw hem edge as described in one of the methods in Chapter 7.**

   Obviously, you want to change out of the dress before attempting to sew.

3. **Place the dress wrong side up on your ironing board and press and pin a ½-inch hem all the way around the hem edge.**

4. **Topstitch the hem, sewing with the right side up and pulling out each pin before sewing over it. (Read more about topstitching in Chapter 5.)**

Now all you need is a party to show off your latest, most fashionable sewing project!

Part VI
The Part of Tens

The 5th Wave   By Rich Tennant

"Maybe a shower curtain wasn't the best thing to try to make into an evening dress."

In this part . . .

This part of the book is the shortest, but it runs long on information. These chapters include fabric and sewing tips and hints that I wish I knew when I was learning to sew. Each one of the tips saves you unwanted mistakes, wasted time, and untold irritation. If you find that just one of these hints gets you through a tricky project or improves your sewing experience, my work here is done!

Chapter 20

Ten Tips for Mixing Prints

In This Chapter

▶ Letting your imagination run (almost) wild

▶ Using contrast to create interest

▶ Making matching easy . . . on the eyes

o you remember Mom telling you not to mix a print with a plaid or put polka dots with stripes? If you follow this rule, *stop*. Pick up any decorating or fashion magazine and see how many beautifully dressed models or decorated rooms break this rule. My goal in this chapter is to give you the confidence you need to play around with prints and mix them up, whether you're selecting fabric for fashion sewing or home décor projects.

Stick with One Base

Many years ago, I found a new sofa on sale that I thought would go with my carpet. Both had shades of mauve and blue (It was the '80s — what can I say?). When I put the sofa fabric together with the carpet, something looked wrong. I later realized that I was putting a warm color base with a cool color base. Even though the colors running through the sofa and the rug were similar, they clashed.

Prevent this dilemma by keeping the same color bases together in your home. Check out Chapter 12 to get the lowdown on color bases, and check out the advice in the following section.

Run a Background Check

When combining print fabrics in an outfit or room, make sure the background color of each fabric matches the others. If the background of one print fabric is white, the background of the other coordinate fabrics should also be white. If the background of one print is off-white or cream, the background of the coordinate fabrics should also be off-white or cream. If you mix crisp white backgrounds with off-white or cream-colored backgrounds, the off-white fabric looks dirty, even though it isn't.

Go Solid and Save Money

Stick with a solid-colored fabric for your big-ticket fashion or upholstered pieces. In fashion, this means a blazer, suit, or pair of dress pants. In home decorating, this translates to your sofa or love seat. The fabric may have several colors woven into it in a pleasing texture, but when you stand back and squint at it, your big-ticket item should look like a solid color. If you choose fabric with an obvious print, you may tire of it before it wears out or is ready for the secondhand store. So go solid, accenting with trendy print fashion or decorating accessories — replacing accessories to update a look is easier and less expensive than replacing the main item.

Mix 'n' Match Manufacturers

Whether your project involves teaming up several prints, like the apron in Chapter 8, or mixing and matching prints in a room, you can use fabrics from different manufacturers as long as they have the same colors and backgrounds in them. I once paired a large-scale black-and-white floral print with a ½-inch black-and-white gingham check. Different manufacturers made both fabrics, but they looked great together because the colors were the same and the scales of the prints were different (see "Weigh the Scales" for more on mixing differently scaled prints).

Stare Down Your Prints

When mixing patterns, stand back and squint. Depending on where you stand, small-scale prints look almost like solid-color fabrics, which can affect the overall color scheme in a room, on a quilt, or in an outfit.

For example, a small red-and-white checked fabric can look like a lighter shade of the red in the pattern — or it may even look pink — when you stand back eight feet. And, although the red of the small check exactly matches the larger red tulip in another fabric, the colors may not look like they match when you check them out from across the room. You may need to choose a slightly different shade or a larger scale print to accomplish the desired look.

Weigh the Scales

When mixing together different patterns such as florals, plaids, or polka dots, don't use designs that have the same scale. From across the room, you can't tell apart two fabrics with the same color scheme that are both printed with 3-inch flowers. For a more interesting contrast, combine scales and patterns. Use a small-scale print with a mid-scale print of a different pattern; for example, try a ½-inch flower print with a 1½-inch windowpane plaid that has the same colors as the floral.

Follow these guidelines to mix your home décor prints in high style:

✔ Use only one large-scale print with a large repeat per room (the repeat is the distance between the same design along the length of a piece of fabric). A 15- to 24-inch repeat is considered large. Using more than one large-scale print confuses the eye. (To see an example of a large-scale print that shouldn't be paired with other large-scale prints, check out the fabric I used in the bedroom makeover in the color section.)

✔ Use the same large-scale print in only one to three areas in the same room.

✔ Complete the room using solid-colored fabrics and smaller scale accents such as florals, stripes, or plaids on throw pillows or an ottoman.

Try Before You Buy

When I see a fabric that I love for a possible fashion sewing project, I usually just imagine what I can make from the fabric and buy the necessary amount. For example, if I find a piece of fabric that would make a great pair of pants, I know that pants take about 1¼ to 1½ yards depending on the width of the fabric, and I buy it to use at a later date. But when it comes to home décor projects, which requires more yardage and may be expensive, I ask the fabric salesperson for a swatch of the fabric to take home to see what it looks like against the tile, carpet, and wall color. If you try this and still can't tell if this fabric is "the one," buy a square of fabric (if the fabric is 54 inches wide, buy 1½ yards of it to make a perfect square), drape it over the sofa or chair, and live with it for a couple of days. See what it looks like in the morning, afternoon, and evening light. If you still like it, buy what you need for your project. Besides getting a chance to try out a fabric in the room before making a serious commitment and buying several yards, you can hem your sample square and use it as a table topper(see Chapter 13 to see how to make one) that works on any size table.

Rely on a Collection

Puzzled by prints? Some fabric manufacturers make it easy on you by designing collections of companion fabrics that work together. When making a fashion sewing project, look at how the fabric store has teamed up the fabrics. If you're making a quilt, many stores have groups of fabric coordinates they call *fat quarters,* quarter-yard fabrics grouped together that are designed to be used in the same project. When it comes to home décor projects, many manufacturers create fabric collections that are perfect complements. Using these fabrics, you can successfully create a pulled-together look in a room and have the color flow effortlessly from one room to the next.

Check out the color section of this book to see how I used a collection in my master bedroom. I used the large-scale print on the duvet and smaller-scale animal print and the coordinate graphics circles for pillow shams and an accent pillow.

Buy More, Use Less

You've heard that less is more, right? That rule applies when planning the number of fabrics for your next fashion sewing project or when sewing for your home, too. After you choose the color scheme and fall in love with just the right primary fabric, find two — not four or five — others that work with it.

Buy enough of each fabric for the coordinating projects you plan to make this month and may want to make next year. Manufacturers frequently drop fabrics from their lines, and dye lots vary, so getting all your fabric at once is the only way to make sure you have enough. When inspiration strikes, you'll already have the fabric you need to make a new throw pillow to replace the one that the dog ate, another table runner to take over for the one that has faded with many washings, a new throw so you can throw away the one with the coffee stain — you get the picture.

Consult a Pro

If you're still unsure about whether one color goes with another or whether the colors you choose create the mood you are looking for in a room, consult a local interior designer, decorator, or a color specialist. When checking someone out, get professional references and see what kind of schooling they've had. Look for one or more of the following credentials:

- ✔ **ASID** (American Society of Interior Designers; college degree required)
- ✔ **CID** (Certified Interior Decorators international; certification required)
- ✔ **CSP** (Certified Staging Professional; training and certification required)
- ✔ **DCC** (Dewey Color Consultant; training and certification required)
- ✔ **IRIS** (Interior Redesign and Home Staging professional; training and certification required)
- ✔ **ODDAA** (One Day Decorating Association Alumni; training and certification required)

Chapter 21

Ten Rookie Sewing Mistakes to Avoid

In This Chapter

▶ Matching your projects to your skill level

▶ Rejecting troublesome fabrics and unflattering styles

▶ Avoiding common sewing pitfalls

▶ Easing up on yourself

Sewing is one of those activities that gets easier and produces better results the more you do it. If you know what common mistakes and pitfalls to watch out for, you're more likely to have an enjoyable sewing experience with positive results. This chapter alerts you to ten of the most common stumbling blocks that I and my students have tripped over.

Attempting a Project Beyond Your Skill Level

I like challenges as much as the next person, but when it comes to sewing, I draw a fine line between challenging and frustrating. The bottom line for your first project: Don't even think about making a suit jacket with notched lapels out of an uneven wool plaid. Starting at that level is a recipe for disaster. You'll probably waste your time and money — and you may never wear the thing after you finish it. You may never even sew again. Instead, look for projects with few seams, such as the pillow cover in Chapter 14 or the tablecloth in Chapter 13, which have just a few seams or hems and don't need fitting; you can make each one in a couple hours or less.

Also know that the first time you make something, you're on a learning curve, and the result probably won't be perfect. In fact, you may never wear or use the project, which is okay. Your skills improve with every project. After you master the basics, you can move on to more challenging projects that have a little bit more style.

Choosing Difficult Fabrics to Work With

Don't choose fabrics that may be too heavy, too fine, too complicated (such as plaids, stripes, and 1-inch gingham checks), or too expensive (with the proviso that using the best fabrics you can afford adds to the tactile experience of sewing). Read the information on fabrics and fibers in Chapter 3, and choose those fabrics that work with your lifestyle, personal style, and comfort requirements.

Also stay away from lightweight slippery fabrics such as polyester faille, silk crepe or charmeuse, sand-washed rayon, acetate linings, and the entire category of microfibers (again, read more about these fabrics in Chapter 3). These fabrics scoot around during cutting, attract static electricity, slip when you pin them together, and need special handling during sewing and pressing.

Because of their *nap,* or fuzzy texture, fabrics such as corduroy and velvet are also challenging because you can lay out and cut the pattern pieces only in one direction. I suggest that when you're ready to make a project out of a napped fabric, choose a fabric such as Polarfleece and make the throw in Chapter 6. When you have a little more experience, go on to the corduroys and velvets. But when you're starting out, stick with easier fabrics like cotton poplin, chambray, and cotton twill.

Choosing an Unflattering Style

When choosing clothing patterns, go for styles that you already know from experience look good on you. Chances are that if elastic-waist, pull-on pants from your local department store don't look good on you, elastic-waist, pull-on pants that you make for yourself won't look good on you, either.

Using the Wrong Fabric for the Pattern

If the pattern says "For knits only" and you decide to use a woven poplin because you love the color, the project won't fit. Knits stretch and contribute to the overall fit of the garment. If you choose a pattern that says "Not suitable for plaids" and you decide to ignore this instruction, you're setting yourself up for failure.

Always read the back of the pattern envelope and choose from the list of recommended fabrics.

Laying Out the Fabric Incorrectly

Have you ever had your pants' legs twist uncomfortably around your legs while walking? And perhaps this same pair of pants makes you look bow-legged even when you carefully press the creases. Chances are good that the fabric was cut off-grain.

Before cutting, lay out the pattern as your pattern guide sheet instructions recommend and read Chapter 4. To avoid costly mistakes, remember the old adage: Measure twice and cut once.

Neglecting to Use Interfacing

I remember my mom complaining about using interfacing in projects. "After all, it really doesn't show," she'd say, "and I don't want to spend the money on it." We agreed to disagree.

Interfacing is a layer of fabric that gives body and oomph to collars, cuffs, and front plackets. It doesn't show on the outside of the garment, but it makes a world of difference in the project's final look. If I'm spending my time and effort making something, I want it to look as professional as possible. Interfacing helps me do that. See Chapter 3 for information about interfacing and plan on using it in your next project. You'll love the results.

Failing to Press as You Sew

I remember one of my favorite college professors at the New York's Fashion Institute of Technology (FIT for short) telling me to "have a love affair with your iron." I never really thought too much about the value of pressing garments-in-progress until he said it, but he was right. When you press a project after each seam, you shape a flat, shapeless piece of fabric into something that fits the forms and curves of whatever is under it — almost like pressing the fabric into submission. To start your own love affair with your iron, follow the pressing tips in Chapter 5.

Using an Old, Beat-Up Sewing Machine

I work with a friend who used to sew and has an oldie but moldy sewing machine. It has been hidden away in the garage, never seeing the light of day for the last 10 to 15 years. Every so often I hear her say, "I think I'll dig out the machine and start sewing again." She never does, and I can only imagine how badly it works after all this time in retirement.

When I sew, part of the joy for me is sitting down in front of the machine, knowing that it works perfectly every time. So, instead of borrowing Grandma's old clunker, get a sewing machine that sews in good working order by

- ✔ Renting or borrowing a machine from your local sewing machine dealer.
- ✔ Taking a sewing class and doing all your sewing on the classroom machines.
- ✔ Buying a new or reconditioned machine from a sewing machine dealer. A used sewing machine sold by reputable dealer has undergone a thorough mechanical inspection so you can be sure it works well.

You don't have to buy one of those $4,000 do-everything models. You just need one that provides good, reliable service. Trade up to a better model as your skills improve and as your budget permits.

When you use a machine that sews in good working order, you also need to maintain it to keep it that way. Read your machine operating manual to see how to care for your machine and then treat yours with the TLC it deserves.

Neglecting to Use a New Needle on Every Project

I once met a woman who complained about her needle unthreading each time she sewed. She brought me the machine so I could diagnose the problem, and I discovered that she'd worn the needle down to the eye! We put in a new needle, and the machine worked perfectly.

I worked with another woman who had a terrible time with skipped stitches. She tried replacing the needle with a different one out of her pincushion, but she experienced the same problem. She was ready to take the machine to the local service center until I insisted that she use a brand-new needle from the package — no more skipped stitches.

Even though the needle looks perfect to the naked eye, the point bends, gets all boogered up, and just plain wears out with use, like a razor blade. So change your needle and throw the old one away after each project.

Refusing to Cut Yourself Some Slack

Remember when you first started riding a bike? You weren't perfect, were you? I spent my first bike-riding summer with scabs on both knees until I figured out what I was doing.

Sewing is like anything new. You can't be perfect from the get-go, so cut yourself some slack. If you can live with a sewing mistake, *don't* rip it out.

Chapter 22

Ten Important Sewing Fundamentals

In This Chapter

▶ Making sewing easier by remembering some basic rules

▶ Getting more pleasure out of sewing by following tips for better results

*I*n this chapter I give you some tips that I wish someone had shared with me when I first started sewing. Post these hints on a the wall in front of you when you sew, or write them on stick-on notes and put them on your sewing machine.

Buy the Best Fabric You Can Afford

Sewing is a tactile craft. For me, one of the pleasures of sewing is working with the best fabric I can afford. Better fabrics are easier to work with; are woven, knitted, or printed on-grain; hold up to frequent washing, cleaning and wearing; and usually produce a better finished product. (See Chapter 4 for more information about fabrics that are printed on-grain.)

Find out if a fabric makes the cut by

- **Checking the fiber content.** Chapter 3 covers fabrics and fiber content. This information (which appears on the end of the fabric bolt) will help you with your fabric purchase so that you buy the right fabric for the project and the way you want to care for it after it's made. If you're a wash-and-wear kind of person, you don't want to buy fabrics that need to be taken to the dry cleaners.
- **Considering what you pay per yard.** Although I can think of exceptions, I've discovered that you usually get what you pay for.

✔ **Examining the fabric's hand.** The way the fabric feels and drapes in your hand or against your body is its *hand.* Gather up a width of fabric in one hand and then drape a length of it over your arm, around your neck, or over one shoulder. Does it drape in smooth folds or bend in stiff creases? Does it bend at all? If it drapes in smooth folds, it has a soft hand. If it bends and creases, or doesn't bend at all, it has a hard or stiff hand. Depending on what you are making, either type may work.

When making a garment, I usually buy the yardage recommended on the back of the pattern envelope because the pattern companies are generous with their recommendations. When it comes to home décor projects, though, I usually buy fabric for one more pattern repeat than I think I need. (See Chapter 4 for determining the pattern repeat in a fabric.)

Understand Your Fabric Terminology

Fabrics have *selvages,* a *crosswise grain,* a *lengthwise grain,* and a *bias.* You need to know these terms in order to understand the pattern layout and cutting instructions, the basic project construction, how to buy the proper amount of fabric, and how to plan your project. Here's the rundown:

✔ **Selvages:** The finished edges of the fabric. Selvages run the length of the fabric.

✔ **Crosswise grain:** The width of the fabric, perpendicular to the selvages.

✔ **Lengthwise grain:** The length of the fabric from one cut end to the other cut end, parallel to the selvages.

✔ **Bias:** The 45-degree angle between the crosswise grain and the lengthwise grain.

See Chapter 4 for more details on these terms.

Know the Difference between Right and Wrong

After one of my two-hour seminars for beginning sewers, a guy stood up in the back of the room and said (with the most perplexed expression on his face), "What's all this about the right and the wrong sides? I think it would be better if you said the top and the bottom or the front and the back. I don't get it."

This experience reminded me never to skip over the basics with someone new to the craft. Here's the lowdown on the right and wrong sides:

- **The right side of the fabric:** The pretty side that faces the outside of the project and usually has the brightest colors and more defined textures
- **The wrong side of the fabric:** The side that faces the inside of the project where the seams are

Some fabrics look the same on both sides. In this case, the right side of the fabric is folded to the inside when it's wrapped on the bolt. Or if you're working with a single knit, it curls to the right side of the fabric when you stretch it across the grain. Other fabrics look similar on both sides, but the wrong side may be a different color combination than the right side, so choose the side you like the best for your project.

When sewing, place the right sides of the fabric together to make a seam. This concept is as basic to sewing as the needle and thread. In other words, place the right side of one piece of fabric against the right side of another piece of fabric (usually matching the notches along the seamline). See Chapter 6 for more information on making perfect seams.

Put Your Foot Down before Sewing

Put the presser foot down, that is. The presser foot firmly holds the fabric under the needle. Without the presser foot, the fabric just flops around and you can't sew straight. When you lower the foot onto the fabric, the upper thread tension also engages so that the stitches form properly.

Lower the foot when you start to sew, and raise the foot to pivot at a corner or to remove your work after you finish sewing.

Remember that your sewing machine comes with several different presser feet designed for different uses. Review your machine's operating manual and Chapter 2 to find out the benefits of sewing with different feet.

Stop and Start Sewing the Right Way

I can't think of anything more frustrating than getting ready to sew a nice long seam, stomping on the foot pedal, and having the needle come unthreaded. The following tips help you stop and start sewing the right way to avoid this problem:

✔ Stop sewing at the end of the stitch cycle, which is when the needle is out of the fabric and the take-up lever is at the highest position. If you don't stop there, the take-up lever pulls out a length of thread for the next stitch and unthreads the needle.

Your machine may have a button that puts the needle up or down when you push it, to be sure that you stop the needle where you want it. If you need to stop your sewing manually, release the foot pedal, and then manually turn the flywheel counterclockwise until the needle is out of the fabric and the take up lever is at its highest position (see Chapter 2 for more on sewing machine parts).

✔ When stitching a corner, stop with the needle in the dead-lowest position before pivoting at the corner to avoid a skipped stitch.

✔ Start sewing by pulling the threads to the right hand side of the presser foot, parallel to the front bed of the machine, and then put your presser foot down on the edge of the fabric. This way the pressure created by the presser foot holding the fabric in place also holds the threads firmly so they don't tangle when taking the first stitch. (See Chapter 5 for more information on taking the first stitch.)

Righty, Tighty; Lefty, Loosey

This little rhyme refers to the tension knobs on your sewing machine and serger. Turning the tension dials to the right makes them tight. Turning them to the left makes them loose — this trick works with pickle and peanut butter jars, too. (You can find more about balancing thread tensions in Chapter 2.) Throughout this book I provide machine settings and occasionally instructions to tighten or loosen the thread tension in order to make a particular sewing technique work better.

Test-Stitch First

When sewing, you want the seams and buttonholes to turn out as flat and as good-looking as possible so that you aren't fighting with them when you press. The best way to make sure that the seamlines behave is to test the stitch you intend to use for the seam on a scrap piece of fabric before you sew the real deal.

After you do a test-stitch, use the following guidelines to help you adjust the stitch length as necessary:

✔ **If your fabric puckers, shorten the stitch length.** Shortening the stitch length puts more thread into stitches so that the fabric stays relaxed in its original shape.

✔ **If your fabric waves out of shape, lengthen the stitch.** Lengthening the stitch puts less thread in the stitch so that the fabric retains its original shape.

Sew from the Bottom Up and from the Center Out

To keep your fabric pattern pieces in good shape for easy pressing and fitting, remember these hard and fast rules when working with vertical seams and horizontal seams on any project:

✔ When you sew a vertical seam (like a side seam on a skirt or a pair of pants), sew from the hem edge up to the waistline.

✔ When you sew a horizontal seam (like a shoulder seam), sew from the outside edges toward the center.

✔ When you sew a collar or facing, sew from the center out to the point or raw edge on one side, and then from the center out to the point or raw edge on the other side.

Press Seams Together and then Open or to One Side

Proper pressing and ironing techniques transform homemade projects into custom-made masterpieces. (To understand the important differences between pressing and ironing, turn to Chapter 5.) Your project's instructions may tell you to press in any of the following ways:

✔ **Press the seam flat and together:** Place the project on your ironing board with the wrong side up (right sides together) and seamline showing — like the seam looks when sewing. Press the iron over the seamline from the wrong side of the fabric. Doing so sets or *blends* the stitches in the fabric. Position the iron so that you press the seam allowance together from the seamline out toward the raw or finished edge.

- ✔ **Press the seam open:** Press a ⅝-inch seam from the wrong side of the fabric so that one seam allowance falls to the right and the other seam allowance falls to the left. The seamline itself ends up centered between the seam allowances. Using a seam roll makes pressing seams open easier (see Chapter 2 for more on pressing tools).

- ✔ **Press the seam to one side:** Press a ¼-inch seam from the wrong side of the fabric to one side or the other so that the crack of the seam faces the back of the project.

Clip with the Tips of Your Scissors

Don't cut a hole in your project where you don't want one! Any time you cut from an edge into a seam allowance (for example, when you clip or notch a curve; see Chapter 6 for info on clipping and notching) and toward a seamline, use the very tips of your scissors or shears. This way, you don't accidentally cut into the seamline.

Appendix

Sewing Resources

• •

The world of sewing includes fabric companies, pattern companies, notion companies, publishers, and organizations that all help you enjoy the craft and sew better. The following lists provide you their contact information to point you in the right direction and help you do further research on the various aspects of the industry.

Sewing Organizations

These organizations bring like-minded sewers together. If interested, contact them and see if they have a chapter in your neighborhood.

American Sewing Guild
Phone 713-729-3000
Web site www.asg.org

Association of Sewing and Design Professionals
Phone 877-755-0303 or 317-848-4950
Web site www.paccprofessionals.org

Sewing and Craft Alliance
Phone 412-372-5950
Web site www.sewing.org

Sewing Publications

These sewing publications keep you up to date with all the latest sewing techniques, fashion sewing trends, tools, and industry events.

Sew News
Phone 303-215-5600
Web site www.sewnews.com

Threads
Phone 203-426-8171
Web site www.threadsmagazine.com

Sewing Community Web Sites

These Web sites are interactive places for sewers to gather, learn, and share. Both include free projects and patterns. The studio DIYStyle also has several how-to videos, designer interviews, a blog, and sewing tips. Most content is free.

DIYStyle
Phone 636-925-1829
Web site www.diystyle.net

BurdaStyle, Inc.
Web site www.burdastyle.com

Sewing Machine Manufacturers

This is a list of sewing machine and serger manufacturers. Visit their Web sites to check out models, or visit the site of the brand of equipment you already use for all the latest product updates and very cool project ideas.

Baby Lock USA
Phone 636-349-3000
Web site www.babylock.com

Bernina of America, Inc.
Phone 630-978-2500
Web site www.berninausa.com

Brother International
Phone 908-704-1700
Web site www.brother-usa.com/homesewing

Elna, Inc.
Phone 847-640-9565
Web site www.elnausa.com

Juki America, Inc.
Phone 305-594-0059
Web site www.juki.com

Pfaff American Sales Corp.
Phone 800-446-2333
Web site www.pfaffusa.com

Singer Sewing Company
Phone 800-474-6437
Web site www.singerco.com

Viking Sewing Machines, Inc.
Phone 800-446-2333
Web site www.husqvarnaviking.com

Pattern Companies

Here's a list of the major pattern companies. Check out their online catalogs for all kinds of project inspiration.

Butterick Pattern Company
Web site butterick.mccall.com

Kwik Sew Pattern Company, Inc.
Phone 612-521-7651
Web site www.kwiksew.com

McCall Pattern Company
Web site mccallpattern.mccall.com

Simplicity Pattern Company, Inc.
Phone 888-588-2700
Web site www.simplicity.com

Vogue/Butterick
Web site www.voguepatterns.mccall.com

National Fabric Stores

The following retailers have a wide variety of fabrics, notions, crafts, and home décor items. To find the location nearest you, use the store-locator function on each Web site. If there isn't a location near you, each site has a shopping cart so you can shop online; and remember to sign up to receive e-mail discounts and valuable coupons.

Calico Corners
Web site www.calicocorners.com

Hancock Fabrics
Web site www.hancockfabrics.com

Hobby Lobby
Web site www.hobbylobby.com

JoAnn Fabrics and Crafts
Web site www.joann.com

Regional Fabric Stores

If you're lucky enough to live near any of these fabric stores, you can find all kinds of inspiration, fabrics, supplies, even some classes to satisfy your most creative whims.

Banasch's Fabrics
Cincinnati, OH
Phone 800-543-0355 or 513-731-2040
Web site www.banaschs.com

Britex Fabrics
San Francisco, CA
Phone 415-392-2910
Web site www.britexfabrics.com

Fabric Depot
Portland, OR
Phone 800-392-3376 or 503-252-9530
Web site www.fabricdepot.com

Fishman's Fabrics
Chicago, IL
Phone 312-922-7250
Web site www.fishmansfabrics.com

G-Street Fabrics
Rockville, MD (Phone 301-231-8998)
Centreville, VA (Phone 703-818-8090)
Falls Church, VA (Phone 703-241-1700)
Web site www.gstreetfabrics.com

Hancock Fabrics of Paducah
Paducah, KY
Phone 800-845-8723 or 270-443-4410
Web site www.hancocks-paducah.com

H & R Sales Fabrics & Supplies
Phoenix, AZ
Phone 602-269-6131
Web site www.handrfabrics.com

Mood Fabrics
New York, NY
Phone 212-730-5003
Web site www.moodfabrics.com

SR Harris
Brooklyn Park, MN
Phone 763-424-3500
Web site www.srharrisfabric.com

Vogue Fabrics
Evanston, IL
Phone 847-864-9600
Web site www.voguefabricsstore.com

Notion Companies

If you love new sewing tools like I do, take a look at what the world of sewing has to offer. These companies have not only sewing notions and tools, but also other gadgets for crafting and creative fun.

Clover Needlecraft, Inc.
Phone 800-233-1703
Web site www.clover-usa.com

Creative Feet (Piping foot and other creative presser feet)
Phone 800-776-6938 or 928-775-3484
Web site www.sewingmachinefeet.com

Prym Consumer USA Inc. (Sewing notions and home décor trims)
Phone 800-845-4948
Web site www.dritz.com

The Snap Source (Sport snaps and snap tools)
Phone 800-725-4600 or 248-280-1411
Web site www.snapsource.com

Velcro USA, Inc.
Phone 603-626-8559
Web site www.velcro.com

Wrights (Trims, belting, and tapes for fashion and home décor)
Phone 888-394-3576
Web site www.wrights.com

Fabric and Notion Mail-Order Companies

Looking for the latest in apparel, home décor, and quilting fabrics, plus very cool tools and sewing notions? Try one of these companies for an excellent selection and pricing.

Clotilde, LLC
Phone 800-545-4002
Web site www.clotilde.com

Nancy's Notions
Phone 800-833-0690 or 920-887-0391
Web site www.nancysnotions.com

Fabric.com
Phone 888-455-2940 or 770-792-8590
Web site www.fabric.com

Thread Manufacturers

Quality thread is important to your sewing success. Check out the different types of thread available for any project you can imagine and some you never even thought of.

American & Efird, Inc.
Phone 800-847-3235
Web site www.amefird.com

Coats & Clark, Consumer Service
Phone 800-648-1479
Web site www.coatsandclark.com

Sulky of America, Inc.
Phone 800-874-4115
Web site www.sulky.com

Index

• Symbols and Numerics •

– (minus sign), for tension control, 34
+ (plus sign), for tension control, 34
1/4-inch seams
  serging, 115–116
  sewing, 114–115
15-minute flanged pillow cover project, 264–265

• A •

accordion pleats, 155
acetate, 38
acrylic, 38
adding
  ribbing, 308–310
  room to waistbands, 315–317
air-soluble marker, 72
all-purpose foot, 30
all-purpose sewing thread, 25
(almost) instant party dress project, 339–344
altering clothing, 305–320
American & Efird, Inc., 366
American Sewing Guild, 361
American Society of Interior Designers (ASID), 350
appliqué foot, 31
appliqués, 109, 323–325
apron (window), 276, 277
apron project, 148–154
armholes
  overview, 15, 197
  raglan sleeves, 203–206
  set-in sleeves, 206–212
  sleeveless
    binding, 201–203
    facing, 197–203
ASID (American Society of Interior Designers), 350

Association of Sewing and Design Professionals, 361
attaching
  buttons, 186–191
  cord-edge trim, 244–245
  cording, 235–245
  elastic on edges, 160–163
  fringe, 235–245
  patch pockets, 221–222
  piping, 235–245
avoiding mistakes, 351–354

• B •

Baby Lock USA, 362
back waist length measurement, 57
background color, 347
backstitch, even, 84
backstitching with sewing machines, 106
ball fringe, 233
Banasch's Fabrics (store), 364
bartracks, 183
base color, 347
basting, 94–95
beading, lace, 48
bedding sets
  custom duvet cover project, 298–301
  overview, 289–290
  pleated bed skirt project, 290–298
Bernina of America, Inc., 362
bias, 63, 356
bias strips, 237–240
bias tape, 46–47
binding
  cutting, 202
  sewing, 202–203
  sleeveless armholes, 201–203
bishop sleeves (curtain), 275
blend fibers, 39
blind hem foot, 31
blind hem stitch, 85, 88
bobbin case, 32
bobbin winder (sewing machine), 32

bobbins
  compared with loopers, 36
  front-loading, 80
  sewing machine, 32
  side-loading, 80
  top-loading, 80
bodkin, 157
bolt ends (fabric), 45–46
boucle fringe, 233
box pleats, 154
box springs, measuring, 291
box-edged pillow project, 270–272
braid, 47, 231
Britex Fabrics (store), 364
broadcloth, 40
brocade, 40
Brother International, 362
bullion fringe, 233
BurdaStyle, Inc., 362
butterfly fringe, 233
Butterick Pattern Company, 363
buttonholes
  attaching buttons, 186–191
  cutting open, 183–185
  marking, 182
  overview, 80
  placement of, 185–186
  sewing, 183
  sizing, 181
buttons
  attaching, 186–191
  moving
    on cuffs, 310–311
    on jackets, 315
  placement of, 185–186
button-sewing foot, 31

● C ●

cable cord, 232, 233, 237–240
cafe rods, 278
Calico Corners (store), 363
canvas, 40
care of fiber, 38
casings
  curtain, 280
  inserting elastic in, 157–160

center back/front (pattern), 61–62
centered zippers, 172–176
centering pattern pieces, 70
Certified Interior Decorators international
    (CID), 350
Certified Staging Professional (CSP), 350
chainette fringe, 233
chair tie, 232, 233
chalk, 9, 22, 72–73
chambray, 40
checking fiber content, 355
chenille, 40
chintz, 40
choosing
  binding fabric, 201
  fabric, 37–46, 247–248, 352
  fabric for table toppers, 247–248
  hand stitches, 82–87
  needles
    for hand sewing, 23–24
    for machine sewing, 24
  stitch length, 89–90
  stitch type, 89
  style, 352
  thread, 25–26
CID (Certified Interior Decorators
    international), 350
circles (pattern), 61
clipping
  seams, 122–124
  tips, 360
closing, 14
clothing
  adding
    ribbing, 308–310
    room to waistbands, 315–317
  (almost) instant party dress project,
      339–344
  altering, 305–320
  choosing style, 352
  coordinating pocket-collage project, 224
  crossover belt, 318–320
  cuffed pajama pants project, 163–169
  eco fashion, 331–344
  facing hems, 306–308
  felted wool hat project, 332–339

letting down hems, 306–308
moving
  buttons on cuffs, 310–311
  buttons on jackets, 315
re-hemming, 306
removing cuffs, 311–313
ruffled apron project, 148–154
shortening jeans, 313–314
taking in waistlines, 317–318
Clotilde, LLC, 366
Clover Needlecraft, Inc., 365
clutch (flywheel), 33
Coats & Clark, Consumer Service, 366
coil, 54
color
  background, 347
  base, 347
  determining color odds, 229–230
  home complexion, 228–229
  overview, 228
  solid, 348
contour darts, 144
conventions, explained, 2
converting stitch lengths, 90
cool neutrals (color), 228
coordinating pocket-collage shirt
    project, 224
cord, 147–148, 232–233
cord-edge trim, 232, 244–245
cording, 49–50, 235–245
corduroy
  overview, 40
  pressing, 98
corners
  sewing, 113–114
  trimming, 124
cornice, 274
cotton, 96
cotton/polyester blends, 39
cotton/spandex blends, 39
cover fit for pillow form project, 258–261
creases, pressing out of fabric, 64
creating
  piping, 236–237
  pleats, 155–156
Creative Feet, 365

crepe, 40
crossover belt project, 318–320
crosswise grain, 63, 356
crosswise matching, 70
CSP (Certified Staging Professional), 350
cuffed pajama pants project, 163–169
cuffs, removing, 311–313
curtains, 274. *See also* window treatments
custom draperies project, 282–287
custom duvet cover project, 298–301
cutter and block, for cutting buttonholes,
    184–185
cutting
  across notches, 71
  bias strips for covering cable cord,
    237–240
  binding, 202
  buttonholes, 183–185
  overview, 12
  pattern pieces, 70–71
  tools for, 8, 20–21
cutting line (pattern), 61
cutting mat, 21

• *D* •

damask, 41
darts
  contour, 144
  defined, 14
  finishing, 145
  marking, 71
  overview, 61, 141–142
  straight, 142–143
DCC (Dewey Color Consultant), 350
decorative stitches, 88–89
decorator trims, 234–235
denim, 41
designs, one-way, 66–67
determining size, 56–57
Dewey Color Consultant (DCC), 350
differential feed (D.F.), 116
directional-stitching symbols (pattern), 62
DIYStyle, 331, 339, 362
dots (pattern), 61

double hemming
  bed skirts, 294–296
  defined, 127
double knit, 41
doubled lower hem (curtain), 280
doupioni, 41
draperies, 274. *See also* window treatments
draperies project, 282–287
drapery headers, 51, 286
drapery heading, 286
dressmaker's chalk, 9, 22, 72–73
dry-clean-only fabrics
  for home décor, 258
  preshrinking, 53
duck, 41
durability of fiber, 38
duvet cover project, 298–301

• E •

easestitching, 207–209
eco fashion
  (almost) instant party dress project, 339–344
  felted wool hat project, 332–339
  overview, 331
edge guide, 31
edges
  attaching elastic on, 160–163
  finishing, 13
  pinking, 104
edgestitching, 120–122
edging, lace, 48
elastic
  attaching on edges, 160–163
  inserting in casings, 157–160
  overview, 47–48, 156–157
Elna, Inc., 362
embroidery foot, 31
embroidery scissors, 20
Etsy, 55, 148
even backstitch, 84
even plaids, 68–69
even slipstitch, 86–87
even stripes, 68
eyelets, 41, 48
eyes, hooks and, 192

• F •

fabric, knit. *See also* fabric
  repairing seams, 322–323
  seaming, 114–115
fabric, woven. *See also* fabric
  finishing edges
    overview, 103
    pinking edges, 104
  lightweight, notching edges in, 123
  mid-weight, notching edges in, 123
  overview, 39
  repairing seams, 321–322
  securing seams
    backstitching, 106
    overview, 105
    tying off threads, 106–107
  standard seam allowances, 105
fabric. *See also* fabric, knit; fabric, woven
  binding, 201
  buying for bed skirts, 292
  cutting for bed skirts, 292–294
  dry-clean-only, for home décor, 258
  fine, average stitch length for, 90
  finishing edges, 104–105
  hand, 356
  heavy-weight, average stitch length for, 33, 90
  home décor, 53, 230–231
  incorrect for pattern, 352
  labels and bolt ends, 45–46
  laying out
    overview, 353
    patterns on, 12
  mail-order companies, 366
  marking
    dark, 72–73
    light-colored, 72
  measuring
    for curtains, 279–282
    for custom draperies, 283
  mid-weight, average stitch length for, 33, 90
  nap considerations
    overview, 43–44
    special care with fleece, 44
  for napkins, 248–249

national stores, 363–364
overview, 9–10
on patterns, 59
for pillows, 257
pivoting, 33
preparing, 64
preshrinking
  dry-clean-only, 53
  home décor, 53
  overview, 11
  washable, 54
pressing
  creases out of, 64
  man-made, 96
  napped, 97–98
  natural fibers, 96
  synthetic, 96
quality of, 355–356
regional stores, 364–365
right/wrong side of, 356–357
seaming
  corners, 113–114
  serging 1/4-inch seams, 115–116
  sewing 1/4-inch seams, 114–115
  sewing straight seams, 111–113
selecting, 37–46, 247–248, 352
types of, 39–43
width considerations, 45
yardage, 45
Fabric Depot (store), 364
Fabric.com, 366
facing
  defined, 119, 198
  hems, 306–308
  sleeveless armholes, 198–201
fake fur, 41
fashion. See clothing; eco-fashion
fasteners. See also buttonholes; buttons
  fold-over clutch with button closure
    project, 192–196
  overview, 191–192
feed dogs/teeth (sewing machine), 32
feel of fiber, 38
felted wool
  defined, 332
  hat project, 332–339

fiber
  categories of, 38–39
  checking content, 356
  defined, 38
  overview, 9–10
15-minute flanged pillow cover project,
  264–265
filler, 39
filler cord, 49, 232, 233
finding pattern pieces, 12
fine fabrics, average stitch length for, 90
finger-basting, 94
finishing
  apron seams, 150–151
  darts, 145
  edges, 13, 103–105
  hem edges
    overview, 128
    Res-Q-Tape, 130
    serger, 130–131
    straight stitch, 128–129
    three-step zigzag/overlock stitch, 130
  sleeveless armholes, facing, 198–201
Fishman's Fabrics (store), 364
flannel, 41
flat rods, 278
fleece
  fleece throw with colorful fringe project,
    107–110
  overview, 41
  preshrinking, 53
  working with, 44
fly-front zippers, replacing, 327–330
flywheel (sewing machine), 33
fold-over braid, 47
fold-over clutch with button closure
  project, 192–196
free-arm (sewing machine), 32
fringe
  attaching, 235–245
  sewing on, 240–244
  types, 233–234
front-loading bobbins, 80
full bust circumference measurement, 57
fusible products, 27

• G •

G-Street Fabrics (store), 364
gabardine, 42
gathering
  over cords, 147–148
  overview, 145
  ruffled apron project, 148–154
  with two threads, 146–147
gimp, 231
glossary (pattern), 60
grainline
  defined, 63
  pattern, 62
grosgrain ribbon, 51

• H •

H & R Sales Fabrics & Supplies (store), 364
Hancock Fabrics of Paducah (store), 364
Hancock Fabrics (store), 363
hand (fabric), 356
hand blind hemming, 133–134
hand needles, 78–79
hand sewing
  attaching buttons, 186–188
  hand blind hemming, 133–134
  selecting needles for, 23–24
  thimbles for, 24–25
hand stitches
  blind hemming, 85
  choosing, 82–87
  even backstitch, 84
  even slipstitch, 86–87
  hand-basting, 83
  hemming slipstitch, 86
  running, 84
  securing, 83
  slant hemming, 85–86
  whip, 85–86
hand wheel (sewing machine), 33
hand-basting, 83, 94
hank, 54
heading (curtain), 280
heavyweight fabrics, average stitch length
    for, 33, 90
hem allowance, measuring, 127–128
hem fold, 126
hemline (pattern), 62

hemming slipstitch, 86
hems/hemming
  allowance calculations, 127–128
  double hemming, 127
  facing, 306–308
  finishing raw edges
    overview, 128
    Res-Q-Tape, 130
    serger, 130–131
    straight stitch, 128–129
    three-step zigzag/overlock stitch, 130
  hand blind, 133–134
  knits, 136–138
  letting down, 306–308
  machine blind, 134–135
  marking placement of, 126–127
  no-sew, 132
  overview, 14, 125
  pinning, 133
  Res-Q-Tape, 130
  securing
    hand blind hemming, 133–134
    machine blind hemming, 134–135
    no-sew hemming, 132
    pinning for hand/machine hemming, 133
  tapered, 135–136
high bust circumference measurement, 57
hip circumference measurement, 57
hip to be square tablecloth, 255–256
Hobby Lobby (store), 364
home décor
  bedding
    custom duvet cover project, 298–301
    overview, 289–290
    pleated bed skirt project, 290–298
  box-edged pillow project, 270–272
  color, 228–230
  cording, 237–240, 244–245
  custom draperies project, 282–287
  custom duvet cover project, 298–301
  easy napkins project, 248–253
  fabric, 53, 230–231
  15-minute flanged pillow cover project,
      264–265
  fleece throw with colorful
      fringe, 107–110
  fringe, 240–244
  hip to be square tablecloth project,
      255–256

overview, 227–228
party-ready lapkins project, 253–254
pattern pieces for, projects, 60
pillows, 257–272
piping, 235–237, 240–244
pleated bed skirt project, 290–298
plush pet bed project, 265–269
repurposed shirt pillow project, 98–101
reversible pillow cover project, 262–264
reversible table runner project, 245–246
sewing for, 15
table toppers, 247–256
trim, 231–235
window treatments
    custom draperies, 282–287
    determining dimensions of, 278–282
    draperies and curtains, 274–276
    overview, 273
    windows and rods, 276–278
Home Decorating For Dummies (McMillan and McMillan), 275
hook and loop fastener, 192
hooks and eyes, 192
hydrophobic, 41

• *I* •

icons, explained, 4
inserting elastic in casings, 157–160
interfacing, 12–13, 52–54, 353
Interior Redesign and Home Staging (IRIS), 350
interlock, 42
Internet resources
  DIYStyle, 331, 339
  Etsy, 55, 148
  fabric and notion mail-order companies, 366
  national fabric stores, 363–364
  notion companies, 365
  pattern companies, 363
  regional fabric stores, 364–365
  sewing community, 362
  sewing machine manufacturers, 362–363
  sewing organizations, 361
  sewing publications, 361
  Simplicity, 10, 56, 332, 363
  thread manufacturers, 366

inverted pleats, 155
invisible zippers, 51–52, 176–180
IRIS (Interior Redesign and Home Staging), 350
ironing
  defined, 96
  iron, 27, 53
  ironing board, 27
  reasons for, 96
  Res-Q-Tape, 130

• *J* •

jacquard, 42
jeans, shortening, 313–314
jersey, 42
JoAnn Fabrics and Crafts (store), 364
joining
  cord-edge trim, 244–245
  fringe ends, 242
  piping ends in casings, 242–244
Juki America, Inc., 362

• *K* •

key (pattern), 60
kick pleats, 155
knife pleats, 154
knit fabrics
  hemming with twin needles, 136–138
  overview, 40
  repairing seams, 322–323
  seaming, 114–115
knit ribbing, seaming, 308–309
knitted interfacing, 52
knots, tying, 80–82
Knuu, Devin (designer), 290
Kwik Sew Pattern Company, Inc., 363

• *L* •

labels (fabric), 45–46
lace, 48–49
lapkins project, 253–254

laying out
  fabric, 353
  one-way designs, 66–67
  patterns, 63–70
  plaids, 66, 68–69
  stripes, 66–68
  twice and cutting once, 70
lengthwise grain, 63, 356
letter of pattern piece, 61
letting down hems, 306–308
light-colored fabrics, marking, 72
lightweight woven fabrics, notching edges
    on, 123
linen, 96
lock stitch, 29
loopers (serger), 36
Lycra, 39

• M •

machine blind hemming, 134–135
machine sewing. *See also* sewing machines
  attaching buttons, 188–190
  machine blind hemming, 134–135
machine stitches
  overview, 87–89
  selecting
    length of, 89–90
    type of, 89
  setting stitch width, 90
  stitching in the ditch, 90–91
  topstitching, 91–92
machine-basting, 94
man-made fabrics/fibers, 38, 96
mandarin, 231
marking
  buttonholes, 182
  fleece, 44
  hem placement, 126–127
  light-colored fabrics, 72
  overview, 12, 71
  tools
    air-/water-soluble markers, 72
    dressmaker's chalk, 72–73
    overview, 9, 22
    pin-marking, 73
master pattern, 60

match points, 22
matelasse, 42
McCall Pattern Company, 363
McMillan, Katharine Kaye and Patricia
    Hart (authors, *Home Decorating For
    Dummies*), 275
measuring
  box springs, 291
  hem allowance, 127–128
  overview, 8
  for patterns, 56–57
  pillow forms, 258–259
  tools for, 18–19
  for window treatments, 278–282
microfibers, 38–39, 42
mid-weight fabrics
  average stitch length for, 33, 90
  notching edges on, 123
middy braid, 47
millimeters (mm), 33, 89
minus sign (–), for tension control, 34
mistakes, avoiding, 351–354
mm (millimeters), 33, 89
molded-tooth zipper, 51–52
Mood Fabrics (store), 365
moss fringe, 233
moving
  buttons on cuffs, 310–311
  buttons on jackets, 315

• N •

name of pattern piece, 60
Nancy's Notions, 366
nap
  considerations
    overview, 43–44
    special care with fleece, 44
  defined, 22
  napped fabrics, pressing, 97–98
napkins
  creating, 248–253
  fabric requirements, 248–249
  as no-sew pillow covers, 253
  serging, 251–253
  sewing, 249–251
national fabric stores, 363–364

natural fibers, 38, 96
natural waistline, 56
needle plate (sewing machine), 32
needle position (sewing machine), 34
needle threader, 78
needle-up/needle-down function (sewing machine), 35
needles
  age of, 354
  hand, 78–79
  machine, 79–80
  overview, 9
  preventing breakage, 94
  selecting
    for hand sewing, 23–24
    for sewing machines, 24
  sewing machine, 30
  threading, 77–80
    hand needles, 78–79
    machine needles, 79–80
    overview, 77
  twin, 136–138
Nice to Have icon, explained, 4
no-sew hems, 132
nonwoven interfacing, 52
notches
  cutting across, 71
  pattern, 61
notching seams, 122–123
notions
  bias tape, 46–47
  braid, 47
  companies, 365
  drapery headers, 51
  elastic, 47–48
  lace, 48–49
  mail-order companies, 366
  overview, 10
  on patterns, 59
  piping and cording, 49–50
  ribbons, 50
  rickrack, 50–51
  twill tape, 50–51
  zippers, 51–52
number of pattern piece, 61
nylon, 38
nylon coil zipper, 51

• O •

ODDAA (One Day Decorating Association Alumni), 350
on-grain, 64–66
One Day Decorating Association Alumni (ODDAA), 350
one-way designs, laying out, 66–70
open arm (sewing machine), 32
organization of this book, 2–3
organizations (sewing), 361
overlap (window), 276, 277
overlock stitch
  finishing hems, 130
  overview, 88

• P •

pajama pants project, 163–169
party dress project, 339–344
party–ready lapkins project, 253–254
patch pockets
  attaching, 221–222
  overview, 215
  unlined
    with curved corners, 218–220
    with square corners, 216–218
patching
  holes with appliqués, 325–326
  holes with patches, 323–325
pattern envelope, 59
pattern guide sheet, 10–11
pattern markings, 61–62
pattern number, 60
pattern pieces
  centering, 70
  crosswise matching of, 70
  overview, 60–62
  pinning and cutting out, 70–71
  placement of, 70
  placing on-grain, 64–66
  storage of, 68
patterns
  companies, 363
  components of, 58–62
  determining size, 56–57
  envelope, 59
  finding pieces, 12

patterns *(continued)*
  laying out, 12, 63–70
  layout guide, 60
  master, 60
  overview, 10–11
  patch pocket, 222–224
  purchasing, 55–56
  step-by-step instructions, 60
  using incorrect fabric for, 352
pet bed project, 265–269
Pfaff American Sales Corp., 362
pill, 38
pillow forms, 258
pillows
  box-edged pillow project, 270–272
  15-minute flanged pillow cover project,
    264–265
  pillow cover project, 258–261
  plush pet bed project, 265–269
  reversible pillow cover project, 262–264
  selecting materials for, 257–258
pin-basting, 94
pincushion, 23
pin-marking, 73
pinking edges, 104
pinning
  hems, 133
  overview, 12
  pattern pieces, 70–71
  tools for, 9, 23
piping
  attaching, 235–245
  joining ends in casings, 242–244
  making, 236–237
  overview, 49–50
  sewing on, 240–244
pivoting fabric, 33
placement of pattern pieces, 64–66, 70
place-on-fold brackets/symbols
    (pattern), 61
plaids
  laying out, 66, 68–69
  seaming, 112–113
pleated bed skirt project, 290–298
pleats
  creating, 155–156
  cuffed pajama pants project, 163–169
  marking, 71

overview, 154
  types of, 154–155
plus sign (+), for tension control, 34
plush pet bed project, 265–269
ply, 26
pocket-collage shirt project, 224
pockets
  coordinating pocket-collage shirt
    project, 224
  creating pocket patterns, 222–224
  overview, 15, 215
  patch
    attaching, 221–222
    overview, 215
    unlined with curved corners, 218–220
    unlined with square corners, 216–218
Polarfleece
  pressing, 98
  working with, 44
polyester, 38–39
poplin, 42
poufs (curtains), 275
preparing fabric, 64
preshrinking
  interfacing, 54
  overview, 11, 53–54
  washable fabrics, 54
press cloth, 27, 64, 98
presser foot lever (sewing machine), 31
presser foot (sewing machine), 30–31, 357
pressing
  corduroy, 98
  cotton, 96
  creases out of fabric, 64
  defined, 96
  fleece, 44
  importance of, 353
  linen, 96
  man-made fabrics, 96
  napped fabrics, 97–98
  natural fibers, 96
  overview, 13
  Polarfleece, 98
  process of, 96–97
  reasons for, 96
  seams, 97, 359–360
  silk, 96
  synthetic fabrics, 96

tools for, 26–28
upholstery velvet, 98
velour, 98
velvet, 98
wool, 96
pressure adjustment (sewing machine), 34–35
preventing needle breakage, 94
prewashing fleece, 44
princess lines, 66
prints, tips for mixing, 347–350
process (sewing), 11–13
projects
  bags
    fold-over clutch with button closure, 192–196
    protective laptop sleeve, 212–214
  clothing
    (almost) instant party dress, 339–344
    coordinating pocket-collage shirt, 224
    crossover belt, 318–320
    cuffed pajama pants, 163–169
    felted wool hat, 332–339
    ruffled apron, 148–154
  home décor
    box-edged pillow, 270–272
    cover fit for pillow form, 258–261
    custom draperies, 282–287
    15-minute flanged pillow cover, 264–265
    fleece throw with colorful fringe, 107–110
    hip to be square table cloth, 255–256
    party–ready lapkins, 253–254
    pleated bed skirt, 290–298
    plush pet bed, 265–269
    repurposed shirt pillow, 98–101
    reversible pillow cover, 262–264
    reversible table runner, 245–246
protective laptop sleeve project, 212–214
Prym Consumer USA Inc., 365
publications (sewing), 361
puddles, of draperies, 274
purchasing patterns, 55–56

• *Q* •

1/4-inch seams
  serging, 115–116
  sewing, 114–115

quilting guide, 31

• *R* •

raglan sleeves, 203–206
rayon, 38
re-hemming pant legs, 306
reading labels and bolt ends, 45–46
regional fabric stores, 364–365
Remember icon, explained, 4
removing cuffs, 311–313
repairing
  patching holes
    with appliqués, 325–326
    with patches, 323–325
  replacing fly-front zippers, 327–330
  by sewing, 16
  split seams, 321–323
  tears, 326–327
replacing fly-front zippers, 327–330
repurposed shirt pillow project, 98–101
Res-Q-Tape, 130
resources
  DIYStyle, 331, 339
  Etsy, 55, 148
  fabric and notion mail-order companies, 366
  national fabric stores, 363–364
  notion companies, 365
  pattern companies, 363
  regional fabric stores, 364–365
  sewing community, 362
  sewing machine manufacturers, 362–363
  sewing organizations, 361
  sewing publications, 361
  Simplicity, 10, 56, 332, 363
  thread manufacturers, 366
return (window), 276, 277
reverse button (sewing machine), 35
reversible pillow cover project, 262–264
reversible table runner project, 245–246
ribbing
  adding, 308–310
  serging, 309–310
  sewing, 309–310
ribbons, 50
rickrack, 50–51
right side of fabric, 64, 356–357
ripper. *See* seam ripper

ripping seams, 116–118. *See also* seam ripper
rods (curtain), 277, 278
rosettes (curtains), 275
rotary cutters, 8, 21
ruffled apron project, 148–154
ruler, 8, 19
running stitch, 84

• S •

satin, 42
satin ribbon, 50
satin stitches, 183
scarf (curtain), 275
scarf (needle), 80
scissors
  clipping with, 360
  overview, 8, 20
  sharpening, 21
seam gauge, 19
seam ripper
  for cutting buttonholes, 183–184
  overview, 25
seam roll, 27
seam sealant, 21
Seam Stick, 96
seamline
  defined, 103
  pattern, 61
seams/seaming
  1/4-inch
    serging, 115–116
    sewing, 114–115
  clipping, 122–124
  corners, 113–114
  finishing edges, 103–105
  fleece throw with colorful fringe project,
    107–110
  knit fabrics, 114–115
  knit ribbing, 308–309
  notching, 122–123
  overview, 113–114
  pillow covers, 259–260
  plaids, 112–113
  pressing, 97, 359–360
  repairing split seams, 321–323
  ripping, 116–118
  securing, 105–107
  sewing straight seams, 111–113

shaping
  edgestitching, 120–122
  overview, 118
  staystitching, 118–119
  understitching, 119–120
  standard allowances, 105
  straight, 111–113
  tips for, 359–360
  trimming, 123–124
securing
  hems
    hand blind hemming, 133–134
    machine blind hemming, 134–135
    no-sew hemming, 132
    pinning for hand/machine hemming, 133
  seams, 105–107
securing stitch, 83
selecting
  binding fabric, 201
  fabric, 37–46, 247–248, 352
  fabric for table toppers, 247–248
  hand stitches, 82–87
  needles
    for hand sewing, 23–24
    for sewing machines, 24
  stitch length, 89–90
  stitch type, 89
  style, 352
  thread, 25–26
selvages, 63, 356
serger thread, 26
sergers
  components of, 35–36
  finishing
    edges, 104–105
    hems, 130–131
  overview, 9, 28–29
  starting and stopping with, 93
  tension knobs, 358
serging
  napkins, 251–252
  ribbing, 309–310
set-in sleeves, 206–212
setting
  sleeves
    in flat, 209–210
    in the round, 210–212
  the square on point, 255
  stitch width, 90

Sew News, 361
sewing. *See also* hand sewing; machine
    sewing
  community Web sites, 362
  organizations, 361
  publications, 361
Sewing and Craft Alliance, 361
sewing gauge, 8
sewing kit checklist, 17–18
sewing machines
  attaching buttons, 188–191
  backstitching with, 106
  bobbin, 32
  components of, 29–35
  feed dogs, 32
  finishing edges, 104–105
  flywheel, 33
  free-arm, 32
  manufacturers, 362–363
  needle, 30
  needle plate, 32
  needle position, 34
  needles, 24, 79–80
  needle-up/needle-down function, 35
  overview, 9, 28–29
  presser foot, 30–31, 357
  presser foot lever, 31
  pressure adjustment, 34–35
  quality of, 353–354
  reverse button, 35
  seams, 118–122
  selecting needles for, 24
  speed control, 35
  starting and stopping with, 92–93
  stitch selector, 34
  stitch-length control, 33
  take-up lever, 35
  tension knobs, 358
  upper tension control, 34
shaping
  darts
    contour darts, 144
    finishing, 145
    overview, 141–142
    straight darts, 142–143
  elastic, 156–163
  gathering, 145–148
  overview, 13–14

pleats, 154–156
seams
  edgestitching, 120–122
  overview, 118
  staystitching, 118–119
  understitching, 119–120
shears
  overview, 8, 20
  pinking, 104
  sharpening, 21
shortening jeans, 313–314
side-loading bobbin, 80
silk, 96
silk ribbon, 50
Simplicity Pattern Company, Inc., 10, 56,
    332, 363
Singer Sewing Company, 363
size
  considerations for laying out one-way
    designs, 66–67
  determining for patterns, 56–57
  pattern piece, 61
  sizing buttonholes, 181
slant hemming stitch, 85–86
sleeves
  moving buttons on cuffs, 310–311
  overview, 15, 197
  protective laptop sleeve project, 212–214
  raglan, 203–206
  removing cuffs, 311–313
  set-in, 206–212
  sleeveless armholes
    binding, 201–203
    facing, 198–201
    finishing, 197–203
slipstitch, even, 86–87
slubbing, 41
The Snap Source, 365
snap tape, 192
snaps, 188, 192
soleplate, 27
solid color, 348
sourcing wool, 332–333
soutache, braid, 47
spandex, 38–39
speed control (sewing machine), 35
spi (stitches per inch), 33, 89
split seams, repairing, 321–323

sport snaps, 188
squares (pattern), 61
SR Harris (store), 365
starting
  with serger, 93
  sewing, 357–358
  with sewing machine, 92–93
staystitching, 118–119
stitch length
  average for fabrics, 33
  choosing, 89–90
  converting, 90
stitch width, setting, 90
stitches
  hand
    blind hemming, 85
    choosing, 82–87
    even backstitch, 84
    even slipstitch, 86–87
    hand-basting, 83
    hemming slipstitch, 86
    running, 84
    securing, 83
    slant hemming, 85–86
    whip, 85–86
  machine
    choosing length of, 89–90
    lock stitch, 29
    overlock, 130
    overview, 87–89
    satin, 183
    selecting type of, 89
    setting stitch width, 90
    stitching in the ditch, 90–91
    straight, 128–129
    three-step zigzag, 130
    topstitching, 91–92
  selecting
    length of, 89–90
    type of, 89
  setting width, 90
stitches per inch (spi), 33, 89
stitching, 13–14
stitching in the ditch, 90–91
stitching line (pattern), 61
stitch-length control (sewing machine), 33
stitch selector (sewing machine), 34

stitch-width control (sewing machine), 33, 90
stopping
  with serger, 93
  sewing, 357–358
  with sewing machine, 92–93
straight darts, 142–143
straight seams, 111–113
straight stitch, 87, 128–129
stretch blind hem stitch, 88
stripes, laying out, 66–70
stuffing for pillows, 258
style, selecting, 352
Sulky of America, Inc., 366
swag (curtain), 275
synthetic fabrics/fibers, 38–39, 96

• T •

table runner project, 245–246
table toppers
  lapkins, 253–254
  napkins, 248–253
  selecting fabric for, 247–248
  tablecloths, 255–256
tablecloth project, 255–256
tailor's ham, 28
take-up lever (sewing machine), 35
tape
  bias, 46–47
  transparent, 22
  twill, 50–51
tape measure, 8, 18–19
tapered hems, 135–136
tassel fringe, 233
tassel tieback, 232
tears, repairing, 326–327
tension control, upper (sewing machine), 34
tension knobs, 359
tension rods, 278
test-stitching, 358–359
thimbles, 24–25
thread
  all-purpose, 25
  manufacturers, 366
  overview, 9
  for pillows, 258
  selecting, 25–26

tying off, 106–107
threading needles
hand needles, 78–79
machine needles, 79–80
overview, 77
Threads, 361
three-step zigzag stitch, 88, 130
throat plate (sewing machine), 32
tiebacks (curtains), 275
Tip icon, explained, 4
toile de jouy, 42
tools
cutting, 20–21
fabrics and fibers, 9–10
importance of having good, 8–9
marking
air-/water-soluble markers, 72
dressmaker's chalk, 72–73
overview, 22
pin-marking, 73
measuring, 18–19
notions, 10
overview, 8–9
patterns, 10–11
pinning, 23
pressing, 26–28
top-loading bobbins, 80
topstitching, 91–92, 120–122
transparent tape, 22
traverse rods, 278
triangles (pattern), 61
tricot, 42
trim
braid, 231
cord, 232–233
decorator, 234–235
fringe, 233–234
for pillows, 258
preshrinking, 53
trim mold (window), 277
trimming
corners, 124
seams, 123–124
tucks, 14, 71
tulle, 42
twill tape, 50–51
twin needles, 136–138
tying off threads, 106–107
tying sewing knots, 80–82

• *U* •

understitching, 119–120
uneven plaids, 68–69
uneven stripes, 68
upholstery velvet, 98
upper tension control (sewing machine), 34

• *V* •

vanishing marker, 22
Velcro USA, Inc., 365
velour, 43, 98
velvet, 43, 98
velveteen, 43
views, 12, 59
Viking Sewing Machines, Inc., 363
Vogue/Butterick, 363
Vogue Fabrics (store), 365

• *W* •

waist circumference measurement, 57
waistlines, taking in, 317–318
warm neutrals (color), 228
Warning icon, explained, 4
warp, 39
washable fabrics, 54
washing fleece, 44
wash-out pencil, 22
water-erasable marker, 22
water-soluble marker, 72
Web sites
DIYStyle, 331, 339
Etsy, 55, 148
fabric and notion mail-order
companies, 366
national fabric stores, 363–364
notion companies, 365
pattern companies, 363
regional fabric stores, 364–365
sewing community, 362
sewing machine manufacturers, 362–363
sewing organizations, 361
sewing publications, 361
Simplicity, 10, 56, 332, 363
thread manufacturers, 366

weft, 39
weft pile, 40
weight, of fiber, 38
whip stitch, 85–86
winding bobbins, 32
window topper, 275
window treatments
  curtains, 274
  draperies
    custom, 282–287
    defined, 274
  measuring dimensions of, 278–282
  overview, 273
  rods, 278
  window components, 276–277
windows
  components of, 276–278
  length of, 277
  rods, 278
  width of, 277
windowsill, 277
woof, 39
wool
  felting, 333
  pressing, 96
  sourcing and preparing, 332–333
worsted, 43
woven fabrics
  finishing seams
    pinking edges, 104
    sewing machine/serger, 104–105

  overview, 39
  repairing seams, 321–322
  securing seams
    backstitching, 106
    overview, 105
    tying off threads, 106–107
  standard seam allowances, 105
woven interfacing, 53
Wrights, 365
wrong side of fabric, 64, 356–357

• Y •

yardage (fabric), 45

• Z •

zigzag stitch, 87, 130
zipper (pattern), 62
zipper foot, 31
zippers
  centered, 172–176
  invisible, 176–180
  overview, 51–52, 171–172
  preshrinking, 53
  replacing fly-front, 327–330

Notes

Notes

Business/Accounting & Bookkeeping

Bookkeeping For Dummies
978-0-7645-9848-7

eBay Business
All-in-One For Dummies,
2nd Edition
978-0-470-38536-4

Job Interviews
For Dummies,
3rd Edition
978-0-470-17748-8

Resumes For Dummies,
5th Edition
978-0-470-08037-5

Stock Investing
For Dummies,
3rd Edition
978-0-470-40114-9

Successful Time
Management
For Dummies
978-0-470-29034-7

Computer Hardware

BlackBerry For Dummies,
3rd Edition
978-0-470-45762-7

Computers For Seniors
For Dummies
978-0-470-24055-7

iPhone For Dummies,
2nd Edition
978-0-470-42342-4

Laptops For Dummies,
3rd Edition
978-0-470-27759-1

Macs For Dummies,
10th Edition
978-0-470-27817-8

Cooking & Entertaining

Cooking Basics
For Dummies,
3rd Edition
978-0-7645-7206-7

Wine For Dummies,
4th Edition
978-0-470-04579-4

Diet & Nutrition

Dieting For Dummies,
2nd Edition
978-0-7645-4149-0

Nutrition For Dummies,
4th Edition
978-0-471-79868-2

Weight Training
For Dummies,
3rd Edition
978-0-471-76845-6

Digital Photography

Digital Photography
For Dummies,
6th Edition
978-0-470-25074-7

Photoshop Elements 7
For Dummies
978-0-470-39700-8

Gardening

Gardening Basics
For Dummies
978-0-470-03749-2

Organic Gardening
For Dummies,
2nd Edition
978-0-470-43067-5

Green/Sustainable

Green Building
& Remodeling
For Dummies
978-0-470-17559-0

Green Cleaning
For Dummies
978-0-470-39106-8

Green IT For Dummies
978-0-470-38688-0

Health

Diabetes For Dummies,
3rd Edition
978-0-470-27086-8

Food Allergies
For Dummies
978-0-470-09584-3

Living Gluten-Free
For Dummies
978-0-471-77383-2

Hobbies/General

Chess For Dummies,
2nd Edition
978-0-7645-8404-6

Drawing For Dummies
978-0-7645-5476-6

Knitting For Dummies,
2nd Edition
978-0-470-28747-7

Organizing For Dummies
978-0-7645-5300-4

SuDoku For Dummies
978-0-470-01892-7

Home Improvement

Energy Efficient Homes
For Dummies
978-0-470-37602-7

Home Theater
For Dummies,
3rd Edition
978-0-470-41189-6

Living the Country Lifestyle
All-in-One For Dummies
978-0-470-43061-3

Solar Power Your Home
For Dummies
978-0-470-17569-9

Internet

Blogging For Dummies,
2nd Edition
978-0-470-23017-6

eBay For Dummies,
6th Edition
978-0-470-49741-8

Facebook For Dummies
978-0-470-26273-3

Google Blogger
For Dummies
978-0-470-40742-4

Web Marketing
For Dummies,
2nd Edition
978-0-470-37181-7

WordPress For Dummies,
2nd Edition
978-0-470-40296-2

Language & Foreign Language

French For Dummies
978-0-7645-5193-2

Italian Phrases
For Dummies
978-0-7645-7203-6

Spanish For Dummies
978-0-7645-5194-9

Spanish For Dummies,
Audio Set
978-0-470-09585-0

Macintosh

Mac OS X Snow Leopard
For Dummies
978-0-470-43543-4

Math & Science

Algebra I For Dummies,
2nd Edition
978-0-470-55964-2

Biology For Dummies
978-0-7645-5326-4

Calculus For Dummies
978-0-7645-2498-1

Chemistry For Dummies
978-0-7645-5430-8

Microsoft Office

Excel 2007 For Dummies
978-0-470-03737-9

Office 2007 All-in-One
Desk Reference
For Dummies
978-0-471-78279-7

Music

Guitar For Dummies,
2nd Edition
978-0-7645-9904-0

iPod & iTunes
For Dummies,
6th Edition
978-0-470-39062-7

Piano Exercises
For Dummies
978-0-470-38765-8

Parenting & Education

Parenting For Dummies,
2nd Edition
978-0-7645-5418-6

Type 1 Diabetes
For Dummies
978-0-470-17811-9

Pets

Cats For Dummies,
2nd Edition
978-0-7645-5275-5

Dog Training For Dummies,
2nd Edition
978-0-7645-8418-3

Puppies For Dummies,
2nd Edition
978-0-470-03717-1

Religion & Inspiration

The Bible For Dummies
978-0-7645-5296-0

Catholicism For Dummies
978-0-7645-5391-2

Women in the Bible
For Dummies
978-0-7645-8475-6

Self-Help & Relationship

Anger Management
For Dummies
978-0-470-03715-7

Overcoming Anxiety
For Dummies
978-0-7645-5447-6

Sports

Baseball For Dummies,
3rd Edition
978-0-7645-7537-2

Basketball For Dummies,
2nd Edition
978-0-7645-5248-9

Golf For Dummies,
3rd Edition
978-0-471-76871-5

Web Development

Web Design All-in-One
For Dummies
978-0-470-41796-6

Windows Vista

Windows Vista
For Dummies
978-0-471-75421-3